5th July 2010

The Complete

To Investigation and Enforcement

A practical Reference Guide for Local Authority Officers, Police Officers, Private Investigators and Industry Investigators.

By
Sarah Owen & Jamie Mackenzie

Introduction

Welcome to, what we hope will become, an indispensable reference to current investigatory best practice for the purposes of enforcement in criminal and civil cases. This book presents the separate stages of investigation in the order in which you are most likely to require them, helping you to quickly and easily consult. In an easy-to-use guide, we will study the origin of law, our current system of law, and how this law is implemented at any given stage of an investigation.

Please note - At the time of going to print this information was as accurate as could be. However legislation changes over time, additionally different organisations have different company policies. A lot of legislation is also summarised only in this book. Therefore we would advise you to check the latest version of the legislation in full (read it in context with your own specific case as well as consulting specific case law), along with your organisations policies. This book is only designed to act as a guide and we can not be held responsible for any harm caused due to out of date or omitted information.

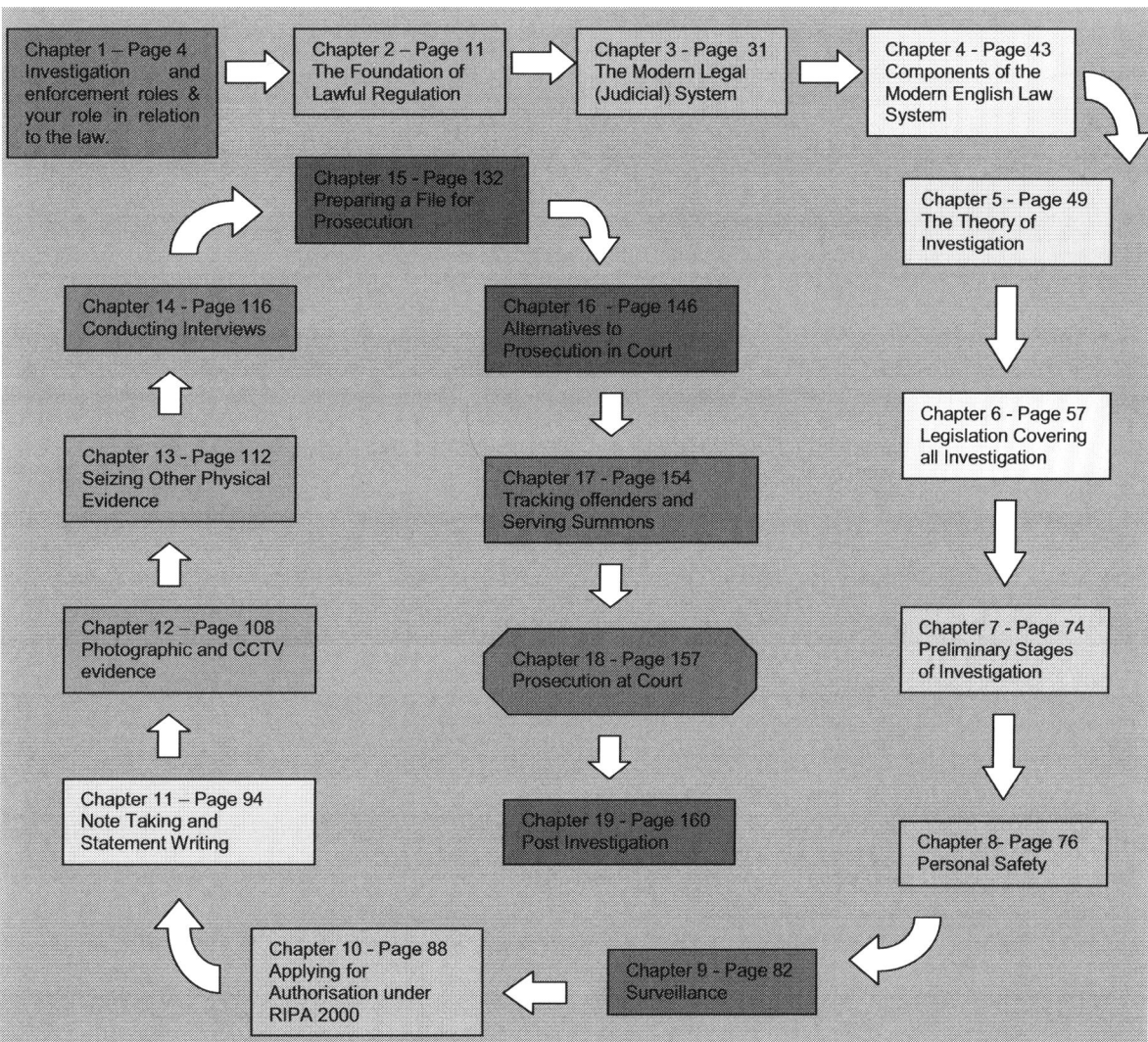

Chapter 1 – Career paths in the investigation and enforcement industry

There are a variety of investigation/enforcement roles within local authority and other agencies. Some of which are listed below;	
	EXAMPLE OF TYPICAL JOB ROLE AND REGULATION OF THE PUBLIC REALM.
Community Safety Officers	<ul><li>ASB Tasking Team dealing with incidents of Community ASB and crime problem solving and/or data analyst (analysing crime figures), crime prevention project development</li><li>Investigation and case management of ASB and crime issues</li><li>Early intervention system with children and young people and referral facility to youth diversion schemes</li><li>Liaising with colleagues and partners on crime and disorder issues</li><li>Links with landlords and RSLs</li><li>Providing mediation referrals</li><li>Monitoring and dealing with community cohesion issues</li><li>Leading on various borough tasking issues, such as brothel closures</li><li>Ensuring compliance with S17 Crime and Disorder Act and various other laws relating to crime and disorder</li></ul>
Local Housing Trust - Homes ASB Team	<ul><li>Enforcing the Council's conditions of tenancy and lease terms in relation to the council's housing stock</li><li>Supporting victims and complainants [including Domestic violence and hate crimes]</li><li>Promoting sustainable communities and social cohesion.</li><li>Promoting incident reporting where there is known to be under reporting e.g. Domestic Violence and racial harassment.</li></ul>
Ranger Patrol/Park Ranger	<ul><li>Parks security and events e.g. - preventing ASB, opening and locking of selected parks</li><li>Education campaigns e.g. against dog fouling</li><li>Undertaking Playground Inspections and engaging the public in Environmental Conservation</li><li>Ensure the parks and Open Spaces are safe and secure where residents and users can enjoy the facilities</li></ul>
Dog Warden	<ul><li>Stray dog service</li><li>Animal welfare education</li></ul>
Street Scene Enforcement / Environmental Crime Officer.	Enforcement of environmental crime activities:<ul><li>Fly tipping / dropping litter inc. cigarettes etc.</li><li>Fly posting</li><li>Dog fouling</li><li>Household & trade waste contraventions and litter</li><li>Licensing of all street trading activities and skips</li><li>Control of footway & highway obstructions</li><li>Cars for sale on highway</li><li>Enforcing waste carrier licence checks.</li><li>Enforcement of licences issued</li><li>Duty of care regulation for trade waste</li><li>Rodent infestation</li></ul>
Highway and Street Scene Maintenance	<ul><li>Licensing with respect to highways, e.g. scaffolding, skips, events and hoarding licences. Some highways agents also issue fixed penalty notices (FPN) for road offences, such as obstruction.</li></ul>

Town Centre Management	<ul><li>Facilitate business against crime partnership</li><li>Reduce crime in town centres</li><li>Reporting of Business rent: Vacancies, Intelligence gathering</li><li>Reporting of business causing problems<ul><li>Bins</li><li>Litter</li><li>Flytipping</li><li>Illegal selling</li></ul></li><li>Facilitating events</li><li>Reporting of public realm defects</li></ul>
Parking Services	<ul><li>The enforcement of traffic and parking restrictions within the borough</li><li>The management of the Councils Car Parks</li><li>The removal of abandoned & untaxed vehicles from streets.</li><li>The issue of Permits and dispensations</li><li>Reducing crime & the fear of crime through Park mark accredited scheme for council car parks</li></ul>
Planning enforcement	<ul><li>Enforcing planning legislation</li></ul>
Benefit Fraud	<ul><li>To investigate cases of suspected benefit fraud in accordance with the law and regulations.</li><li>To receive and log referrals of suspected benefit fraud.</li><li>To undertake investigations of suspected benefit fraud and make recommendations</li><li>To undertake interviews under caution in accordance with the Police and Criminal Evidence Act.</li><li>To undertake any surveillance activity in connection with a suspected benefit fraud in accordance with the relevant codes of practice.</li><li>To carry out visits to claimant's, landlords and employers.</li><li>To deal with correspondence arising from the work of the verification and investigations sub section.</li></ul>
Trading standards	<ul><li>Investigate cases of rogue traders, consumer protection issues, weights and measures and good descriptions.</li></ul>
Immigration and border control	<ul><li>Enforce and investigate immigration issues</li></ul>
DVLA	<ul><li>Investigate and carry out enforcement on driver offences, vehicle offences etc.</li></ul>
DWP / Pensions service	<ul><li>Investigate sickness benefit fraud, pension fraud etc.</li></ul>
Private sector - Banks	<ul><li>Anti fraud and money laundering</li></ul>
The Office of Fair Trading	<ul><li>Consumer protection</li></ul>
Private investigator	<ul><li>Various private investigation jobs, as set by clients, usually short term contract work.</li></ul>
Customs and excise	<ul><li>Tax inspectors</li><li>Enforcing compliance with the Minimum Wage</li><li>Corporation and Environmental taxes, personal tax, tax Credits</li><li>Investigate VAT and Customs Duty invasion (Often includes items smuggled through customs).</li></ul>

Legal investigator / Background investigator	- Mainly working for solicitor firms, investigate cases, usually for the defence / Provide background checks for people on behalf of employers.
Investigative journalist	- Journalist conducting investigations and reporting on findings.
Tracing services	- Trace and track down people to issue court summons
Fire investigations officer/Arson investigator	- Investigate cases of arson
Store detective	- Protecting stock within the store, maybe involved in investigations of theft amongst employees.
Police staff - civilian investigator	- There are now many civilian positions, including investigation roles, where you will conduct basic investigations and take statements, under the supervision of a Police sergeant.
Police	- There are also many specialist police roles which you can apply to go into, once you have completed your training/probation period. Such as; Fire arms Special branch - Counter terrorism etc.
British Transport Police	- Police the transport network.
VOSA	The Vehicle and Operator Services Agency (VOSA) was created in 2003 as a result of the merger of the Vehicle Inspectorate and the Traffic Area Network Division within the Department for Transport. VOSA is an Executive Agency under the auspices of the DfT. Its primary functions are to enforce current legislation and standards for heavy goods vehicles and public service vehicles by means of licensing and testing. VOSA is responsible for supporting the work of the Traffic Commissioners relating to operator licensing for public service vehicles (PSVs) and heavy goods vehicles (HGVs) as well as PSV registrations. Enforcement includes; enforcing vehicle standards and drivers' hours for HGVs and PSVs via annual and spot checks, providing veichle checks, investigating vehicle defects and recalls, assisting the police with accident investigations, and conducting research related to these VOSA also carries out enforcement checks, in which potentially non-compliant vehicles are identified on the roads and brought in to a roadside inspection site for examination. The Traffic Commissioners hear appeals against the impounding by VOSA of illegally-operated goods vehicles.
Security Industry Authority Investigator	- Investigates complaints against security professionals.
Public carriage office	- Taxi & mini cab licensing enforcement
Debt collector	- Often working on behalf of HM Courts to collect unpaid fines or on behalf of private companies etc.

Security manager

Personal protection specialist

Secret service special agent

Crime prevention specialist

Data security specialist

Information systems security (Infosec) manager

Computer forensic specialist

Probation/parole officer

Environmental health - Food inspector (also see environmental crimes officer).

Licensing Enforcement Officer.

Quality assurance/consumer safety inspector.

Compliance safety and health officer

Health and Safety executive – Investigator

Aviation Safety Inspector

Postal Inspector

Building & construction inspector

Loss control representative

Security consultant

Qualification;

There are various investigation and enforcement courses and qualifications available, including;

    BTEC in public services
    Certificate in terrorism studies
    Certificate in counter terroism
    BSc (Hons) Criminology and Criminal Justice
    BSc (Hons) Criminology and Forensic Studies
    BSc (Hons) Criminology with Psychology

    FdA Investigation and Evidence
    FdA Police Studies
    BSc (Hons) Counter Fraud and Criminal Justice Studies
    BSc (Hons) Crime and Criminology
    BSc (Hons) Risk and Security Management

    MSc Criminology and Community Safety
    MSc Criminology and Criminal Justice
    MSc Criminology and Criminal Psychology
    MSc Criminology and Crime Cultures
    MSc Security Management
    MSc International Criminal Justice
    MSc Policing, Policy and Leadership

    MSc Counter Fraud and Counter Corruption Studies
    MSc Criminology and Community Safety
    MSc Criminology and Criminal Justice
    MSc Criminology and Criminal Psychology
    MSc Security Management

    Doctorate in Criminal Justice (D.Crim.J.)

    LLB Law and Criminology
    BSc (Hons) Sociology and Criminology
    BSc (Hons) Digital Forensics
    MSc Forensic Information Technology
    MSc Forensic Accounting
    MSC Community safety and crime prevention
    MSc Countering Organised Crime and Terrorism

To work in the field of investigations and enforcement, most employers will expect you to have a sound knowledge of investigation techniques and:

- Police and Criminal Evidence Act 1984 (PACE) http://police.homeoffice.gov.uk/operational-policing/powers-pace-codes/pace-code-intro/
- Criminal Procedure and Investigations Act 1996 http://www.opsi.gov.uk/acts/acts1996/ukpga_19960025_en_1
- Regulation of Investigatory Powers Act 2000 http://www.opsi.gov.uk/acts/acts2000/ukpga_20000023_en_1
- Data Protection Act http://www.ico.gov.uk/what_we_cover/data_protection.aspx

If you want to specialize in fraud, the well know fraud qualification is *professionalism in Security (PinS)*. This is a modular course, with 7 parts. Once you have completed the modules you will be awarded Accredited Counter Fraud status (This course is equivalent to level 4 NVQ).

Society, Freedom and the necessity of Law

Your role as an officer, in relation to the letter of the law;

Why do we even need enforcement officers? Why, for that matter do we need a structure of law? Would society perhaps profit from a reduction in regulation, where people are left to settle their own disputes as they see fit? Well, some people think so. As an investigator or enforcement officer, you will deal with a wide variety of people all of whom have their own ideas about how best society should be governed. Are you more qualified than they to say they are right or wrong? The answer is invariably 'no'. However, you do have a job to do and that job is ensure that the law, as currently written, is fairly applied and strictly adhered to, whether you always agree with them or not.

Your job is to enforce the law and therefore you have to be equal and consistent and treat everyone the same, and if someone breaks the law you will need to take action, according to the letter of the law and not your own beliefs. That said, depending on the legislation and the situation there is sometimes room for discretion and you will have some choice over how you enforce the law (as we will see later on, in the chapter 16 'What action to take'). It is important to note this is a great deal of responsibility and power that you have, therefore you should act accordingly. Especially as any inappropriate actions you may take will have not only implications on you but implications on your colleagues and their reputation. It is important to be consistent and fair.

As an investigator the personal qualities that you should have are;
- Empathy
- Respect for the law, the offender and the victim
- An inquisitive mind - things are not always as they seem and the investigator needs to be determined to get to the truth. The investigator must be persistent in seeking out the truth and shouldn't except things on face value.
- An objective approach
- Be clear, calm and authoritative when giving instructions
- Be honest, fair, consistent & trustworthy
- You need to set a good example and must be an upstanding citizen, who does not break the law (after all how can you enforce the law in you are in the wrong yourself).

Before we go further, study the following questions and decide for yourself if you think the answers are correct…

Reasons for the law

Why do we have laws?
Laws provide the framework within which a healthy, safe and fair society can operate. Without them, we would have no way of regulating or governing the more extreme aspects of human behaviour.

Couldn't we just deal with things as and when they occur?
We could, but the system would be inherently unfair. How would we ensure each and every person was treated in a similar way for a similar crime?

We could write down previous punishments for crimes and apply them to similar cases.
Absolutely. But for this to work we would have to know when a crime had been committed.

We could set down rules to let people know what they can and can't do.
Congratulations, you've just written a law!

Of course, the above is a simplified version of how things work, but it can clearly be seen that if a number of people want to live together in a community, law must exist for the community to function. It is not only desirable, but inevitable and natural.

For peaceful society to exist, we will always require law.

So how did the structure of UK law come about? And how are laws made today?

Chapter 2 - The Foundation of Lawful Regulation

2.1 The Rule of Law - An Historical perspective.

The English legal system has developed gradually over time. The system whereby a case would be decided on the basis of adopted or accepted law can be traced back many centuries. Indeed, it can be argued that the historic settling of any tribal dispute through adjudication by the tribal leader, with perhaps advice from tribal elders, is not too disimilar from the basic system of today where a judge will hear evidence brought before him and direct a jury of twelve people to reach a decision. However, while the principle may remain the same, the method most certainly has not. Any changes have been slow. Nevertheless, there are many interesting landmark incidents along the way.

Our English legal system can certainly be dated back from the local customs of the Anglo-Saxons, traces of which survived until 1925..

The oldest law currently in force is the Distress Act 1267, part of the Statute of Marlborough. (The Statute of Marlborough was a set of laws passed by King Henry III of England in 1267. There were twenty-nine chapters, of which four are still in force. The full title was Provisions made at Marlborough in the presence of our lord King Henry, and Richard King of the Romans, and the Lord Edward eldest son of the said King Henry, and the Lord Ottobon, at that time legate in England).

Three sections of Magna Carta, originally signed in 1215 and a landmark in the development of English law, are extant, but they date to the reissuing of the law in 1297. The law seek to govern the recovery of damages ("distresses") and make it illegal to obtain recompense for damages other than through the courts, and c.23 (the Waste Act 1267), seeks to prevent tenant farmers from "making waste" to land they are in tenancy of.

There have many different systems of law and customs along the way, from………..

Compurgation, which was a ritualistic procedure in which accused persons might clear themselves of an alleged wrongdoing by taking a sworn oath denying the claim made against them, and corroborating the denial by the sworn oaths of 12 other persons, usually neighbours or relatives. If an accused person failed to provide the requisite number of compurgators, he or she lost. The number of compurgators was the same as the number of jurors later empanelled to hear criminal cases under the common law. In the United States, the Sixth Amendment to the Constitution required that all criminal trials be prosecuted before 12 jurors—until 1970, when the Supreme Court ruled that six-person juries were permissible (*Williams v. Florida*, 399 U.S. 78, 90 S. Ct. 1893, 26 L. Ed. 2d 446).

Through to….

Trial by ordeal, which was a superstitious procedure administered by clerics who subjected accused persons to physical torment in hopes of uncovering divine signs of guilt or innocence. The most common forms of ordeal involved boiling or freezing waters and hot irons. In the ordeal of freezing water, accused persons were thrown into a pool to see if they would sink or float. If they sank, the cleric believed they were innocent, because the water would presumably reject someone with an impure soul. Of course, persons who sank to the bottom and drowned during this ordeal were both exonerated of their alleged misbehaviour, and dead.

And…

Battle, which was another form of primitive trial that was thought to involve divine intervention on behalf of the righteous party. The combatants were armed with long staffs and leather shields, and fought savagely until one party cried, "Craven," or died.

Trial by battle, though in many ways as barbaric as trial by ordeal, foreshadowed modern trials in several ways. The combatants fought in an adversarial arena before robed judges who presided over the battle. The accused person was required to put on a defence, quite literally in the physical sense, against an opponent who was trying to prove the veracity of his or her claims. Some parties to a battle, particularly women, children, and older individuals, were entitled to hire stronger, more able champions to fight on their behalf. This last practice sheds light on the more recent phrase *hired guns*, which is sometimes used to describe U.S. trial attorneys.

But the main landmarks in the English legal system, to note, are as follows;...............

AD43 - The Romans invade Britain

Roman law was heavily influenced by Greek teachings. Roman law, in the days of the Roman republic and Empire, was heavily procedural. However, there was no professional legal class. Instead, a lay person was chosen to adjudicate. This lay person was, theoretically at least, unconnected to the plaintiffs. Each case was decided afresh from the laws of the state - that is, no precedents were reported. No previous case decision could be used as a way of helping victory in a separate case.

AD449 - Anglo Saxons invade England

When the Anglo-Saxons invaded England, they brought with them their local customs and rules. This period also heralds the beginning of the period known as the Dark Ages. In European history the Dark Ages ran from around the end of the 5thC to approximately AD1000.

C6th AD   The Emperor Justinian codifies and consolidates the laws that exist in Rome

The remains of the collected and simplified law was one twentieth of the mass of the original legal texts. This consolidation into one easily managable tome became known as the *Corpus Juris Civilis*.

Note: ***Roman law was lost through the Dark Ages. In the eleventh century AD medieval legal scholars at the University of Bologna rediscovered the texts of the Corpus Juris Civilis and began to use the concepts to interpret their own laws. Some other countries still use Roman law.***

AD 871-901 - Alfred the Great, King of England

Alfred, argued by a number of scholars to be the greatest of England's Kings, is perhaps most well regarded for his Law Code. This book of laws, or Dooms was taken from the long established laws of Kent, Mercia and Wessex, areas over which Alfred's father, Ethelwulf, had ruled. These laws blended differing strands of Mosaic law (the laws of Moses), Celto-Brythonic law (the traditional laws of the tribes and communities of England, and old Germanic customs introduced by the Anglo Saxons.

AD1066 - Willam the Conqueror invades with his Norman army

King William's conquest of England introduced not only Norman, but also the first Islamic legal concepts, possibly carried from Bologna.

Note: **After the invasion of William the Conqueror, the Chancery division of the High Court was established. The Chancery is a long standing court and administrative department of the British political and legal system**

(After the Norman Conquest the feudal courts of the barons and the ecclesiastical (church) courts grew up beside the existing Anglo-Saxon courts. From the king's council developed the royal courts, presided over by professional judges, which gradually absorbed the jurisdictions (legal powers) of the baronial and ecclesiastical courts. By 1250 the royal judges had amalgamated the various local customs into the system of common law – that is, law common to the whole country. A second system

known as equity developed in the Court of Chancery, in which the Lord Chancellor considered petitions).

AD1154 - The Accession of Henry II

In 1154, Henry II changed the legal system forever when he set about the process of applying one set of legal rules, the common law, throughout the country. Possibly following the example of Alfred, this action proved to be one of the most important influences on the shape of the current legal system. At first, travelling the length and breadth of the country, the King's representatives would only check on the procedures in the local courts. Gradually, however, these checks became more thorough. In time, representatives came to judge the proceedings, eventually trying their own cases, and recording their decisions. Importantly, these decisions could then be followed by other judges to decide similar cases in an entirely separate part of the country. In a classic example of the evolution of the law, the first precidents - otherwise referred to as case law - had now been set.

Note: *Predictably, there were some significant flaws with this system. Legal action could only be commenced through the issue of a writ. Political pressure from Barons led to the passing of a statute that prevented new writs from being issued. If this did not work, it was very easy to use any slight defect in the wording of the writ to ensure the content became unenforceable.*

In consequence, anyone who found themselves unable to seek a solution to their claim under the rigid procedure of common law could instead petition the Chancellor, the highest ranking clergymen in the country, asking him to intercede on their behalf. The Chancellor at this time had almost unlimited power and if he so wanted, could simply issue an injunction to stop a person behaving in a particular way.

Before long, justice dispensed by the Chancellor became known as Equity. It was not designed as a rival system to common law but merely to supplement it. However, with corruption it quickly became a rival system, leading, in effect, to two separate systems of court and laws. The higher, that of the Chancellor, was used for the application of Equity when any conflict between decisions arose.

The two systems were eventually merged but not until 1875 under the Judicature Acts, over seven hundred years later!

Lex Mercatoria - Also in medieval times a Europe wide *lex mercatoria* was formed. This enabled traveling merchants to trade using familiar standards, rather than the many splintered types of local law. A precursor to modern commercial law, the *lex mercatoria* emphasized freedom of contract and the alienability of property; that is, the right of property transfer from one person to another.

The Law Merchant, or *Lex Mercatoria*, was originally a body of rules and principles laid down by merchants themselves to regulate their dealings. It consisted of usages and customs common to merchants and traders in Europe, with slightly local differences. It originated from the problem that civil law was not responsive enough to the growing demands of commerce: there was a need for quick and effective jurisdiction, administered by specialized courts. The guiding spirit of the merchant law was that it ought to evolve from commercial practice, respond to the needs of the merchants, and be comprehensible and acceptable to the merchants who submitted to it. International commercial law today owes some of its fundamental principles to the Law Merchant as it was developed in the medieval ages. This includes choice of arbitration institutions, procedures, applicable law and arbitrators, and the goal to reflect customs, usage and good practice among the parties.

The Law Merchant was administered by merchant courts, set up along trade routes and trade centers. A distinct feature of the Law Merchant was the reliance by merchants on a legal system developed and administered by them. States or local authorities seldom interfered, and surrendered some of the control over trade within their territory to the merchants. In return, trade flourished under the Law Merchant, increasing tax revenues.

The Law Merchant was the product of customs and practices among traders, and could be enforced through the local courts. However, the merchants needed to solve their disputes rapidly, sometimes on the hour, with the least costs and by the most efficient means. Public courts did not provide this. A trial before the courts would delay their business, and that meant losing money. The Law Merchant provided quick and effective justice. This was possible through informal proceedings, with liberal procedural rules. The Law Merchant rendered proportionate judgments over the merchants' disputes, in light of "fair price", good commerce, and equity.

Judges were chosen according to their commercial background and practical knowledge. Their reputation rested upon their perceived expertise in merchant trade and their fair-mindedness. Gradually, a professional judiciary developed through the merchant judges. Their skills and reputation would however still rely upon practical knowledge of merchant practice. These characteristics serve as important measures in the appointment of international commercial arbitrators today.

12thC medieval - The Exchequer formed - The financial and accounting office for England

The Exchequer obtained its name from the fact that accounts were calculated by means of counters on a chequered table in its Westminster HQ. It existed of upper and lower exchequer.

AD1215 - The Magna Carta signed at Runnymede

Arguably the most significant early influence on the extensive historical process that led to the rule of constitutional law today in the English speaking world. Magna Carta heavily influenced the development of the common law and has had further influence on many other constitutional documents, including that of the United States.

Magna Carta required King John of England to proclaim certain rights (to Barons, Church and Freemen), respect certain legal procedures, and accept that his will could be bound by the law. It forced King John to submit to the law and succeeded in putting limits on feudal fees and duties. An earlier example of a similar notion was the Islamic law of the Middle East which recognized the equal subjection of all classes, including Caliphs and Sultans, to the ordinary law of the land.

Magna Carta also explicitly protected certain rights of the King's subjects, whether free or fettered — most notably the writ of habeas corpus.

Note: *The importance of the writ of Habeas Corpus should never be underappreciated. This writ allows for an imprisoned man or woman to be brought before a court so that the court may decide whether the detention is lawful or not. Prior to this, a man could be locked in a cell unlawfully, and have no means by which to prove his innocence.*

In England, the issuing of the Magna Carta was a prime example of the 'rule of law'. Perhaps the most important application of the 'rule of law' is the principle that governmental authority is legitimately exercised only in accordance with written, publicly disclosed laws. These laws are adopted and enforced in accordance with established procedural steps that are referred to as due process. The principle is intended to be a safeguard against arbitrary governance, whether by a totalitarian leader or by mob rule. Thus, the rule of law is hostile to both dictatorship and to anarchy.

Many clauses of the Magna Carta were renewed throughout the Middle Ages, and continued to be renewed as late as the 18th century. By the second half of the 19th century, however, most clauses in their original form had been repealed from English law.

AD1420 - Treaty of Troyes signed.

This was an agreement between the French & British monarchies to establish claims and successions to the thrones of each country, it was signed on 21 May 1420 during the 100 year war. The terms of the treaty allowed for the French King, Charles VI, to betroth his daughter Catherine to Henry V, it also made Henry regent of France, Henry V then died leaving his son Henry VI

AD1689 - The Bill of Rights

'Commoners' i.e. non-baronial representatives at parliament, were traditionally summonsed to appear. In the sixteenth century, the Commons had acquired its permanent meeting place in Westminster. In the Glorious Revolution of 1688, William of Orange and his wife, Queen Mary, were invited to ascend the throne of England subject to certain conditions. These conditions were presented to the future monarchs as the Declaration of Rights, in a more or less take-it or leave it proposition. Unsurprisingly, having been handed the throne of England, William and Mary took it. Control over taxation and free speech had been won by the Commons and was subsequently laid down in the Bill of Rights.

The Bill of Rights laid out the certain basis rights all Englishmen could expect. It helped to bring about the change from absolute monarchy to constitutional monarchy and can be seen as the forerunner of the American Bill of Rights, and even an early form of the European Convention on Human Rights (much more of which later). The Bill granted the people of England certain civil and political rights for the first time in history, amongst which were:

> Freedom from Royal interferrence with the law
>
> Freedom from taxation without the consent of parliament
>
> Freedom to elect those members of parliament without interferrence
>
> Freedom from cruel and unusual punishment
>
> Freedom from fine and forfeiture without a trial

Until now, the monarch had more or less ruled the country with parliament acting as advisors. Only here do we see the true emergence of a dedicated political forum consisting of the monarch, the house of lords and the house of commons, all three based in the Palaces of Westminster, London. From now on, no single person or group could change policy or enact law without the consent of the other two arms of government. It is this system of checks and balances which allows for a truly balanced legislature today.

In the 17th and 18th centuries common law absorbed the Law Merchant, the international code of mercantile customs. During the 19th century virtually the whole of English law was reformed by legislation; for example, the number of capital offences was greatly reduced.

AD 1911 - Parliamentary Act

Asserted the supremacy of the House of Commons, those members of governemnet voted for by the people of England, over the House of Lords, the hereditary house, thereby ensuring that the majority of the population held the balance of power in their own legislature. No Act of Parliament can be passed without the consent of the House of Commons and the House of Commons is created by the voting public. Therefore, no law can be passed that does not carry the majority support, and no law can be enforced that does not exist…

AD 1994 - Police and Magistrates' Court Act 1994

In the interest of fairness, any system of law enforcement has to be impartial. For many years, Police and judges were allowed (and often exercised) a considerable degree of freedom when deciding how to enforce the law. However, eventually there arose a significant concern that this freedom was not necessarily in the public interest, and furthermore, did not necessarily always fit in with the policies of the government of the day. As a result, two new acts were passed to try to 'bring into line' with government expectations, the objectives of the Police and of the Judiciary. In 1994 the Police and Magistrates' Court Act was passed. This Act required Police to attain a number of objectives which would be set for them by the Home Secretary. The Association of Chief Constables would still be able to set further objectives designed to run alongside of those imposed by the Home Secretary, but they would have no choice but to follow the Home Secretaries requirements. This ensured that the major objectives of the Police would from now on be Government controlled. The second of the two Acts, the 1997 Crime (Sentences) Act introduced a range of mandatory sentences for a series of crimes, including murder and domestic burglary. This had a similar effect on the Judiciary, at once removing at least a fraction of the freedom previously enjoyed by judges to set their own sentences for such crimes.

1998 - The Human Rights Act 1998

The Human Rights Act 1998 gives further legal effect in the UK to the fundamental rights and freedoms contained in the European Convention on Human Rights.

2000 - The Regulation of Investigatory Powers Act 2000 (RIPA)

This legislation was implemented as a result of the Human Rights Act, to ensure the powers are used lawfully and in a way that is compatible with the European Convention on Human Rights

A brief note on - THE HISTORY OF THE POLICE FORCE

While military organizations have existed as long as governments themselves, a standing police force is relatively modern. Medieval England's system of traveling criminal courts, or assizes used show trials and public executions to instil communities with fear and keep them under control. The first modern police were probably those in 17th century Paris, in the court of Louis XIV, although the Paris Prefecture of Police now claim to have been the world's first uniformed policemen. In 1829, after the French Revolution and Napoleon's dictatorship, a government decree created the first uniformed policemen in Paris and all other French cities, known as sergents de ville ("city sergeants"). In Britain, the Metropolitan Police Act 1829 was passed by Parliament under Home Secretary Sir Robert Peel, founding the London Metropolitan Police (refereed to as 'Peelers' or 'Bobbies' after their founder). Robert Peel first entered Parliament in 1809, became a minister a year later, and served as chief sectary for Ireland from 1812-1818 before becoming Home Secretary in 1822. In 1829 he went against his previous views and persuaded Wellington to grant Roman Catholic Emancipation, he became leader of the party in 1834 and later Prime minister, he introduced income tax for the first time in peace time and repealed the Corn Laws in 1846, however his party split which led to the end of his government.

2.2 - The Legislature

A Legislature is a type of representative assembly with the power to make and amend or repeal laws. In England the Legislature is the government (Parliament), based at Westminster. The government of the day is formed by the political party which wins a majority of seats in the house of commons, government departments such as the ministry of defence propose legislation for approval. The government consists of the prime minister, cabinet and junior ministers.

Legislatures perform their function via;
- Debate
- Committees
- Questions

The primary components of a legislature are one or more *chambers* or *houses*: assemblies that debate and vote upon bills. A legislature with only one house is called unicameral. A bicameral legislature possesses two separate chambers, usually described as an upper house and a lower house, which often differ in duties, powers, and the methods used for the selection of members. Most political systems have two bodies, or two debating chambers. For instance, in the UK we have the House of Commons and the House of Lords. The United States have the Senate and the House of Representatives; the French the *Sénat*, Much rarer are those who have trilateral legislatures.

In most parliamentary systems, the lower house is the more powerful house while the upper house is merely a chamber of advice or review. The government can act only with the consent of Parliament and this gives the House of Commons the majority power, being able to pass a notion of 'no confidence' in extreme circumstances and thus requiring the Prime Minister to resign.

As the most powerful body, it is the legislature which appoints the executive branch of government. Once this appointment is made, the legislture is in place to scrutinize or check the actions of the executive.

2.3 - The Executive

The executive in a legal system refers to the government's centre of political authority. In parliamentary systems, like Britain, the executive is the cabinet, composed of members of the legislature. The executive is chosen by a Prime Minister or a Chancellor, who holds power only while holding the confidence of the legislature. Because elections appoint a political party to govern, the leader of the party can change without the need for a Genral Election. The Head of State, Her Majesty, Queen Elizabeth the Second, is considered seperate to the executive. She lacks any formal political power but continues to symbolically enact laws and acts as a representative of the nation.

The executive branch of government is further split into the following 2 areas.

1. Politicians (members) – Prime Minister, cabinet and junior ministers. The Prime Minister is the chief executive. He or she is called upon by the Head of State to form a government, taking the proposal for government policy from the party manifesto on which basis the party were elected by the public.

2. Paid permanent officials (officers)
   These act at the consent of parliament, who can, at the house of commons pass a motion of 'no confidence' requiring the chief executive (prime minister to resign).

The ministers/civil servants will examine issues in depth and report their conclusions to the full cabinet.

The executive will initiate or propose the majority of legislation and propose the agenda of government. Executives are responsible for foreign relations, the military and police, and the bureaucracy. Ministers or other officials head a country's public offices, such as a foreign ministry or interior ministry.

The **executive** is the branch of government responsible for the day-to-day management of the state. In many countries, it is referred to simply as the ***government***, but this usage can be confusing in an international context. The executive branch contains the head of government, who is the head of this branch. Under the doctrine of the separation of powers, the executive is not supposed to make laws (role of the legislature), nor to interpret them (role of the judiciary); rather, their purpose is to enforce them. In practice however, this separation is rarely absolute. The executive is identified by the Head of Government.

In general, the legislature has a supervisory role over the actions of the executive, and may replace the Head of Government and/or individual ministers by a vote of (no) confidence or a procedure of impeachment. On the other hand, a legislature which refuses to cooperate with the executive, for example by refusing to vote a budget or otherwise starving the executive of funds, may be dissolved by the Head of State, leading to new elections.

The legislature usually delegates some legislative power to the executive, notably to issue regulations or executive orders which complete a piece of legislation with technical details or points which might change frequently (e.g. fees for government services). The executive may also have powers to issue legislation during a state of emergency.

The term 'core executive' refers to those bodies, agencies, or procedures that are responsible for co-coordinating policy and managing conflict within national government, in the UK, the core executive is made up of; the prime minister, the cabinet and cabinet committees, the treasury, the cabinet office, government departments and informal.

The Executive Branch acts by and with the advice and consent of the Legislation made by the Legislature and thus is subject to the Legislative Branch. The judiciary acts as a competent administrator to ensure compliance with the laws crafted by the Legislative Branch.

The laws which apply specifically to the executive are known as administrative law, although this should not be taken to imply that the executive is exempt from other laws such as human rights or the rules of war. The Executive Branch may be challenged in court for failure to comply with the decisions of the Legislative Branch. The idea of judicial review is that the competent administrators in the judiciary have the responsibility to review compliance with Legislation wherever there is a party claiming injury. The Legislature Branch has the responsibility to supervise the execution of its laws and the compliance of the judiciary and the Executive branch with them.

The Legislature makes decisions and the Judiciary and the Executive Branch enforce its decisions with the help of the forces funded by the Legislature to enforce its laws (e.g. police force, prison service). The Legislative Branch is responsible for providing funding for courthouses, establishing and paying the salaries of judges: The Executive Branch is responsible for getting them built and staffed as instructed. The competent administration of the judicial system is the responsibility of the justice minister, also referred to as the attorney general.

The Legislative Branch makes laws and the Executive branch executes them as instructed. In the Department of Justice the Attorney General oversees the staff responsible for taking legal action in the public interest, for example enforcing Civil Rights, Public Safety, policing corporations, prosecuting them as any other criminal and protecting the interests of those who cannot defend themselves (e.g. children or the mentally handicapped). The authority to perform these functions is delegated by the legislature to be both the executive Branch and the judiciary as required. The executive is responsible for the day-to-day management after the Legislature decides to provide the necessary infrastructure and pay the necessary salaries.

The G8 meetings are composed of representatives of each country's executive branch

Under 'Royal Prerogative' the governments have the ability to act in a number of matters without having to consult with parliament, i.e. for declarations of war. Reforms have been brought in to elements of accountability to the Royal Prerogative i.e. The Intelligence Act 1994.

Parliamentary democracies do not have distinct separation of powers. The executive (often a prime minister) and the Cabinet ("government") are drawn from the legislature (parliament). This is the principle of responsible government. However, although the legislative and executive branches are connected, in parliamentary systems there is usually a independent judiciary.

Most countries have safeguards to protect the independence of the judiciary from the executive, such as the impossibility of the executive to dismiss a judge. Similar safeguards may apply to other categories of government employees, in order to allow them to conduct their functions without undue political pressure. In return, judges and government employees may be expected not to take part in active politics themselves.

Local government may be funded through local taxes (often property taxes), through a grant from the central government or through a combination of the two. The head of the local executive of a municipality is usually known as the mayor; various terms exist for the head of the executive at other levels of local government. The local executive is usually supervised by an elected council, which is responsible for setting the rates of local taxes (where these exist, and often only to a limited extent) and for approving the budget of the local executive. The central government may also have a supervisory role, which may go as far as the power to dissolve the local government completely in exceptional cases.

As mentioned above, it is essential to consider the different roles of local (or State) government when comparing the roles of the executives in different countries: the provision of public education is an executive function whether it is provided by the local education authorities.

2.4 - Passing legislation - The Creation of New Law

Before a law can be passed and become an Act of Parliament it must first passed through the parliamentary process. There are several stages to passing an Act of Parliament. All new Acts will begin life as a proposal and this proposal could come from one of a number of sources. A proposal can be made by:

> A government department in Whitehall
>
> By a minister or civil servant
>
> Through a special commission
>
> As the result of an official enquiry

Following a report submitted by the Law Commission (The law commission is a permanent body is set up to review areas of law which might need to be changed).

The idea, or inspiration, for a piece of legislation could come from a variety of sources, including:

> political parties (often as part of their election manifesto)
>
> interest groups and research organizations
>
> consumer or trade associations
>
> other expert bodies

Sometimes a piece of legislation is introduced in order to incorporate an International Treaty or Directive from the European Union - that is to make this treaty or directive a part of United Kingdom law.

The Cabinet - that is the group of ministers chosen to represent the government on the most important areas of policy - will decide what the priorities are for each legislative session. A Legislative Session lasts about a year, usually starting around November. It is at this time, each year, when the main aims of the Governement will be announced by Her Majesty at the annual opening of Parliament. (We can see here the continued importance of the Monarch in the Parliamentary process. Indeed, the governemnt of the day, although democratically elected by the people, must still be invited to form a governement by Her Majesty the Queen - an example of the checks and balances which serve to ensure the UK remains free from the tyranny of unchecked power). There is room for only a limited number of major Bills in each each Legislative Session session. The Parliamentary timetable generally allows for between 15-20.

Due to this tight timeframe, where possible, Government departments try to think ahead, commissioning research, seeing how other countries tackle similar problems, and holding discussions with relevant European Union bodies and International Organizations in order that the best solutions can be found. However, this is not always possible and some legislation will be introduced as a reaction to recent events, either for the public interest or because the public have demanded it, or both. An example of legislation passed quickly in reaction to a series of events is the Criminal Justice (Terrorism and Conspiracy) Bill (comprising 10 clauses) passed on 2 September 1998, in one day, this was passed following the Omagh bombing. As the threat has evolved, Since Labour came to power in 1997, it has introduced five major pieces of terrorism legislation: the Terrorism Act 2000; the Anti-Terrorism, Crime and Security Act 2001; the Prevention of Terrorism Act 2005; the Terrorism Act 2006; and the Counter-Terrorism Act 2008. This is in response to the changing world we live in.

On top of this need to meet the important issues of public demand and national security, the Cabinet must also balance manifesto commitments (the promises made to the public), the demands of individual government departments, and many other demands (often private sector). Once the decision has been taken to go ahead with a particular proposal there are a number of stages before it becomes law.

The 9 stages for translating a proposal into law

1. Initial Papers (Green and White)

Once a department has decided to ask Parliament to pass legislation on a certain topic it will undergo a consultation process with interested parties. The people and organizations consulted vary according to the subject matter of the Bill. They generally include experts, trade organizations, unions, MPs and other politicians, the Treasury and other government departments and international agencies.

This formal consultation process is done in the form of papers, prior to passing a bill, there are two types of papers, green and white.

Note: ***Ministers and their civil servants are responsible for the content of Bills. Ministers determine the overall scope of a Bill, Civil Servants are responsible for working out the detail.***

The consultation document is known as a *green paper* and it states what the government wants to do and requests interested parties, such as organizations and members of the public to put their point of view forward.

A white paper is then produced setting out the proposal in more detail and the reasons for the legislation.

A White Paper is a statement of fairly definite legislative intentions, where as a Green Paper (or consultation document) is more exploratory, and is often issued when the government has not made a firm decision on what action to take, if any.

These stages are not fixed stages and there is no set rule about the order in which these stages should be conducted, although it is usual that a White Paper follows a Green one. Both may be debated in Parliament before the government proceeds any further with the proposed legislation.

Only once this stage is complete can the next step of writing the Bill begin.

2. Drafting the Bill

Before the White Paper is put to the House of Commons it is first passed to the Parliamentary Council. Parliamentary Council is made up of Solicitors/Barristers and Civil Servants. The Parliamentary Council will check the wording before drafting the Bill. They have to make the Bill as precise and clear as possible so that everyone knows exactly what is meant, and also to ensure the Bill does not contain any loopholes.

A controversial Bill may go to the Cabinet, or to one of its Committees, for further discussion, and Bills are increasingly being published in draft form to allow more time for public scrutiny and consultation.

When the Bill has been drafted, agreed by Ministers, and consulted upon, it is ready to be introduced into Parliament for its first reading.

Note: ***There are different types of Bills; public Bills, private Bills or private members Bills. Most Bills are public - these will affect the whole country. Private Bills affect only a local area or institution, for example a company. Private members Bills are public Bills proposed by back benchers rather than Ministers.***

3. **First Reading**

Once the paper has been drafted it goes to Parliament for the first reading. This is merely an announcement of the intentions of the Bill - there is no debate at this stage. After this stage the Bill is printed and put forward for the Second Reading.

Although there is no debate, and it is not until the Second Reading, that debate on the Bill will commence, the Bill presented to Parliament for its first reading is not a 'rough draft'. It is a refined version - in effect, the closest to the Bill the Governement hopes to have passed by Parliament.

Note: *Government Bills can be introduced in either the House of Commons or the House of Lords. Most controversial Bills, and all those concerned with finance, start their life in the Commons. This account of the legislative procedure assumes a Bill has been introduced in the Commons.*

4. **Second Reading**

After the Bill has been read to the House for a second time, a debate is held. This debate is general and wide-ranging. Members of the House will discuss the principles and scope of the Bill. The length of a debate can range from a few hours to many days although on average a Bill is usually debated for a full Parliamentary day (approx. 6 hours). Particularly complex or controversial propsals can extend the debate and the House will not allow an unpopular measure to pass simply in order to get home early.

At the Second Reading, Ministers and their Opposition counterparts make the opening and closing speeches, whilst the rest of the debate will consist of speeches by backbench MPs from each side of the House, MPs with a special interest in the subject, and MPs whose constituencies are most affected by the Bill.

If the Bill is at all controversial, the debate concludes with a Division, or vote. As the Bill is no more than halfway to being passed at this stage, it is very rare for a Government Bill to be defeated at second reading. This is due to the fact that such a Bill will almost certainly represent government policy, and the government's MPs, the majority of the House, are relied on to support it. However, a controversial Bill can still divide the House significantly, and although the Bill may pass the Second Reading, it might only be so that significant changes can be made to it before the third and final reading.

Following the Second Reading, the Bill now proceeds to the Committee Stage for approval by the cabinet committee.

5. **Committee Stage**

A detailed examination is then carried out of the Bill. This is normally carried out by a specially-appointed standing committee of 18 to 25 MPs, selected in line with party strengths in the Commons. The Minister responsible for the Bill and his or her opposition counterparts are always members, and occasionally junior ministers as well. There are two Whips (MPs who ensure their colleagues vote with the party leadership), one each from the government and opposition parties. The remaining members are backbenchers from each side of the House, often with special expertise or interest in the subject concerned. Amendments can be made at this stage as long as it doesn't affect the principals of the Bill. The committee can be made up of a small number of MPs, the whole house of lords or a select committee.

This stage can take anything from a single meeting to several months. On a major Government Bill the standing committee will meet at least ten or twelve times over about six weeks. A senior backbencher - not necessarily from the ruling party - chairs the committee and remains impartial during the discussions. For lengthy Bills, two backbenchers (one from each side of the House) will take this role.

What does the committee do?

The job of a standing committee is to discuss and approve every clause of the Bill. It does not debate its overall scope and purpose. Discussion is usually based on amendments to individual clauses. Any member of the committee may propose an amendment. The Opposition, or backbenchers from either side of the House, may want to alter a specific part of the Bill; the government may respond to improvements suggested during the second reading debate, or to arguments submitted by outside organizations or interest groups, and decide to make changes itself.

Since MP's usually vote with their parties, the government's built-in majority ensures that usually only those amendments acceptable to it are passed. On the whole, these consist of second thoughts by the government, technical amendments such as improvements to the wording, and minor concessions on detail. Significant changes can only be made if opposition members combine with backbenchers who disagree with their government.

Who else can take part?

Sometimes, the committee stage is taken 'on the floor' in a 'Committee of the Whole House', enabling every MP to take part in the discussion. This time-consuming procedure is usually only used for some parts of the annual Finance Bill and for Bills dealing with major constitutional questions. A Bill that needs to be passed urgently will be sent to a Committee of the Whole House, to avoid spending time setting up a standing committee. It is possible to split a Bill, so that some provisions are dealt with in Committee of the Whole House, with the remainder going to a standing committee.

Once the Bill has passed through this rigorous process, it can move on to the report stage, the House, are often appointed to chair the committee.

6. Report Stage

This stage (also known as 'the Consideration') is a detailed examination of the Bill as amended in committee. This time, all MPs can take part in the discussion. Fresh amendments and clauses are discussed and voted on. Many of these are introduced by the government in response to commitments made during the committee stage. Amendments already rejected in committee are not normally discussed again. The report stage can last from a few minutes to several days.

Basically this is where changes to the proposed bill are considered by the full house of commons and either approved or rejected.

The Bill then goes back to the floor of the House of Commons for the Third Reading.

7. Third Reading

This is a final debate on the overall content of the bill as amended in the house of commons. It is often very short and frequently held immediately after the report stage. If it passes this stage it goes through the whole process again in the House of Lords.

8. **The House of Lords**

In the House of Lords, discussion proceeds on broadly similar lines. A formal first reading is followed by a major general debate at second reading. Then come detailed discussions with amendments at the committee and report stages, followed by a concluding debate at the third reading.

But there are a number of important procedural differences between the two Houses. For example the committee stage in the Lords almost always takes place on the floor of the House, not in a standing committee, so any Peer may speak or suggest amendments.

If a Bill passes through the House of Lords unchanged, it is immediately submitted for Royal Assent. But, if any amendments have been made, the Bill returns to the Commons, which then debates each Lords amendment. The Commons can accept the amendment, replace it with another amendment of its own, or reject it. If it takes any of the last three options, the Bill returns to the Lords once again, accompanied by a statement of 'reasons' for the Commons action.

At this stage the Lords generally accepts the situation (so acknowledging the pre-eminence of the Commons as determined in the Parliamentary Act of 1911). This is not always the case though, and if the Lords insist on any of its amendments the Bill will continue to be passed between the two Houses until agreement is reached. If the Houses ultimately fail to agree, the Bill falls. This has only happened on a very few occasions since 1945.

There are two important restrictions on the legislative power of the Lords. First, it may not delay a Bill for more than one Parliamentary session. A Bill lost in the Lords in one session and passed by the Commons the following session will automatically receive Royal Assent even if the Lords opposes it the second time around. Second, the Lords does not consider so-called 'money Bills', i.e. Bills dealing with taxation or that vote money to the government. These pass formally through the Lords without discussion. Both these restrictions assert the pre-eminence of the democratically elected Commons over the unelected Lords.

All of the stages must be completed in one parliamentary session or it will need to start from stage one all over again.

Once the Bill has cleared the Lords, it is sent to Buckingham Palace for Royal Assent.

9. **Royal Assent**

As one of the three branches of Parliament, the Sovereign formally signifies assent to the Bill, which now becomes an Act and part of the law of the land. The words used are the Norman French 'La Reyne le veult' ('The Queen wishes it').

As soon as the Queen has given the Royal Assent, the Bill becomes an Act of Parliament. All that remains is for the Act to be implemented.

2.5 - Implementing the Law

The timescale for when an Act comes into force depends on its wording. In some cases, its provisions apply immediately. In others, a starting-date is laid down in the Act (or more than one if different parts of the Act come into force at different times). In other cases, a Commencement Order must be made to activate the Act, or certain parts of it.

Once the Act has been implemented it is the law of the land. The lengthy and thorough process of legislation has finally come to its conclusion.

Some legislation, once passed, is automatically to be enforced by the Police and Local Authority. Other legislation, or parts of it need to be adopted by the Local Authority before they can use the legislation/carry out enforcement action.

Any Act can be amended, superseded by another Act, or repealed.

2.6 Judicial Review

"Judicial review represents the means by which the courts control the exercise of governmental power. Government departments, local authorities, tribunals, state agencies and agencies exercising powers which are governmental in nature, must exercise their powers in a lawful manner. Judicial review has developed to ensure that public bodies which exercise law making power or adjudicatory powers are kept within the confines of the power conferred. Judicial review is concerned with the legality of the decision made, not with the merits of the particular decision." (Barnett 2000 p. 1007)

In other words, Judicial review is the means by which the acts of public bodies are 'kept in check' by the courts to ensure that they are lawful.

The process of judicial review can involve assessing Acts of Parliament passed by the legislature to ensure they are compatible with the countries constitution. But the UK is different to many countries in that it does not have a written code of conduct. because of 'parliamentary sovereignty' (as asserted by the Parliamentary Act 1911), Acts of the Parliament of the UK cannot be overturned, even by judicial review. For this reason, Judicial Review has a more limited scope in the UK when applied to Acts of Parliament. However, as well as scrutinizing Acts of Parliament, Judicial Review will also scrutinize actions and decisions taken by the legislature, executive or other tiers of government, for instance, a decision by the local council can be considered at Judicial Review.

An application for judicial review needs to be based upon one or more of the recognised 'grounds' for review. :
In Council of Civil Service Unions v Minister for the Civil Service [1985] AC 374, Lord Diplock summarized the grounds for reversing an administrative decision by way of judicial review as follows:

- Illegality
- Irrationality (Unreasonableness)
- Procedural impropriety

The first two grounds are known as substantive grounds of judicial review because they relate to the substance of the disputed decision. Procedural impropriety is a procedural ground because it is aimed at the decision-making procedure rather than the content of the decision itself. The three grounds are mere indications: the same set of facts may give rise to two or all three grounds for judicial review.

1. Procedure
2. Standing
3. Public Body
4. Illegality
5. Ultra Vires
6. Improper purpose
7. Irrelevant consideration
8. Discretion
9. Irrationality
   a) Wednesbury
   b) Proportionality (derived from European Law)
10. Legitimate expectations
11. Procedural impropriety
    i. Fair hearing
    ii. Bias

Procedure

This refers to any legal procedures which were supposed to be followed by the public body and were not e.g. consultations / time period of decision making etc.

Standing

This refers to the position of the applicant i.e. that is s/he has 'sufficient interest' in the decision / action made by the public body. The test of 'sufficient interest' has been defined by the courts and is not always consistent. Generally, the test is fairly wide. For example, in 1995 the 'World Development Movement' (a political organisation) was granted 'standing' to a case judicially reviewing the actions of the British Government in relation to its investment in the Pergau Dam project in Malaysia. The test of standing is stricter for cases involving the Human Rights Act 1998 that for other cases.

Public Body

This test is to ensure that the action / decision complained about has been made by a 'public body'. The Court will look at the 'source' of the body's powers and the functions which it carries-out to decide if the body is a public body. It should be noted that definitions under European Union law are different to those under UK law. Generally in the UK this will include central and local government, public companies, and regulatory bodies.

Illegality

There are 4 broad classifications of 'illegality':

a) ultra vires – this is where the public body has taken / not taken an action / made a decision which is outside its legal powers. An example is provided in *R v Richmond Upon Thames Council ex parte McCarthy and Stone Ltd (1992).* Here the local planning authority introduced a scheme of charging £25 for some informal consultation between corporation officers and property developers. The Court held that this was unlawful as the charge was not authorised by statute and was not incidental to the planning function.

Another example is *Hazell v Hammersmith & Fulham Council (1992)* where the Council entered into 'interest rate swaps' as part of its financial investments activity. The Court held that such speculative investment was outside the Council's legal borrowing powers.

b) improper purpose – this is where the public body has taken an action / made a decision for a purpose other than that required by statute. In some cases this is relatively clear to ascertain as the purpose is explicitly specified in statute; in others statute may not specify the legal purpose and the courts are able to infer one. In the latter case, the courts will presume that statute did not have any purpose 'in mind' which would interfere with citizens fundamental / human rights. At other times, there may be mixed purposes to the public body's actions / decisions and the courts will decide which was the main purpose to see if this corresponds with the 'proper purpose' under statute. Some cases will illustrate these situations:

R v Ealing LBC, ex parte Times (1986) – The statutory requirement was for Ealing LBC to provide a comprehensive and efficient library service. Ealing LBC had taken the decision not to stock 'The Times' or 'The Sun' newspapers in its library in support of the print workers who were on strike against the owner of these papers (Murdock). The court held that this was an improper purpose and the purpose of the statute was clear.

R v Somerset CC, ex parte Fewings (1995) – The statutory requirement under the Local Government Act 1992 was for Somerset CC to manage its land for the development of the area. Somerset CC was held to have acted unlawfully when it banned stag hunting from its land. The court found that this was for an improper purpose and not the purpose of statute, which was clear.

Padfield v MAFF (1968) – This case concerned the Milk Marketing Scheme which had established both a Board to inform producers of milk how much they could charge, and a Commission to investigate complaints by any producers that prices had been set too low by the Board. The Secretary of State reserved the power to decide whether complaints by producers were to be investigated by a committee of investigation. A complaint by a group of farmers was not investigated, based on a decision by the Secretary of State. Whilst there was no stated 'purpose' in statute as regards the Secretary of State's powers, the court inferred that his powers were for the purpose of 'ensuring complaints are investigated' and the Secretary of State was therefore acting illegally by not exercising his powers for their proper purpose.

Congreve v Home Office (1976) – The Television Act required all television users to have television licences. When the Government decided to increase the licence fee from £12 to £18, various sections of the media encouraged people to buy their licences in advance of the price increase. In response, the Home Secretary revoked all television licences so that the increased fee would have to be paid. The courts found that the Home Secretary had been acting for an improper purpose as the purpose of the licence fee was clearly not to raise taxes, which had been the motivation behind the Home Secretary's actions.

Raymond v Honey (1983) - The Home Secretary made a Regulation, under the Prison Act, which provide prison governors with the power to prevent mail being sent outside of the prison in certain circumstances. Mr Raymond's letters to his lawyers were stopped as a result. The Court held that statute would never have intended to interfere with Mr Honey's fundamental (human) rights and ruled that the Home Secretary's action had been an illegal one for this reason.

Irrelevant Consideration

This is either where the public body has failed to take account of a relevant consideration or has taken into account an irrelevant consideration. The Courts are able to decide what is relevant and what is not. An example case is provided:

> *Tower Hamlets ex parte Chetnick (1998)* – The Chetnick company had been incorrectly charged rates for one year and were entitled to a refund. However, Tower Hamlets decided not the pay the refund for two reasons: firstly that the Chetnick company had enough money to pay and; secondly because the authority believed that the Chetnick company should have ensured it had better legal representation. The Court held that these were irrelevant considerations and that the refusal to refund was illegal.

An example of how an irrelevant consideration could be taken into account under the Licensing Act 2003 would be if a Licensing Authority made a decision / took an action based upon consideration of 'public health', which is not one of the four 'licensing objectives' contained in the Licensing Act 2003.

> *More likely is that Licensing Authorities may be open to accusations of not having taken into account 'relevant considerations' especially with regard to the policy statement consultation process. To guard against such accusations Licensing Authorities are advised to detail their consultation process carefully, recording all representations and how they were taken into account. It may also be that Licensing Authorities are accused by some of not having taking into account the Statutory Guidance provided by Government. It is therefore advised that Licensing Authorities detail where they have / seem to have departed from Statutory Guidance and set-out clearly there reasons for this. It should be noted that the Draft Statutory Guidance itself states: "…so long as the Guidance has been properly and carefully understood and considered, licensing authorities may depart from it if they have reason to do so. When doing so, licensing authorities will need to give full reasons for their actions."(2.3).*

Discretion

Where a public body has been granted some statutory discretion, the general rule is that the public body must not delegate these powers. Some example cases are provided:

> *Barnard v National Dock Labour Board (1953)* – The local authority was found by the Court to have illegally delegated its disciplinary powers to the Port Manager (who had sacked a number of dockers who had taken part in industrial action).

> *Lavender and Sons v Minister of Housing (1970)* – The legal power to grant planning permission resided with the Minister of Housing, however, the latter had stated that he would not agree to any planning permissions unless the Minister of Agriculture consented. The Court found that this was an illegal abdication of statutory power by the Ministry of Housing.

Key for any public body which makes its decision based upon a 'policy' is that the policy must not be so rigid as to mean that the public body is not using its statutory discretion. **The case where the Court first set-out its considerations on this matter is *Ex parte Kynoch (1919).* A more recent example cases follows:**

> *A-G ex rel Tulley v Wandsworth LBC (1981)* – The Council decided that it would not house mothers with children, as a result of what the Council believed was an abuse of its housing policies. The Court held, however, that this 'blanket' rule was unlawful and that each case needed to be decided on its merits.

> *R v Secretary of State ex parte Brent LBC (1983)* – The Secretary of State made a policy that he would automatically cut the Government's rate support grant to Councils if they overspent. The Court held that this was too strict a policy and that each Council's case should have been decided on its own merits.

It should be noted that in <u>R (on the application of Chorion plc) v Westminster City Council (2002)</u> the Court held that a 'strong presumption' was possible as part of the Authority's policy.

Irrationality

It can be said that there are two types of 'irrationality' as regards the actions / decision of public bodies being viewed by the Courts as unlawful acts. These are referred to as 'Wednesbury unreasonableness' and 'proportionality'.

a) Wednesbury unreasonableness (or 'perversity') – this type of 'irrationality' derives from <u>Association Provincial Picture Houses Ltd v Wednesbury Corporation (1948)</u>. Here the Court held that the key test as to whether the public body had acted 'illegally' was whether it had acted, or reached a decision, in a manner *"so unreasonable that no reasonable authority could have come to it"*. This test is quite a strict one and a number of judges have exemplified this in their definitions: Lord Greene in <u>Wednesbury</u>: *"so absurd that no sensible person could ever dream that it lay within the powers of the authority"* and Lord Diplock: *"...so outrageous in its defiance of logic or of accepted moral standards that no sensible person who had applied his mind to the question to be decided could have arrived at it."* (in <u>Council of Civil Service Unions v Minister for the Civil Service (1984).</u>

Further development of this doctrine can be seen in <u>Smith & Grady v UK (1999)</u> where Sir Thomas Bingham, the Master of the Rolls in the Court of Appeal commented *"the court may not interfere with the exercise of an administrative discretion on substantive grounds save where the court is satisfied that the decision is unreasonable in the sense that it is beyond the range of responses open to a reasonable decision-maker. But in judging whether the decision-maker has exceeded this margin of appreciation the human rights context is important. The more substantial the interference with human rights, the more the court will require by way of justification before it is satisfied that the decision is reasonable in the sense outlined above."*

b) Proportionality – Whilst the Wednesbury test is a strict one the Courts also now utilise a test favoured by European law (including the European Court of Human Rights) which involves a consideration of 'proportionality' i.e. are the means by which the public body used to secure its aim, any more than strictly necessary? This is generally used by the courts where there are questions of human rights involved in the case. Some example cases follow:

> *R (Daly) v Secretary of State for the Home Department (2001)* – In this case the House of Lords allowed an appeal concerning a prisoner's rights to confidentiality and respect for his/her legal correspondence. It was held that the Secretary of State had exceeded his powers to make rules regarding prisons by instituting a blanket rule that all legal correspondence of prisoners could be inspected by staff, and without the prisoner's presence. This was held to be an excessive intrusion, not justified by the statutory power the Secretary of State had to make rules for the discipline and control of prisoners i.e. it was a rule disproportionate to the aim of the relevant legislation (Section 47(1) of the Prison Act 1952).

> *Smith & Grady v UK (1999)* – In this case, which was eventually referred to the European Court of Human Rights in Strasbourg, the two applicants had been dismissed from the Royal Air Force on the basis of their homosexuality. Their dismissals were a result of Ministry of Defence policy against the membership of homosexuals in the armed forces. In the Court of Appeal, The Master of the Rolls, Sir Thomas Bingham, stated that the action of investigating a person's sexuality and consequently dismissing him/her from his/her employment was likely to contravene that person's human rights (see Articles 8 and 9) of the European Convention on Human Rights and Fundamental Freedoms. However, it may be that the policy against homosexuals in the armed forces was a proportionate response to the legitimate aim pursued by the Ministry of Defence which constituted a 'pressing social need'. However, he held that these were questions for the European Court of Human Rights, and not the Court of Appeal.

> *R v Home Secretary ex parte Brind (1991)* – In this case the House of Lords would not accept the concept of proportionality as the Human Rights Act 1998 had not yet incorporated the European Convention on Human Rights and Fundamental Freedoms into domestic law.

However, Lord Ackner's query as to whether the Secretary of State had "used a sledgehammer to crack a nut" by banning the broadcasting of statements by prescribed Northern Irish organisations, is exemplary of the type of reasoning behind the 'proportionality' test.

R v Barnsley Metropolitan Borough Council ex parte Hook (1976) – This case, again, was pre Human Rights Act 1998, however 'proportionality' type reasoning was utilised. Here, a market stall holder had his licence revoked for urinating in public. Lord Denning MR had the decision quashed, partly on the grounds that the loss of his licence was disproportionate to the offence.

In this regard Licensing Authorities should be careful not to promise licence applicants / objectors anything which cannot be delivered upon; this is perhaps particularly important for Licensing Committee members to bear in mind.

Legitimate Expectations

This is generally where an individual has applied to the Government for some 'benefit' on the basis of previous Government policy, and where the Government has then changed its policy, and thus refused the application. In some situations the applicant is said to have had a 'legitimate expectation' to a hearing at the least. The case law is not particularly consistent in this area but two cases provide examples of the general notion:

R v North East Devon HA ex parte Coughlan (1999) – Ms Coughlan was very badly injured in a road traffic accident and needed 24 hour attendance. The Health Authority had persuaded her to go into a residential home based upon assurances that it would be a home for the rest of her life. Twelve months later the Authority wanted to move Ms Coughlan but the Court stated that this would be an 'illegal' act as the citizen was entitled to her 'legitimate expectations'.

A-G v Hg Yuen Shiu (1983) – The Attorney General of Hong Kong had promised a number of individuals that each of them would be consulted by an immigration official before being deported. As no consultation by such an official took place the Court held that the Attorney General had acted illegally and that the individuals were entitled to their legitimate (procedural) expectations.

Procedural Impropriety

This is based upon Constitutional Law i.e. domestic case law and the European Convention on Human Rights and Fundamental Freedoms incorporated into UK law via the Human Rights Act 1998. It occurs where either a fair hearing has not taken place or where there is an appearance of bias.

a) Fair hearing – Some cases explain this well:

Cooper v Wandsworth Board of Works (1863) – A statute prohibited any building being erected without giving seven days notice to the Board of Works. Mr Cooper started putting up a house without giving notice and thus, the Board demolished the building. Whilst the Board was within its statutory powers in carrying-out the demolition, the Court held that the individual did have a right to a 'fair hearing' before the decision was taken.

Ridge v Baldwin (1964) – A Police Constable was dismissed without having been given a hearing by his superiors. This was held by the Court to have been 'illegal' as he was entitled to a fair hearing before any decision was made.

For a 'hearing' to be 'fair' a number of conditions must be satisfied including the right for the individual to know the opposing case; generally the right to call witnesses; the ability to question witnesses; the right to legal representation; and generally the right to be given reasons for any decision made. Sometimes a 'written' hearing will suffice and no 'oral' hearing is required.

Licensing Committees will therefore need to follow clear procedures to ensure hearings take place and are / seen to be fair.

b) Bias – Generally the rule is that there need be no proof of actual or potential bias for there to be 'procedural impropriety'. It is sufficient that there is an 'appearance' of bias. This is demonstrated in the case of *R v Bow Street Magistrates ex parte Pinochet (No 2) (1999)* where Lord Hoffman disqualified himself as a judge in the case of the extradition of General Pinochet as Lord Hoffman had connections with Amnesty International, one of the parties to the case. However, it should be noted that in *Dallaglio (1994)* Lord Bingham suggested that the test was not based upon an 'appearance' of bias but only if there is *actual* bias. In this case the coroner had said that some of the relatives / parents of the people who died in the Marchoness sinking were 'unhinged'. However, Lord Bingham said as there would be no real/actual bias then the coroner could continue with the case.

'Bias' also includes the situation where it is felt that the decision-maker has pre-judged the case based upon his/her own prejudices – for discussion of this see *Locabail UK v Bayfield Properties (2000)*.

Wednesbury Unreasonableness; Associated Picture houses – v- Wednesbury Corporation (1948) 1 KB 223; established that decisions must be relevant and fair and supported by reason.;
1. Take into account all relevant factors
2. Ignore irrelevant factors
3. Make a rational balanced decision based on the evidence.

Legitimate Expectation;
A promise that you will do something before you make a decision;
Lord Justice Simon Brown said that it can mean;
1. A substantive right;
2. An expectation that a right or benefit will not be withdrawn unless a fair procedure is followed;
3. An expectation that a particular procedure which has been followed in the past, or has been promised will continue to be followed and
4. A fair procedure itself.

Rules Of Natural Justice;
1. The other party must be informed of the substance of the objection or allegation being made against them.
2. All parties must be given a chance to put their case forward.
3. A person who has an interest in the matter must be disqualified from considering it

The Principal of Proportionality – restrictions on individual rights must be proportionate to the legitimate aim they pursue, i.e. must not go beyond what is strictly necessary to achieve that purpose.

Occasionally a statute indicates that - A person must have knowingly committed an offence before a prosecution can succeeded.

Interestingly, almost all of the above principles will remain important and relevant considerations to make later, when deciding on how to proceed with individual cases. It can be seen then, how the law works in a similar manner at different scales, the same principals being applied at each stage of creation, enforcement, and prosecution.

Chapter 3 - The Modern Legal (Judicial) System

So we have seen how the basic structure of the law has evolved over time and how law is made. But how does the current legal system operate on a day-to day basis? And what, in all of this, should you expect your role as an enforcement officer to be?

Before we can look at how we enforce the law and carry out investigations to identify breaches of it, we must firstly understand the detail of the legal framework we are working within. Only then can we understand our duties and carry them out effectively...

Wikipedia, the online encyclopedia defines law as follows;

"Law is a system of rules, usually enforced through a set of institutions. It shapes politics, economics and society in numerous ways." – *The Law Society.*

Law manifests itself throughout the community in many more ways, and serves as the foremost social mediator of relations between people. "The rule of law", wrote the ancient Greek philosopher Aristotle in 350 BC, "is better than the rule of any individual."

So taking the defintion listed above we can see that law is enforced through a set of institutions. But what law, *precisely*, are we talking about...?

Well, unlike other European countries, the law in England and Wales has not been set down in one complete set of written codes. Instead, as seen in Chapter 2, it is drawn from a variety of different sources, all of which bring their own influence to the decision making process. It can therefore be said that the UK has a truly flexible constitution - one that can always be altered further and by normal law making processes. Significantly, the UK system can be altered slowly, over time, bit by bit as and where necessary.

We can see from the briefest of timelines in Chapter 2 that the law was first collated and distributed as a series of 'common laws' throughout the land. Afterwards, as parliament grew in importance, so laws came to be passed as 'statutes'. Both of these law making processes continue to run alongside of one another until the present day. But what exatly is the difference?

3.1 - Sources of Contempory Law

In English law as well as the growing body of European Community Law, there are two main sources of law, statute and common law. The majority of our law is derived from common law rather than statute. In many cases, law contained in statues was originally made by precedents derived from the application of common law.

Note - Common Law is sometimes referred to as Case Law

A. Statute Law

A statute is the ultimate source of law. Created by an Act of Parliament (ref: Chapter 2), a statute will over-rule any other rules of law which conflict with it, including earlier statutes. Furthermore, statutes remain in force indefinitely until they are repealed. A statute loses none of its authority even if it remains unused for many years. A popular example of this is the case R v Duncan (1944). Here, a defendant was convicted of fortune telling under the Witch Craft Act 1735, even though the statute had long since fallen into disuse. Similarly, an old Act will still retain all of its original force in law, an example being the legislation used to regulate Hackney Carriages. The Town Police Clauses Act was passed in 1847, yet is used widely even today.

A further point of note is that Judges may not consider the validity of statutes, and they must apply them. In British Railways Board v Pickin, a gentleman whose land had been compulsory purchased under the British Railways Act 1968, Mr Pickin tried to argue that the statute was invalid on the grounds that parliament had been fraudulently mislead in passing it. The House of Lords subsequently ruled in what became a **landmark** ruling that such an argument was invalid and should no longer be considered in any court.

Statute law is often composed of a number of pieces of law collected together and presented as a new Act. Often, a new act will be compsed primarily of precendents - that is, previous case law. This usually happens when such case law has become so complicated and extensive that it is deemed necessary to reduce the decisions and precents to their companent parts - an easily readable and understandable version of all the precedents laid down so far. This is often the case if a particular set of offences are all linked by similar cause, i.e. The Sale of Goods Act 1979 was made by collecting together the precedents of countless nineteenth century judges. and when Parliament passed the original Sale of Good Act, in 1893, it was designed to codify all the existing precedents.

However, long before we reach this stage (and often this amalgamation never occurs) precedents will instead be applied as common law...

B. Common Law (Case Law)

1. As previously discussed, Common Law, often referred to as precedent or case law, relies on the judgement of past cases. In the past most of the legislation was made this way. It refers to law and the corresponding legal system developed through decisions of courts and similar tribunals, rather than through legislative statutes or executive action. The majority of criminal law is made in this way, whereas a lot of business law is derived from statute.

The common law has been, and is **continuously**, created and refined by judges. A decision in the case currently pending depends on decisions in previous cases and affects the law to be applied in future cases. This means that a court should consider what happened in a previous similar case. When there is no authoritative statement of the law, judges have the authority and duty to make law by creating precedent.

In common law systems this type of precedent is granted more or less weight in the deliberations of a court according to two main factors.

1. Most important is whether the precedent is "on point," that is, does it deal with a circumstance identical or very similar to the circumstance in the instant case?

2. When and where was the precedent decided? A recent decision in the same jurisdiction as the instant case will be given great weight. Next in descending order would be recent precedent in jurisdictions whose law is the same as local law. Least weight would be given to precedent that stems from dissimilar circumstances, older cases that have since been contradicted, or cases in jurisdictions that have dissimilar law.

This body of precedent, or common law, binds future decisions. In future cases, when parties disagree on what the law is, a court applying common law will look to the past decisions of any relevant courts. If a similar dispute has been resolved in the past, the court is bound to follow the reasoning used in the prior decision. This principle is known as *stare decisis*. Under the doctrine of *stare decisis*, (The full legal term is "stare decisis et quieta non movere", which is Latin meaning "stand by decisions and do not move that which is still"), a lower court must honor findings of law made by a higher court **providing that** the higher court is within the appeals path of cases the lower court hears.

However, if the court finds that the current dispute is fundamentally distinct from all previous cases (as determined by the 2 factors above), it will decide the case instead as a "matter of first impression." Thereafter, this new decision becomes precedent, the decision again binding future courts under the principle of *stare decisis*.

When a precedent establishes an important legal principle, or represents new or changed law on a particular issue, that precedent is often known as a **landmark** decision.

The decisions of a court are binding only in a particular jurisdiction, and even within a given jurisdiction, some courts have more power than others. Interactions between common law, constitutional law, statutory law and regulatory law also give rise to considerable complexity when applying, or attempting to apply, the law in a fair and even manner. It is for this reason the principle of *stare decisis* is so important, providing the framework whereby all courts should, theoretically, reach similar results when hearing cases involving similar factors. This consistent application of principals lies at the heart of all common law systems.

In most jurisdictions, decisions by appellate courts are binding on lower courts in the same jurisdiction and on future decisions of the same appellate court, but decisions of non-appellate courts are only non-binding persuasive authority.

Common law legal systems are in widespread use, particularly in those nations which trace their legal heritage to Britain. This includes most of the United States of America, Canada, Australia, New Zealand and other former colonies of the British Empire. This common/case law derived from judicial decisions, in the United States, is also referred to as presidential law because it operates by application of precedent.

C. Comparison

The common law is far less rigid than statutory law. Common law courts are not absolutely bound by precedent, but can (when extraordinarily good reason is shown) reinterpret and revise the law, without legislative intervention, to adapt to new trends in political, legal and social philosophy. As has been demonstrated, Common Law evolves through a series of gradual steps - each step gradually working out all the details so that, over a decade or more, the law can change substantially but without a sharp about turn. It is this gradual change that helps to prevent excessively disruptive effects. In contrast, the legislative process is very difficult to get started: legislatures do not act until a situation is totally intolerable. Because of this, legislative changes tend to be large, jarring and disruptive (either positively or negatively).

In common law jurisdictions, legislatures operate under the assumption that statutes will be interpreted against the backdrop of the pre-existing common law case law and custom, and so may leave a number of things unsaid. For example, in most U.S. states, the criminal statutes are primarily codification of pre-existing common law. (Codification is the process of enacting a statute that collects and restates pre-existing law in a single document - when that pre-existing law is common law, the common law remains relevant to the interpretation of these statutes.) In reliance on this assumption, modern statutes often leave a number of terms and fine distinctions unstated -- for example, a statute might be very brief, leaving the precise definition of terms unstated, under the assumption that these fine distinctions will be inherited from pre-existing common law. For this reason, even today American law schools teach the common law of crime as practiced in England in 1789, because the backdrop of centuries-old English common law is necessary to interpret and fully understand the literal words of the modern criminal statute.

Where a tort is rooted in common law, then all traditionally recognized damages for that tort may be sued for, whether or not there is mention of those damages in the current statutory law. For instance, a person who sustains bodily injury through the negligence of another may sue for medical costs, pain, suffering, loss of earnings or earning capacity, mental and/or emotional distress, loss of quality of life, disfigurement and more. These damages need not be set forth in statute as they already exist in the tradition of common law. However, without a wrongful death statute, most of them are extinguished upon death.

3.2 - Judicial interpretation

It is not only Common Law that is open to interpretation, although it is only from Common Law that precedent can be decided. All laws are open to interpretation depending on the evidence produced and this means judges are involved in law making as the law will be dependant on the way they interpret it. This is known as judicial activism. Judges also have security of tenure and are protected by the fact that an address of the house of parliament and the queen has to be made before they can be sacked, this is to protect them from political pressures to act in a certain way, also as Judges aren't elected and are in a way isolated from direct accountability, there are measures put in place to limit their discretionary powers to a more acceptable level, and therefore protect peoples rights, these are in the way of; political intervention (legislation sets out mandatory sentences), juries off set the political bias, furthermore decisions can be appealed and set aside via revisions to the law or amendments to the constitution.

Law is open to interpretation and the way that legislation is interpreted in the courts affects future decisions.

To interpret a law a judge must think logically of the purpose of that piece of legislation. What did parliament intend when they passed the legislation and what outcome would be reasonably fair?

Some judges make take the literal approach, giving words in a statute their ordinary, literal meaning, which can be dangerous when some statutes are badly worded and the literal approach may mean interpreting legislation in a way that it was not meant to be interpreted, where as other judges may take the purposive approach, meaning that they will give the words in statute their ordinary, literal meaning as far as possible, but only to the extent that this would not produce absurd reports. Another rule of statutory interpretation is the *mischief rule* this says that any judge can take into account what 'mischief' the statute set out to remedy, for example, in Smith v Hughes, the lord chief justice, Lord Parker, had to consider whether prostitutes who were soliciting from balconies and from behind windows were soliciting 'in the street' within the meaning of section 1 of the street offenders act 1959. Using the *mischief rule,* he had little difficulty in deciding that they were. The prostitutes were not literally soliciting 'in the street', but their behaviour was just the kind which the Act sought to prevent.
The *ejusdem generic rule* (of the same kind rule) means the general words which follow specific words must be given the same type of meaning as the specific words, for example, the Betting Act 1853, prohibited betting in any 'house, office, room or other place'. In *Powell v Kempton Racecourse Company,* the court held that the Act did not apply to a racecourse. The specific words 'house, office, room' were all indoor places, and so the general words 'or other place' had to be interpreted as applying only to indoor places.
The rule *expression unius est exclusion alterius* (to express one thing is to exclude another) means that if there is a list of specicifc words, not followed by any general words, then the statute only applies to

the specific wods mentioned, for example in, *R v Inhabitants of Sedgeley,* a statute that raises taxes on 'lands, houses, tithes and coalmines' did not apply to other types of mines.

Until recently, judges interpreting statues, were not allowed to consider the speeches which MPs made when the statute was being debated. However, in *Pepper v Hart (1993),* a landmark decision, the House of Lords held that *Hansard* could be consulted if this was the only way to solve ambiguity.

The record of events and public statements of legislators that explain the reasons for the law and its expected meaning are called "legislative history". Often, this will include formal speeches or writings made by the bill's sponsors and chief critics. Courts often refer to legislative history in interpreting legislation, in order to discern "legislative intent" - or what legislators meant for the law to mean.

The doctrine of Judicial precedent holds that the judges in lower courts are absolutely bound to follow decisions previously made in higher courts. The highest level of all is the House of Lords, they are not bound by any previous presidents, although they do tend to follow their own previous decisions unless there is any reason not to. The judges also hear appeals from the commonwealth countries, this is known as the Privy council, technically these privy council decisions are not binding on English courts, although they due usually tend to be regarded as having the same authority as the House of Lords decisions. The courts of appeal is the next rung down the ladder and as well as decisions being binding on lower courts they are binding on future court of appeal judges. The there is the High Court, they are bound by decisions by the House of Lords and the Court of Appeal. If there is only one judge sitting in a High Court case, the Judge's decision is not binding on other high court judges, however, in a Divisional Court of the High Court more than one judge sits, therefore the decision of the Divisional Courts are binding on other High Court judges. However such cases can never be binding if there is a more recent statute or higher ranking precedent (such as an EC article), to the contrary.

The binding part of the case – Most cases are lengthy and therefore it is the Lawyer's task to sort out the important parts of the case, known as the *ratio decidendi (the reason for the decision* - often abbreviated to *Ratio),* this is the part that is binding on other judges, the reason for the decision will be looked at by other judges in the future when they are deciding if its relevant to apply to their case. Statements of law which did not form the basis of the decision, are known as *obiter dicta* (other things said), they are not binding like a president but if judges in House of Lords all express the same *obiter* then a lower court judge would usually follow this in the absence of a president. Appellate courts, usually have more than one judge (and an odd number), if the decision is unanimous, for instance the court of appeal decides 3:0 for the defendant, then the *ratio* of the case can be found in the judgement of any of the three judges. If the court decided for the defendant 2:1, then the *ratio* must be found in the decision of the two judges in the majority. The decision of the judge in the minority maybe persuasive as *obiter,* but it cannot form a *ratio* which will bind future courts.

When case law and statue conflicts statute takes precedence because of **Parliamentary Sovereignty**, which dictates that parliament can make or repeal any law it chooses and therefore it can't be bound by the decisions of the court, or by its own earlier decisions. Although this has been affected by the combined impact of the growth of delegated legislation, devolution and international law, which has somewhat impacted upon the parliamentary powers.

3.4 Further Sources of Law

Delegated Legislation – Parliament has not got time to pass all of the necessary legislation into statutes. It therefore delegates to ministers the power to make some legislation. This legislation is theoretically concerned with minor, administrative matters, such as traffic regulations, rather than with politically contentious matters such as privatising the public utilities. If the Minister of Transport is asked to make a new traffic regulation he will first pass the task onto the branch of Civil Service which he supervises, The Department of Transport. The Civil Servants will draw up the legislation and the Minister will then present it to Parliament. MPs vote such regulations through 'on the nod' which means without having a debate or a proper vote on them. Once delegated legislation has been passed, it ranks alongside a statute as a source of law superior to any other president. The court can only interfere if the legislation was not formed in a proper manner.

European Law is passed by The European Parliament in Brussels and applied by The European court of Justice in Luxembourg. The European Communities Act 1972 states that European law takes

precedence over our domestic law. Although International treaties do not take precedence over domestic law and it is also true in English law that no piece of legislation can be binding on future legislations, in that no law can be passed that affects the law making process in so far as that legislation can not be amended and changed.
As European law takes precedence over UK law it can be argued that this has undermined

Parliamentary Sovereignty, however as it is an act of parliament that applies the European law to the UK it can be repealed like any other, by a future parliament on a simple majority, however that said because a greater majority is needed to repeal it, it is unlikely to happen.

Most European law comes is adopted into UK Legislation via delegated legislation, which is scrutinised by a committee in parliament, this law is then interpreted and applied by the domestic courts in the same way as any other legislation. A good example of this is the Human Rights Act, this act adopts The Human Rights Convention into English law, prior to this the convention could only be enforced in the European Court of Human Rights in Strasbourg (and not in the UK). The European Court of Human Rights is in fact separate from the European legal system, it was created by the council of Europe. The decision of the courts are not binding in the UK, although parliament would change the legislation to become into line with the decision of the court or risk expulsion from the council of Europe. It is also expected that any current legislation is interpreted in a way in which is compatible with the convention, 'in so far as it is possible to do so' (If this is not possible the higher courts will make a 'declaration of incompatibility' this will not affect the continuing validity of the law and therefore parliamentary sovereignty is retained, but as fore mentioned, it is expected that parliament will normally amend legislation which is incompatible with the convention).

The ECHR was set up by the Council of Europe (which was set up by the leading European Countries). It was set up after the second world war in order to prevent atrocities of the war happening again by committing each country to the provisions of the bill of rights. The Human rights act is the first time that a written bill of rights has been made enforceable in the courts since 1689. The early bill of rights in 1689 was not to set out the rights of individuals but was intended primarily to restrict the powers of the monarch to control parliament.

Because the UK had no written rights, like in the US constitution it doesn't mean that there were no rights. Instead the constitution was an unwritten one, or an assumed one, with the assumption that all citizens enjoy complete freedom except where it has been specifically and lawfully taken away, i.e. a 'negative concept of rights', i.e. you have the right to do anything unless there is a law to say that you can't. It can be said that English law has a flexible constitution because it can be altered by normal law making processes, the legislation plays a key role in the process of changing a countries constitution.

The convention rights are broad and as with any law it is the role of the judges to interpret it by weighing up the rights of the individual and the impact upon society.
The convention allows the each country a margin of appreciation to allow for political, cultural and historical differences between the countries .

Any public organisation is bound by The Human Rights Act, therefore when carrying out investigations you need to be aware of this. However at certain times it may conflict with the domestic law and your investigation, for instance you may need to breach the right to privacy, The Regulation of Investigatory Powers Act 2000 (RIPA) allows certain public organisations to breach this right if it falls within the necessary criteria and is necessary and proportionate, for instance the Police may be allowed to breach someone's right to privacy if it is in the interest of national security.

Legislation is law which has been promulgated (or "enacted") by a legislature or other governing body. This includes **Primary legislation** (This is legislation passed by the executive under authority set out in statutes that gives the executive discretionary powers) & **Secondary legislation** (Delegated legislation – This now accounts for a lot of legislation and demonstrates the growing power of the executive and lessening role of Parliament).

Devolution Legislation – Since 1998 Scottish Parliament and Northern Ireland Assembly (Since the Good Friday agreement, which was part of the peace process, paved the way for a directly elected Northern Irish assembly) have been given law making powers in certain areas of policy i.e. Education (this is known as Primary legislation). The Welsh assembly have less power and can only pass secondary legislation under authority from Westminster.

International law/International treaties

The United Kingdom joined the European Community, the common market, in 1973. In order to be admitted as a member, the UK parliament passed the European Communities Act 1972. Under this statute the united kingdom aggress to apply EC law in British courts. It was also agreed that If there was any conflict between EC law and UK domestic law then the EC law would prevail. British statutes would have to be interpreted in a way which was consistent with Community law. Although there is a margin of appreciation that allows for political, cultural and historical differences between countries and therefore there have been wide differences between types of trial and pre trial procedures in civil and common law systems.

It could be argued that this has affected Parliamentary Sovereignty and goes against the principal of our legal system that no law can be binding, however even though Parliament is subject to laws made by the European Community and therefore no longer free to pass whatever statute it wants, it is still still supreme because the European Communities Act is just another statute, and like any other statute it can be repealed by future parliament. At the time of joining the EC law was a very small percentage of English law, but it is gradually growing and eventually could replace English law?

The treaty of Rome – This original treaty was signed in 1957, long before the United Kingdom joined the community. On joining the UK agreed that it would be bound by all the articles of the treaty, there are 248 Articles, which makeup the primary legislation of the EU. The secondary legislation of the EC is found in three types of rules; 1. Regulations (These are directly applicable in all member States without the approval of the Parliament of those states & no Parliament can pass a statute that which conflicts with a regulation), 2. Directives (These are not immediately binding, but require member States to pass legislation which bring them into effect, within a reasonable time). 3. Decisions (They bring in broad new policies, they are immediately binding on those they address, usually member Governments or corporations).

Bye Laws (Bye laws are laws that are made by a particular authority that has been given permission to make those laws and that particular authority is the only ones authorised to enforce those particular bye laws – for instance certain councils adopt bye laws for hackney carriage drivers also British Rail have their own bye laws enforced by British Transport Police). Local government act 1972, grant local authorities and other regulatory bodies the power to make byelaws for which specific provision is not otherwise made.

Custom can be described as the established patterns of behavior that can be objectively verified within a particular social setting. A claim can be carried out in defense of "what has always been done and accepted by law." Generally, customary law exists where a certain legal practice is observed and the relevant actors consider it to be law (*opinio juris*).

2.4 The Distinction between Civil and Criminal Law

In the UK there are two main types of legal frameworks, the is the criminal legal framework and there is the civil legal framework, in addition to this there is military law which governs military personal.

Areas of law - Criminal and Civil law

The law is categorized into two different areas and the offences and ways that these can be enforced vary according to the area of law it falls into and the severity of the offence.

There are two main areas of law, which defines how the law is imposed; these areas are Criminal law & Civil law. The distinction between civil and criminal liability is fundamental to English law. The courts are divided into civil and criminal courts.

Please note; The civil court system, is not to be confused with the civil legal system which many countries operate under, just like we have a common law legal system some countries have a civil law legal system, this is different to our terms of civil law, which we use to classify an area off our common law system, as apposed to it being a separate legal system within itself. 'Civil law' as a legal system refers to a legal systems usually based around one or several codes of law, which set out the main principles that guide the law, although some of these systems are uncodified.

This form of Civil law or Romano-Germanic law or Continental law is the predominant system of law in the world. Civil law as a legal system is often compared with common law. The main difference that is usually drawn between the two systems is that common law draws abstract rules from specific cases, whereas civil law starts with abstract rules, which judges must then apply to the various cases before them.

In common law jurisdictions, case law is created by the courts' interpretations as a result of the principle of *stare decisis*;

In civil law jurisdictions, courts interpret the law, but are, at least in theory, prohibited from *creating* law, and thus, still in theory, do not issue rulings more general than the actual case to be judged; in practice, jurisprudence plays the same role as case law;

Scotland is often said to use the civil law system but in fact it has a unique system that combines elements of an uncodified civil law dating back to the Corpus Juris Civilis with an element of common law long predating the Treaty of Union with England in 1707 (see Legal institutions of Scotland in the High Middle Ages). Scots common law differs in that the use of *precedents* is subject to the courts seeking to discover the principle which justifies a law rather than to search for an example as a *precedent* and that the principles of natural justice and fairness have always formed a source of Scots Law. Comparable pluralistic (or 'mixed') legal systems operate in Quebec, Louisiana and South Africa.

France, which is fairly typical of European countries, has a Civil law system, as it has a codified system of law, all of the criminal law is contained in the Penal code and all of the Civil law is contained in the Civil Code. They do not operate judicial interpretation as French judges are civil servants rather than lawyers and do not feel compelled to interpret the codes according to previous decisions until those decisions have for some time unanimously interpreted the codes in the same way.

Civil law in the UK as an area of law

However when we refer to civil law, instead of referring to a legal system in itself, it is used to explain an area of law that is separate to a criminal one and instead of concerning itself with punishing people for committing crimes it is designed to compensate people who have been injured or wronged by others, where as the criminal court system is there to punish people who have committed a crime. It is possible that the same wrongful act can give rise to both civil and criminal liability. For instance in a car crash the instigator of the crash, if caused by dangerous driving, may get punished by the state for dangerous driving but may also be sued by the injured party, who will sue under the tort of negligence and he/she may have to pay compensation to the injured party. In civil cases the levels of compensation to be awarded will be viewed in terms of what is needed rather than how serious the wrongful act was, for instance if the person in the car crash was injured so badly they needed permanent care, the compensation awarded may reflect this and be such an amount to cover the costs of that care where as if the person was not injured there would be no claim and if they subsequently died the compensation would cover the funeral costs, but would therefore be less than if seriously injured as there would be no need for so much money as the injured party would injure no further costs, such as those needed for permanent care, unless however a dependant spouse could argue that they were now missing out on the income from their spouse, but in most cases this would not be accepted.

Civil law can be sub divided into;

- Contract liability – Liability in contract is undertaken voluntarily as you undertake the contract, this is strict liability, for instance if you don't do what you agreed to do in the contract then you will be liable. The level of compensation awarded in the breaking of a contract is to concerned with putting the injured party in the position that they would have been in, if the contract had been performed.

Contracts include business contracts between businesses, consumer law and employment law. Although there is no legal definition of a consumer there are many important statutes, each of these statutes define, in themselves, who they afford protection to, for instance, The Consumer Credit Act 1974, specifies that it protects borrowers up to a certain amount, providing that they are not companies.

- Tort Liability i.e. trespass, libel and negligence.

The liability in tort is imposed by the courts and this liability is based on fault, for instance, a person maybe liable if his/her conduct does not match up to a objective, reasonable standard. For instance a driver who injured another will only be liable if it can be shown that he/she drove badly and failed to take reasonable care and that resulted in the crash, even if there was a crash, no matter how bad it was, if it could not be proven that the person drove badly then he/she will not be liable. The compensation awarded is done so with the view to put the person in the position he/she would have been in had the tort never been committed, for instance the injured party in the car crash would be compensated for any medical expenses, for pain and suffering, for any loss of wages and damage to personal property such as clothes worn at the time and vehicle damage etc. The person affected by the tort may sue for damages to be compensated from a tort taking place, or for an ongoing tort may sue for an injunction for them to stop the person committing the tort from doing so. Almost all common law in tort is fault based meaning that a person will not usually be liable in tort unless he/she was inn some way at fault, however an increasing number of statutes are imposing liability without fault, this is known as strict liability and basically means that even if you are not responsible of causing harm by your actions, if something is caused harm as a result of you failing to take action to prevent it, even though the harm was not caused as a result of your actions you will be automatically liable.

An injunction can also be sought to prevent person from breaking a contractual agreement, although these are very rarely granted.

IMPORTANT! - **For negligence to take place it must be proven that:**

A) duty of care was owed

B) that the care was breached

C) that an individual was harmed as a result.

In the UK civil law is not concerned with the public, and therefore not enforced by the state i.e. a contract between two individuals, where as in some countries civil law is the laws observed by that county, for instance in some Arabic countries the law of the land is Sharia law.

In English law you are innocent until proven guilty, although this burden of proof can be reversed meaning that you have to prove your innocence in certain situations, for instance, The Health & Safety at Work Act 1974 (section 40) reverses the burden of proof in health and safety prosecutions, meaning you are classified as guilty until you can prove your innocence. However as stated in Art 6(2) ECHR [2004] EWCA Crim 1025 Ct of Appeal **AG Ref No 1 of 2004** - Where a reverse burden of proof exists the prosecutor must still prove the circumstances of the offence and the easier it is for a defendant to prove a fact within his knowledge the more likely a court is to require him to do so.

In the case of Robertson v Bannister -ALL ACTS [1973] RTR 109 EVIDENCE- BURDEN OF PROOF HELD If matter at hand is particularly within knowledge of defendant then it is for him/her to prove exemption, this decision is binding.

Criminal cases, depending on the offence, are enforced by the Police and Local Authorities, most serious criminal offences are arrest able and therefore dealt with by the Police. In the case of serious offences, usually those where an individual has harmed another and may cause further harm or perhaps take flight the Police will charge the accused immediately and keep him/her under arrest and in custody, if it is less serious they will be released on Police bail and later summonsed to appear in court. The courts will need to decide at a fist hearing if there is enough evidence for a trail to go ahead, they will also need to decide (if the person is still in Police custody) whether to grant bail or not until the time of the trail, if no bail is granted the accused will remain in Police custody until the time of the trail. The Police will submit their evidence to the Crown Prosecution Service who will decide whether to go ahead with the prosecution or not, this will be decided based on the quality of the evidence and whether or not it is in the public interest to go ahead with the prosecution. With local Authority cases it will be dependant on the local polices of that authority as to weather to take a prosecution forward or not, usually the investigator will take advice from the in-house legal department or employed solicitor.

At the start of the trial the charges will be read out to the defendant , who will be asked to make a plea, if he/she pleads guilty there will be no trial and the case will go to the judge to pass sentence, if he/she pleads not guilt the trial will begin.

Civil disputes will either be heard in the county court or high court, disputes concerning less than £50,000 are usually heard in the county court, where as disputes concerning more than £50,000 are usually heard in the high court (Disputes in which the claim amount is less than £1,000 will be heard in 'arbitration' in a small claims court). Commercial disputes don't always get to court, they can sometimes be settled by arbitration, in this instance it is resolved by an impartial referee, an arbitrator, who takes over the role of the court. In addition there are ombudsmen and other dispute resolution schemes. Other disputes, such as those relating to employment law, go before tribunals. Tribunals are courts, but the members are not judges.

Law can be broadly categorized into various different categories;

- Domestic Statute & Secondary Legislation (e.g. the Licensing Act 2003, Statutory Guidance & Regulations) & Domestic case law (pre Licensing Act 2003 case law will apply where statute is not clear)
- Contract law regulates everything from buying a bus ticket to trading swaptions on a derivatives market.
- Property law (classified into **Real** property; this is property that can not be moved, and is limited to land and things attached to the land & **Personal** property; this consists of 2 types of property; tangible items such as cars, and intangible items such as copyright, debts or patents.
- Trust law applies to assets held for investment and financial security, such as pension funds.
- Tort law allows claims for compensation when someone or their property is injured or harmed. If the harm is criminalized in a penal code, criminal law offers means by which the state prosecutes and punishes the perpetrator.
- Financial law governs lenders and borrowers and includes topics such as security for loans etc.
- Constitutional law provides a framework for creating laws, protecting people's human rights, and electing political representatives. Constitutional Law (includes domestic case law + statute e.g. the Human Rights Act 1998 which incorporates the European Convention on Human Rights and Fundamental Freedoms, into UK law)
- Administrative law relates to the activities of administrative agencies of government.
- International law regulates affairs between sovereign nation-states in everything from trade to the environment to military action, and includes both international treaties e.g. the Geneva Convention and European Union Law incorporated via the Single European Act 1972 which takes the form of case law from the European Court of Justice as well as Regulations & Directives.

The influence of these types of law varies, and the following provides some indication of the relative influence of each:

> 12. Domestic Statute takes primacy over both secondary legislation and domestic case law. As such, the Licensing Act 2003 takes primacy over the Statutory Guidance.
> 13. International Law (e.g. treaties) is not binding upon UK courts, except with regard to European Union Law in the form of case law from the European Court of Justice, Regulations and Directives.
> 14. The Human Rights Act 1998 does not fully incorporate the European Convention on Human Rights into UK law: courts are not able to 'overrule' UK Statute although they can make 'declarations of incompatibility'. However, case law will incorporate the provisions of the European Convention on Human Rights, primarily by interpreting the actions of public bodies in light of the Convention Articles.

Outside the UK

Even outside England and Wales English law may be applicable i.e. When two foreign business make a contract with each other, for example a Germany company buys from a Japanese one, it is common for a term of the contract to state that in the event of a dispute English law should apply. In addition to the duties imposed to individual citizens, the law also places addition laws on businesses, such as The Trade Description Act.

The privy council (established in the sixteenth century), now largely ceremonial, (membership is granted to those who have obtained high office) still holds the power to administer legal disputes from Britain's overseas dependencies, including capital punishment cases.

In socialist law, the primary responsibility for interpreting the law belongs to the legislature.

Chapter 4 - Components of the Modern English Law System

As an enforcement officer it is your job, should your case go as far as court, to help the magistrate or judge to reach the most informed decision based on the facts of the case.

You will called as witness to present the evidence you have gathered (the methods of which, more later) and this evidence will almost certainly be presented to the court by a solicitor or barrister. But what's the difference? And what's a lawyer?...

4.1 - Solicitor or Barrister?

Firstly, a lawyer is the catch-all term to describe a solicitor or a barrister, where as in America, for instance, a lawyer is often referred to an an advocate, or an attourney. In the UK, for the prosecution of criminal cases we will usually refer to a solicitor or barrister. Though the distinction between these two fields is no longer as strictly defined as it once was (discussed below in further detail) as a mark of professional courtesy you should do your best to use the correct form of address to each, and wherever possible, avoid the use of the non-descript 'lawyer'.

Unlike other European countries, England has two different types of lawyers. These are **Barristers** and **Solicitors**; The main job of the barrister is to argue cases in court, they also give written opinions in which they state what they consider the law to be, they tend to be specialist, either working in the criminal area, or a particular specialist branch of civil law. A barrister can only be hired by a solicitor, under the 'Cab rank' rule a barrister, like a taxi is meant to provide his/her service to whoever requests them, nowadays solicitors have *right of audience, in the crown court, following a recent statute* (previously they could only argue a case in magistrates or county courts).
A solicitors scope is much wider than a barristers, they have more of a wider knowledge of the law, although once they have completed their training they can decide to specialise in a particular area of law (especially if they work in a larger firm), as apposed to barristers they work with their clients over a longer period of time, be it an individual defendant or working with a prosecutor/investigator, giving advice on individual cases.

Solicitors and Barristers give their clients advice about their legal rights and duties, and represent them in court. As the European Court of Human Rights has stated, the law should be adequately accessible to everyone and people should be able to foresee how the law affects them. In order to maintain professionalism, the practice of law is typically overseen by either a government or independent regulating body such as a bar association, bar council or law society. An aspiring practitioner must be certified by the regulating body before undertaking his practice. This usually entails a two or three year programme at a university faculty of law or a law school, earning the student a Bachelor of Laws, a Bachelor of Civil Law or a Juris Doctor degree. This course of study is followed by an entrance examination (e.g. admission to the bar). Some countries require a further vocational qualification before a person is permitted to practice law. A year's pupilage under the oversight of an experienced barrister is required of those wishing to become a barrister. Beyond the requirements for legal practice higher academic degrees may be pursued. Examples include a Master of Laws, a Master of Legal Studies or a Doctor of Laws.

Once accredited, a lawyer will often work in a law firm, in chambers as a sole practitioner, in a government post or in a private corporation as an internal counsel. In addition a lawyer may become a legal researcher who provides on-demand legal research through a commercial service or through freelance work. Many people trained in law put their skills to use outside the legal field entirely. Significant to the practice of law in the common law tradition is the legal research to determine the current state of the law. This usually entails exploring case-law reports, legal periodicals and legislation. Law practice also involves drafting documents such as court pleadings, persuasive briefs, contracts, or wills and trusts. Negotiation and dispute resolution skills are also important to legal practice, depending on the field.

If a lawyer in court makes a statement of law, he must provide authority for this statement by quoting the case or statute which makes the law, therefore the lawyers need to be familiar with current cases, statutes, past rulings, and precedents set etc.

No lawyer knows all of the law, although they have to have a basic overall knowledge, some specialize and will know a particular area of the law in great detail.

In English law the Solicitors or Barristers are adversaries, arguing to win the case for the clients they represent. Whereas most other countries have an inquisitorial system of trial - a system which allows for the judge to ask his own questions in order to probe and discover the truth, in English Law, the judge is not an inquisitor, but is instead present to apply the law to any relevant facts that are submitted to the court by the adversaries before him. Under English Law, a judge must apply the law in this way regardless of whether or not this leads to the fairest outcome. As previously discussed, the judge is bound by judicial precedent, the hierarchical system whereby a judge in a lower court is bound to follow legal principals which were previously formulated in higher courts. If a Jury is present, it is the role of the judge to direct the jury as to whether or not they should accept evidence, i.e. the judge determines the eligibility of evidence based on the law. The jury, composed of members of the public, are not expected to have any understanding of the legal system. It is therefore vital that the judge aid them in this way to prevent them from being led astray or confused as to the truth by cunning and wily advocates…

A brief note on CHAMPIONS OF JUSTICE -

> While the solicitors or barristers on each side 'fight' each other in trying to win judgement for their client, today the battle is metaphoric. However, in the middle ages many disputes were resolved with a trial by actual battle - a battle in which the parties would fight each other, hand to hand, toe to toe. It was believed that God would grant victory to the righteous but if the defendant was too young, old or disabled then they would be allowed to hire champions to fight on their behalf (it presumable being thought that God would favour the champion of the righteous). We have since moved on but the set up with the solicitors and barristers as 'champions' and the judge overseeing the 'battle' is still, give or take the bloodshed, the same..

4.2 - The Different Types of Court

In the UK, all but the most serious or difficult civil and criminal cases are handled by separate court systems: civil cases by tribunals and county courts (complaints of maladministration i.e. accusations of incorrect procedures followed to arrive at a decision, maybe dealt with by the ombudsman), criminal cases by magistrates' courts and Crown Court centres. In England and Wales, more serious cases, and some appeals, are handled by the High Court. Appeals from the High Court and, in some cases, from subordinate courts are heard in the Court of Appeal. In Scotland the Court of Session combines the roles of the High Court and Court of Appeal. Appeals from the Court of Appeal and Court of Session may be heard in the House of Lords.

A. **County Court**

The county courts hear most civil litigation, particularly financial matters like non-payment of debt, and disputes over land boundaries. The small claims court system is a division of the county courts, but with a streamlined claims procedure and a fixed upper limit on the size of the claim. Cases that cannot be resolved in the county courts, or which are appealed, will usually be heard in the High Court. Most cases of up to £50,000 are heard here, where as smaller cases are heard in the small claims court.

B. **Magistrates' Court**

The Magistrates Court usually consists of a bench of 3 lay magistrates. Magistrates are generally employed on a part time basis and are not required to have any specific knowledge of the legal system. Instead, they will have a qualified clerk to advise them on any points of law and also, once the case has been heard, on the types of sentence they may impose, if any.

***IMPORTANT** - Some Magistrates Courts have a single District Judge in place of the 3 Magistrates. The District Judge is a professional with full knowledge of the relevant law.*

Magistrates act as judge and jury. Firstly, they hear the case before them. The case will be presented to the magistrates by the Solicitor or Barrister acting for each side. In cases where one side is a private individual accused of a minor misdemeanour, it is not unusual for one side to present their own case, dispensing with expensive professionals altogether. In this instance, the clerk can advise on points of procedure or etiquette. They will be advised accordingly by the clerk. They will then usually retire from the courtroom into an adjoining chamber to discuss the case in private. Once they have reached a decision, they will return to the courtroom to pronounce judgement. There is no jury in a Magistrates Court. Cases heard in the magistrate court can be referred to the crown court for sentencing, if the magistrate feels this is appropriate.

Cases that can be heard in the magistrates courts are, summary only or either way offences, these are less serious cases (the more serious indictable cases are heard at the Crown court and not the magistrates court), therefore as most cases are of a less serious nature, magistrates courts, hear most criminal cases initially. Either way offences can be heard in the magistrates or the crown court, some may be referred to the Crown Court for jury trial or for sentencing, (this process is called `committal for trial') or they may be heard in the magistrates court, who may then ask a judge from the crown court to deal with sentencing, (this is known as `committal for sentencing').

Magistrates' courts also hear a number of civil actions, particular relating to licensing, and some may deal with family matters. These latter include the grant of maintenance, protection, and custody orders.

Magistrates are not necessarily professional lawyers, but lay magistrates - residents of the local community in good standing, they normally sit as a panel of 3 with a `Clerk to the Justices' (a solicitor, , or barrister, of five years' standing) to provide guidance to the magistrates on points of law and precedent, and manages the administrative work of the court. The Clerk does not normally get involved with the judgement itself. Some sessions will have a single judge (previously called Stipendiary magistrates), they sit in busy urban courts and hear cases alone. The magistrates play the role of judge and jury, they cover a certain area and are independent to that area. Their max. powers of sentence are to issue a max of 6-12 months custodial sentence and their fines are limited to £5,000 (some offences heard in the magistrates court) may warrant higher fines, in which case it may need to be referred up to the next court.

C. **Crown Court**

A Crown Court is perhaps the type of court most people would think of if asked to imagine how they think a court would look. A Crown Court consists of a Judge, a number of clerks, and a jury of 12 ordinary people. The case is presented in the same manner as   The judge decides the sentencing and the procedures of the case, issues such as what evidence is admissible. In a crown court, where evidence is required in order to reach a decision on admissibility, it is heard in a trial-within-a-trial, called a 'voire dire', this takes place in absence of a jury and both sides address the judge.

Crown Courts hear most of the more serious criminal cases, and cases appealed from the magistrates' courts on points of fact. They may also determine sentence in cases where an offender has been found guilty by a magistrates' court, but the magistrates don't have sufficient powers to sentence appropriately. Decisions may be appealed to the Court of Appeal or `by way of case stated' to the Divisional Court of the Queen's Bench Division. It is not clear whether Crown Court decisions are binding on magistrates' courts; this is difficult to test because Crown Court decisions are not recorded in the Law Reports so precedent is not always clear. The court consists of a judge and lay jury of 12 people, the judge decides on sentencing and the procedure of the case i.e. what evidence can be used. The Old Bailey is the central criminal court and is the Crown Court for the City of London. It is not typical because it is staffed only be senior judges and hears most of the serious criminal cases in London.

D. **High Court**

The High Court hears the more serious civil cases, and most appeals from the county courts. It also hears some appeals from magistrates' courts, as will be discussed later. The High Court has three Divisions: `Queen's Bench', `Family' and `Chancery'. This is based in the Royal Courts of Justice, London, high court judges also travel around the country to hear cases. Its is divided into three divisions;

this is where the most serious civil cases are heard, this is split into 3 sections;
5. The Queens Bench Division (QBD)
6. Chancery Division
7. Family Division

1. The Queen's Bench Division (QBD) hears cases concerning contract law, tort law, commercial law, and admiralty. The Divisional Court of the Queen's Bench Divisional has a somewhat distinct role from the Queen's Bench Division itself, and is discussed separately. This Division is headed by the Lord Chief Justice, who is also head of the Criminal Division of the Court of Appeal.

2. The Family Division deals with divorce and similar family matters, particular those relating to the care of children, adoption, and complex medical conditions, such as life support. It also contains the Probate Registry. The Division is headed by a President.

3. The Chancery Division deals with equities and trusts, wills, companies and issues relating to patents.

Cases appealed from the High Court are heard in the Court of Appeal.

E. Divisional Court of the Queen's Bench Division

This court is formally part of the Queen's Bench Division of the High Court, but is concerned with criminal, not civil, cases. It hears appeals from the magistrates court *on points of law*, not on points of fact. This type of appeal is called an appeal `by way of case stated'.

F. Coroners' Court

Although historically the Coroners' Court had extensive powers, it is now concerned primarily with determining cause of death and the identity of the deceased. Coroners' Courts are often involved when death is suspicious, violent, or `unnatural', or takes place in a prison or mental institution. If a person has been formally accused of causing a death, the Coroners' Court formally adjourns until sentence is passed, and no verdict is offered.

Coroners' Courts have a number of roles which are less well-known. For example, they decide on the disposition of valuables discovered with no known owner.

G. Court of Appeal

The Court of Appeal deals entirely with appeals from other courts. It has a Criminal Division, which deals with appeals from the Crown Court and the Queen's Bench Divisional Court, and a Civil Division for appeals from the High Court, county courts, and tribunals. Decision made in the Court of Appeal are binding on all other courts except the House of Lords. Decisions of the Criminal Division are binding on the Crown Court and magistrates' courts, and *may* be binding on the QB Divisional Court (this is uncertain at present). Decision of the Civil Division are binding on the county courts and High Court. The Criminal Division is headed by the Lord Chief Justice, the Civil Division by the Master of the Rolls. The judges of the Court of Appeal are formally known as Lords Justice of Appeal.

H. Courts Martial Appeal Court

The court that hears appeals from courts martial (military courts). Despite its business (or perhaps because of it) this court is not presided over by military personnel, but by the same judges that sit in the Criminal Division of the Court of Appeal.

I. House of Lords

The judicial function of the UK House of Lords is entirely separate from its role in government; the judicial work is done by a number of senior judges colloquially called `Law Lords'. They hear appeals from the High Court and the Court of Appeal and are, in effect, the final resort for appeal in the UK legal system. House of Lords rulings are binding on all other courts.

4.3 - The Court System

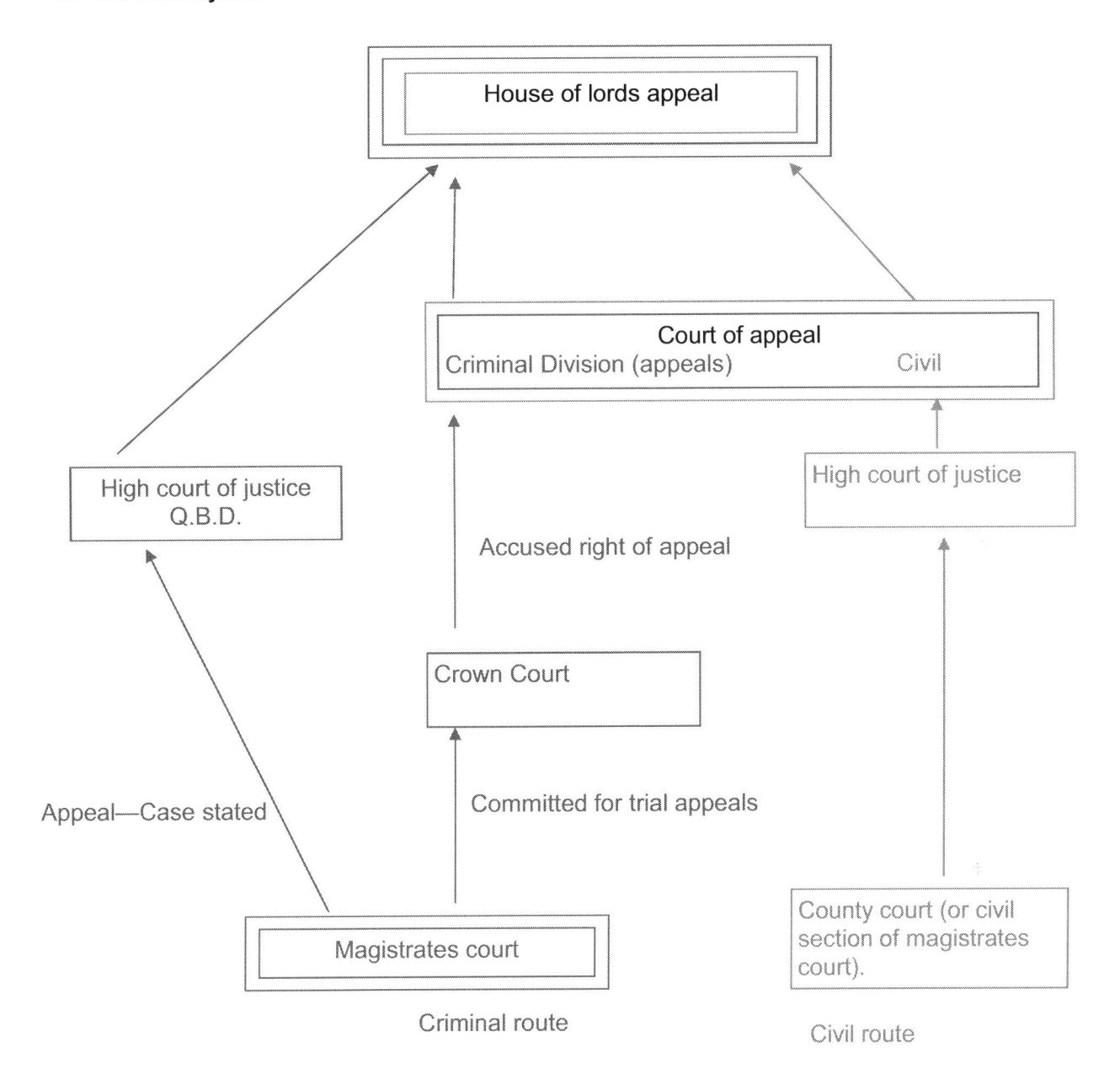

```
                    ┌─────────────────────────┐
                    │  House of lords appeal  │
                    └─────────────────────────┘
                       ↑         ↑          ↑
                       │         │          │
                       │    ┌────────────────────────────────┐
                       │    │        Court of appeal         │
                       │    │ Criminal Division (appeals)    Civil │
                       │    └────────────────────────────────┘
                       │              ↑              ↑
                       │              │              │
            ┌──────────────────────┐  │      ┌──────────────────────┐
            │ High court of justice│  │      │ High court of justice│
            │       Q.B.D.         │  │      └──────────────────────┘
            └──────────────────────┘  │              ↑
                       ↑         Accused right of appeal
                       │              │
                       │        ┌─────────────┐
                       │        │ Crown Court │
                       │        └─────────────┘
                       │              ↑
                Appeal—Case stated    │
                       │    Committed for trial appeals
                       │              │              │
                    ┌─────────────────────┐   ┌──────────────────────┐
                    │  Magistrates court  │   │ County court (or civil│
                    └─────────────────────┘   │ section of magistrates│
                                              │ court).              │
                                              └──────────────────────┘

                        Criminal route                 Civil route
```

Chapter 5 - The Theory of Investigation

5.1 - Concepts of Investigation and Enforcement

We looked at some of the legal principals in chapter 2 when discussing Judicial Review. It can now be seen how the principals should be applied at the investigative stage, to ensure that results of your investigation (evidence) stands up at court, rather than being thrown out of court, for the correct principals not being followed.

Wednesbury Unreasonableness; Associated Picture houses – v- Wednesbury Corporation (1948) 1 KB 223; established that decisions must be relevant and fair and supported by reason.;
4. Take into account all relevant factors
5. Ignore irrelevant factors
6. Make a rational balanced decision based on the evidence.

Legitimate Expectation;
A promise that you will do something before you make a decision;
Lord Justice Simon Brown said that it can mean;
5. A substantive right;
6. An expectation that a right or benefit will not be withdrawn unless a fair procedure is followed;
7. An expectation that a particular procedure which has been followed in the past, or has been promised will continue to be followed and
8. A fair procedure itself.

Rules Of Natural Justice;
4. The other party must be informed of the substance of the objection or allegation being made against them.
5. All parties must be given a chance to put their case forward.
6. A person who has an interest in the matter must be disqualified from considering it

The Principal of Proportionality – restrictions on individual rights must be proportionate to the legitimate aim they pursue, i.e. must not go beyond what is strictly necessary to achieve that purpose.

Remember! - Occasionally a statute (such as The Licensing Act 2003) indicates that a person must have knowingly committed an offence before a prosecution can succeeded. Where as the standard rule for most legislation is that ignorance to the law is no defence.

A brief note on gathering evidence in general:

When conducting an investigation and gathering evidence it MUST be done in a fair and open manner and in accordance with the law. The manner in which any evidence is obtained can affect the admissibility, reliability and credibility of the evidence, and consequently the weighting that it will hold in any criminal proceedings. If evidence is gathered in an unlawful way the judge may declare it to be inadmissible, and depending on your reliability on that evidence you may lose the case.

5.2 Investigations and Gathering evidence

You can only investigate offences or incidents that fall under your particular sphere of powers i.e. those you are authorised to investigate. When beginning your employment you will be informed of your authority, the limits to your authority, and the Acts under which you are authorised to carry out investigations. It is useful to study at least the basics of the legislations that you have been granted the authority to enforce, and to be aware of the limitations of these legislations. That said, it would be a well read enforcement officer who knew by heart every paragraph of every act! You will always have reference books on hand to study the detail of legislation and you should refer to these as often as necessary. The beginning to any enforcement investigation is to take the initial allegation or evidence and to study the legislation to decide whether any offence has been committed. Only after this stage will you have any indication of your next steps.

At the scene of the crime it is important to secure early evidence.

Take photos of graffiti so that you can secure the tags, collect spray paint cans so that they can be fingerprinted (depending on the severity of the graffiti i.e. is it racist etc). Drinking cans, saliva from spit, cigarette butts, body fluids etc. are all good ways to secure DNA. Descriptions, registration numbers and CCTV are all good ways of securing identification.

In order to use evidence at court you must have continuity of evidence i.e. the act was seen, the evidence was gathered, sample was taken and sealed and statements can account for the whole chain of the evidence.

5.3 Conducting Investigations

Everything must be investigated, all complaints and enquiries, nothing should be assumed or taken for granted, if you investigate everything, without taking shortcuts you will be seen to do your job and if things go wrong can not be criticised. If you take a short cut, or assume something is not important and don't investigate it, if something goes wrong you will be asked why you didn't act on the complaint/enquiry.

Once you have details of the offence/suspected offence that has occurred and have familiarised yourself with the legal framework and relevant legislation for this offence and the authority for which you have to investigate this. You can start to undertake the investigation;

Firstly you will need to establish who may be responsible, this sounds obvious but it may be more than one person and can be quite complicated if it is an offence in the business i.e. operating without a licence and the owner of the business, or who is responsible for running it is unclear.

Once you have established who the responsible person(s) is/are you will have to prove that the defendant is was capable of committing the offence, for instance was involved or carried out some sort of action or failed to take action that therefore resulted in a crime or breach in regulations taking place, this is known as 'ACTUS REUS' the guilty act, you will also have to prove that the defendant had the state of mind to be involved, this is known as 'MENS REA' the guilt mind, some crimes may have a statutory defence, where as others may have strict liability. In the case of strict liability 'MENS REA' will not need to be proved.

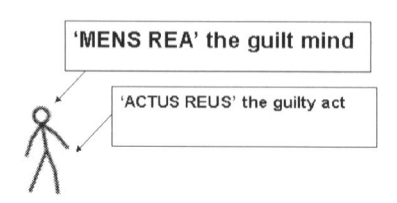

'MENS REA' the guilt mind

'ACTUS REUS' the guilty act

Every crime has its own mens rea, which can be ascertained from its statutory definition, or from case law. It is usually expressed, stated or implied. The defendants state of mind or his surrounding circumstances can affect his defence. If the law says 'knowingly' it is implying that the defendant with his state of mind should have known what he was doing. Criminal liability for most serious offences depends on the defendant having acted intentionally, recklessly, or dishonestly. Although a few criminal offences, such as careless driving, can be committed by negligence.

You will also need to be aware what the standard of proof is for the particular offence that you are investigating. In most criminal cases the prosecution will have to prove the case beyond reasonable doubt, although in some exceptional cases the defendant may have to prove his defence on a balance of probabilities, such as what was reasonably practicable to do.

You will also need to look at the possible defences and what, if any defence they have, they maybe able to proved due diligence and you may therefore decide not to prosecute them or to take alternative action as a result. Or you may decide to continue to prosecute but if you are aware of defences they may use and you have considered these your case will be stronger, or you will at least have some idea of how the defence solicitors may attack your case and can therefore build your case appropriately.

In many cases the defendants defence will be that of actus reus or mens rea, for instance that the defendant either didn't commit the crime or was not in the right frame of mind to know what he was doing, there may also be mitigating circumstances, or the defence of consent (this is an implied defence and is not set out in law, for instance the deference of 'self defence' – see Section 3 of the Criminal Law Act) or in some cases there may be a statutory defence, this are set out in law and in limited circumstances they are able to escape liability. For instance under the Licensing Act 2003, section 139, there is a defence of due diligence and under the Water Resources Act 2003 provides the defence for causing pollution to the water, if the defendant had a consent or licence to do so.

However there are some crimes which do not require mens rea to prove the offence, these are known as strict liability. These are usually statues where the social benefits of stringent enforcement outweighs the harm of punishing a person or organisation, such as the case in some H&S legislation. If the statue is silent it is presumed that mens rea will be presumed to be necessary, although the statutes rarely expressly rule out mens rea, therefore you will need to look at what the words indicate, for instance the words, "cause" or "use" indicate strict liability, where as words that imply a mental element was necessary i.e. "allow", "knowingly", or "wilfully" require some degree of mens rea rather than strict liability.

Standard of proof, as already mentioned in a civil case (including employment tribunals) the standard of proof is one of the balance of probability, this include, in health and safety cases, some civil defences such as reasonably practicable. In criminal cases the prosecution have to prove the case beyond reasonable doubt, exceptionally, even in some criminal cases, the defendant may have to prove his defence on a balance of probabilities (rather than the prosecution proving his guilt beyond reasonable doubt), as we have already seen this known as a reverse burden of proof and relates to some health and safety statutes.

In summary, when conducting investigations you also need to be aware of points to prove (actus reus & mens rea) and possible defences, what the liability is, and the burden of proof / standard of proof for that Act and ensure that you gather all of the necessary evidence in a lawful manner, and keep the appropriate notes, to prove that offence. If in doubt as to the standard of proof always assume that you are working to the criminal standard, as if you have enough evidence to prove your case against this you should be able to prove your case against any other standard.

When carrying out an investigation always gather evidence with a prosecution in mind so that if it does go to court you have the necessary evidence. It is important to be clear what is evidence and what is hearsay. Always write up your statements and take statements from witnesses as soon as possible so that the memory is fresh and the information is accurate even if it seems like a minor offence you still need to investigate it fully and make the appropriate notes as it may lead onto something else or you may need to go to court with it.

5.4 Aggregating and Mitigating Circumstances – Decisions affecting the outcome of an investigation are often influenced by aggravating or mitigating factors. It is therefore important to recognise and document these. Aggravating circumstances mean that the offence committed was worse, for instance if;
- The offence was committed over a lengthy period of time
- Large sums of money or valuable goods
- It was planned / highly sophisticated, and organised team involved
- There was related damage or victims and victims were particularly vulnerable or the defendant was an adult and the victim involved a child.

An example is Burglary, it is aggravated burglary when a thief breaks in knowing people are in the house i.e. at night.

Mitigating circumstances are almost the opposite to aggravating, rather than meaning the situation is worst, it means they may have a 'reason' why to make the offence less serious, for instance they didn't understand what they were doing.

5.5 Types of Evidence

Oral evidence – the statement of a witness made orally in court
Witness of fact – someone giving evidence of what they have seen, heard, done etc.
Expert evidence – An expert witness is entitled to give opinion on evidence because of their experience or qualifications. The Criminal procedure rules apply.
Real evidence – this usually takes the form of material objects such as CCTv footage, samples etc.

Documentary evidence – Documents produced for inspection by the court.
Photographic evidence – Photographs.
Circumstantial evidence – Evidence used to draw a picture of the circumstances i.e. it was raining.
Witness Statements – all evidence that you want to put to the court needs to be in the form of a witness statement, these are shown to the other side before the trial. When you go to court you will be asked to give orally evidence based on your witness statement, therefore it must be comprehensive, clear, accurate and easy to refer to.
Bad Character evidence – The Criminal Justice Act 2003 allows bad character evidence if in accordance of Criminal Procedure Rules 2005.

5.6 Evidence Collection

To make the collection of evidence more effective it is important to distinguish between issues, facts and inferences. Any evidence or documents collected must be recorded as to who removed them, from whom and the date and time and a note should be made as to where the items are stored etc. Where possible evidence should be placed in a sealed evidence bag, it must be logged and given a number at the very least, obviously when it is returned a detailed record should also be made.

When gathering evidence and making decisions think about what is admissible in court, the admissibility is a question of law for the judge. In order to be admissible evidence must be sufficiently relevant, although this does not mean that all relevant evidence is admissible. Obviously all evidence must be collected in accordance with RIPA & PACE, if it isn't it may be inadmissible, also there is a whole load of other reasons why a judge may deem evidence inadmissible, as it is at the judges discretion evidence may be excluded on the grounds that it is more prejudice rather than probate.

Therefore if someone has given you evidence you may not be able to use it, if it has not been gathered in an appropriate way. You also have to be aware that by giving them specific instructions about how evidence should be gathered, and asking them to gather specific information, may mean you are asking them to act as a CHIS.

5.7 Identifying the Offender;

It is important to correctly identify the offender or offenders, as there maybe multiple offenders. The offender may not only be an individual, but maybe a company, a company officer, or a parent company.

If you are prosecution a company you should check with companies house web site to see the status of the company, if the company is insolvent you may need permission from the high court to prosecute.

It is important to determine the legal status of a proposed defendant. A company or other body corporate may be prosecuted in its own right as it has a distinct legal personality. In other cases, it will be necessary to proceed against the
individual(s) responsible for the undertaking, for example the partners in a partnership.

It is also important to be exact in identifying the correct defendant. To include the wrong defendant on the information or summons will invalidate the document and such an error is normally incapable of being corrected by amendment. A new information or summons will need to be issued.

A brief note on - ENTRAPMENT

The following are the opinions of the lords of appeal for judgment, with regard to entrapment, made by Lord Nicholls of Birkenhead, Lord Mackay of Clashfern, Lord Hoffmann, Lord Hutton and Lord Scott of Foscote, on 25 OCTOBER 2001, in which Lord Nicholls of Birkenhead stated that:

> *'In some instances a degree of active involvement by the police in the commission of a crime is generally regarded as acceptable. Test purchases fall easily into this category. In Director of Public Prosecutions v Marshall [1988] 3 All ER 683 a trader was approached in his shop in the same way as any ordinary customer might have done. In breach of his licence he sold individual cans of lager to plain-clothes police officers'.*

More specifically he goes onto say that;

> *'In Nottingham City Council v Amin [2000] 1 WLR 1071 a taxi was being driven in an area not covered by its licence. The driver accepted plain-clothes police officers as fare paying passengers. Police conduct of this nature does not attract reprobation even though, in the latter case, the roof light on the taxi was not illuminated. The police behaved in the same way as any member of the public wanting a taxi in the normal course might have done. Indeed, conduct of this nature by officials is sometimes expressly authorised by Act of Parliament. The statute creating an offence may authorise officials to make test purchases, as in section 27 of the Trade Descriptions Act 1968. Thus, there are occasions when it is necessary for the police to resort to investigatory techniques in which the police themselves are the reporters and the witnesses of the commission of a crime. Sometimes the particular technique adopted is acceptable. Sometimes it is not. For even when the use of these investigatory techniques is justified, there are limits to what is acceptable. Take a case where an undercover policeman repeatedly badgers a vulnerable drug addict for a supply of drugs in return for excessive and ever increasing amounts of money. Eventually the addict yields to the importunity and pressure, and supplies drugs. He is then prosecuted for doing so. Plainly, this result would be objectionable. The crime committed by the addict could readily be characterised as artificial or state-created crime. In the absence of the police operation, the addict might well never have supplied drugs to anyone.'*

Using the SARA Model

When investigating, try keeping an open mind. Look at the evidence from all sides and do not ignore any angles, you may use problem solving models to help you.

One problem solving model commonly used in many ASB cases is the SARA model of problem solving;

The SARA model has four phases: Scan (descriptive exploration of the problem), Analysis (identifying the underlying causes of the problem), Response (addressing the problem by action), Assessment (measuring the effectiveness of the response).

1. Scan the problem, looking at all angles inc. info from:
- Witnesses (neighbours)
- Victims
- Alleged Suspects
- Police – CAT, PCSOs, Safer Schools Officers
- Local Authority - Various departments (street cleaning – youth service – housing, ASB teams – Community Safety, RSLs, Park Patrols, Noise Teams, Environmental Health, Trading Standards)
- Police
- Schools
- Local shopkeepers - Customers
- Residents Associations
- Neighbourhood Watch
- MP & Councillors
- Conduct an environmental visual audit (see Appendix 6 for more information on EVAs).

Once you have scanned what the problem is, or ascertained what crime has been committed, what legislation has been breached etc. You will need to look into it in more detail to determine who the potential offenders are and what action should be taken. This next stage of the investigation, the fact finding process is known as the analysis stage. Further chapters in the book go into more exact details of carrying out a full investigation.

2. Analysis may involve collecting information about offenders and victims, the time of occurrence, location and other details of the physical environment, the history of the current problem, the motivations, gains and losses of involved parties, the apparent (and hidden) causes and competing interests, and the results of current responses.

For example, scanning might have revealed that there were many thefts from shops in a particular area, but analysis will provide the hour, day or month that the thefts took place and from which particular shops. This detailed information will form the basis of your investigation.

Police and other practitioners may need to talk to colleagues, partners, local businesses, or to members of the community to better understand the problem. As well as police data, information held by other organisations such as insurance companies, hospitals, local authorities, probation and schools may be useful.

Another tool which can be used at this stage is the Problem Analysis Triangle (PAT) which appears to derive from the Routine Activity Theory developed by Cohen and Felson (1979) and Felson (1994). PAT breaks incidents down into three constituent elements:

- the features of the incident's location
- the features of the caller/victim
- the features of the offender or of the source of the incident.

It helps to be as precise as possible in defining the problem, having identified the incidents to be included in the analysis. It is crucial to establish what it is about the place, caller or victim, and the offender or source of the problem that causes it to arise, and how and when happens. This may need some lateral thinking to define the factors behind a problem.

Analysis

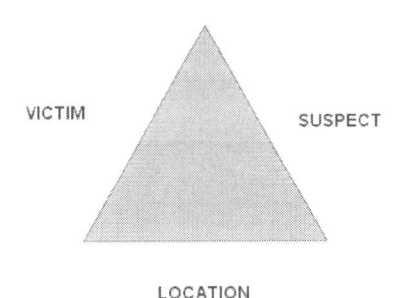

```
        VICTIM    △    SUSPECT
              LOCATION
```

Every case of anti social behaviour has a victim, a suspect and a location.
Removing any one element of the 'triangle' will solve the problem

It is important that we do not assume that the complainant is always the victim and those who shout the loudest should not get a better service than the quiet or weak & CCTV is not the answer to all crime and disorder problems.

3. Response - Once we have conducted the investigation and established the offences and the offender that has committed them you will need to look at what your response will be, how you will respond, what enforcement action you will take, will you give a warning or prosecute? (For more information on this see Chapter 16 - Determining the level of enforcement action to take – Alternatives to prosecution).

4. Assessment - Once you have done this, it is not all over, you will then need to assess (evaluate) the action you have taken, was it successful, what would you do differently next time. For instance you may have got a successful prosecution but the fines may have been small as the offence may have seemed minor i.e. dropping litter, however this may have a wider impact on the community and it may be a big problem in that area, therefore you may decide to do an impact statement, with your next prosecution for litter, explaining to the magistrates the wider impact on the community, thus hoping that they may take a firmer stance on this issue.

There are 6 Measures of Success for any case

1. Total elimination of the problem
2. Partial elimination – Fewer incidents
3. Incidents remain the same but less serious/harmful
4. Incidents remain the same but better response by agencies
5. Find more appropriate agency to deal with problems
6. Assist victims to better deal with problems themselves

Points to note
1. We should not assume that the complainant is always the victim
2. Those who shout the loudest should not get a better service than the quiet or weak
3. Sometimes people's expectations of what we can achieve are too high
4. CCTV is not the answer to all crime and disorder problems

Chapter 6 - Legislation covering all investigation

As well as the legislation under which an offence may have been committed, there is a further consideration to be made as to whether other statutory legislation will in any way affect your investigation. This section contains some of this other legislation. These Acts may affect your investigation even if it is not the legislation under which you may prosecute.

6.1 Human Rights Act (HRA) 1998

All investigations need to be carried out in accordance with the Human Rights Act, 1998 Whilst no Act could be said to be more important than another in law, this is the single most all encompassing Act you will come across. It has a bearing on **everything** you do. Ignore the HRA at your peril!

The act is very extensive and sets out many rights but here are some of the main rights that may be affected by you action or lack of action:

Article 1*	-	Protection of property – every person is entitled to the peaceful enjoyment of his possessions and may not be deprived of their possessions (which include things of economic value) except in the public interest
Article 2	-	Right to life
Article 3	-	Prohibition of torture including inhuman or degrading treatment or punishment
Article 5	-	Right to liberty and security
Article 6	-	Right to a fair trial
Article 7	-	No punishment without law
Article 8	-	Right to respect for private and family life
Article 9	-	Freedom of thought, conscience and religion
Article 10	-	Freedom of expression
Article 11	-	Freedom of assembly and association
Article 14	-	Prohibition of discrimination (sex, race, colour, language, religion, political or other opinion, national or social origin, association with a national minority, property, birth or other status)

*Also known as the First Protocol

As you can no doubt imagine, the scale of this Act is vast - far too much to reproduce here. Instead, the following questions can be asked when beginning an investigation to determine whether further consultation with the Human Rights Act is necessary before proceeding...

Are the actions or inactions you may take prescribed by law?

Can the affected rights be **legitimately** interfered with?

> *Some articles, such as Articles 1 and 8, will contain information on when it is permissible to interfere with the right.* **The occasions when a right can be interfered with are very specific in their application and any instruction must be followed to the letter**

Is there a limitation contained within the affected Article relating to a specific right?

> *Some rights are limited dependent on…*

What aim are you seeking to pursue? What relevant considerations are taken into account e.g. personal circumstances of the people affected?

> *Is what you are doing or not doing necessary in a democratic society? Does it pursue a pressing social need? Is it proportionate and are there relevant and sufficient reasons for it?*
> *You may suspect someone of a breach of law but is your investigation likely to be so intrusive as to undermine the democratic ideal of freedom and right to a fair trial that you are supposed to be upholding?* **Never allow personal feeling to cloud your judgment!**

Of course, the Human Rights Act only applies in those countries who have signed up to it. The **European Convention of Human Rights** is the adoption of the Human Rights Act within European Law. When dealing with Local Authority enforcement issues within EU member states, investigators will consider the following articles of the ECHR in virtually every case:

> **Article 6** of the European Convention of Human Rights states that everyone has the right to a fair trial. This right extends to the pre-trial investigation stage as the court has to take article 6 into account when looking at any evidence. They may declare this evidence inadmissible if it was not gathered in a lawful manner.
>
> **Article 8** of the European Convention of Human Rights protects every persons right to a private and family life. In some cases this may be breached, for instance, under certain types of surveillance. The Regulation of Investigatory Powers Act 2000 (RIPA), designed to allow for surveillance that will not breach Article 8, will be covered in more detail later.

Since the Act came into force it has unlawful for any public authority, including a court or tribunal, to act (including a failure to act) in a manner which is incompatible with a Convention right.

> *The definition of "public authority" is at section 6 (3) of the Human Rights Act. It includes -*
> - *A court or tribunal, and*
> - ***any person certain of whose functions are functions of a public nature***

Furthermore, if the results of an investigation are presented before a Court or Tribunal (criminal or civil), that court or tribunal will itself be a "Public Authority" under the Human Rights Act. The Court or Tribunal will therefore be under a duty to ensure that in relation to its dealings with the individual(s) before it, the individual's human rights are not breached. As stated above, the European Court of Human Rights has declared that fair trial procedures apply in the pre-trial investigation stage. The Court or Tribunal will have to take human rights into account when considering questions of admissibility of evidence and exclusion of any evidence they deem to have been obtained in breech of this Act.

A brief note on SECONDARY PARTIES –

> *Be aware that secondary parties may be affected by your decisions. You will need to record who is likely to be affected and what actions you have taken to minimise the effects on them/or the reasons for carrying out the actions. This should be recorded on the investigation file, in order that you can justify your actions.*

6.2 Police and Criminal Evidence Act (PACE) 1984

The Police and Criminal Evidence Act was introduced in 1984 to establish a balance between the powers of the British Police and the rights of members of the public. PACE contains codes of practice which govern how evidence is collected and gathered in criminal investigations. PACE also governs how interviews of witnesses and suspects should be conducted in order to ensure that evidence is gathered in a fair manner.

The codes run from A to H. The codes used in association with enforcement procedures, both Local Authority and Police, are listed below. There are many occasions on which a private investigation should also take guidance from PACE 1984...(although it is not compulsory for none public body officers i.e. civil investigators and private detectives to adhere to PACE, if they do not then any evidence they have gathered will not be admissible in a court of law, and therefore can not be used in a prosecution.

Code A: Deals with the exercise by police officers of statutory powers to search a person or a vehicle without first making an arrest. It also deals with the need for a police officer to make a record of such a stop or encounter. On 1 January 2009, Code A was amended to remove lengthy stop and account recording procedures, requiring police to only record a subject's ethnicity and to issue them with a receipt.

Code B Covers the practise for searches of premises and seizure of property, this should be taken as best practise even when carrying out searches by consent or when empowered to ask for the production of documents.

Code C Covers the detention, treatment and questioning of suspects.

Code D Concerns the main methods used by the police to identify people in connection with the investigation of offences and the keeping of accurate and reliable criminal records.

Code E Covers audio recorded interviews with suspects and witnesses.

Code F Deals with the visual recording with sound of interviews with suspects.

Code G: Deals with statutory powers of arrest.

Code H Was brought out in July 2006 to take account of the Terrorism Act. And deals with the detention of terrorism suspects

It is important that these codes are adhered to at all times. Code C is probably the most widely used as it dictates that you must caution a person before asking them any questions relating to an offence. Therefore if you suspect an offence has taken place or that the suspect is about to reveal details of their possible involvement in a crime you should caution them immediately before any further questions are put (and preferably, though not always practicably, before the suspect admits his or her guilt). If you do not do this whatever they say may be inadmissible in court and therefore of no use. **It is not necessary to caution a person merely to establish their identity.** The wording of the caution will be explained in further detail later.

Again, to reproduce the entire text of PACE 1984 would take up far too much space. Later we will discuss the practical application of PACE in conducting interviews of witnesses and suspects. It is enough here to draw your attention to the existence and importance of the Act.

6.3 Regulations of Investigatory Powers Act (RIPA) 2000

The main purpose of the Regulations of Investigatory Powers Act 2000 is to ensure that surveillance (and other intrusive investigation techniques) undertaken are a justified infringement of Article 8 of the European Convention on Human Rights (ECHR) - **the right to privacy**.

RIPA lays down the circumstances and the methods with which it is **sometimes** permissible to interfere with the rights laid down in the ECHR. The two Acts are therefore inextricably linked. The first (RIPA) would not exist were it not for the second (ECHR).

As previously mentioned, Article 8, ECHR provides as follows:

(1) Everyone has the right to respect for his private and family life, his home and his correspondence.

It is further stated:

(2) There shall be no interference by a public authority with the exercise of this right except such as is in accordance with the law and is necessary in a democratic society in the interests of national security, public safety or the economic well-being of the country, for the prevention of disorder or crime, for the protection of health or morals, or for the protection of the rights and freedoms of others.

From (2) above we can see that when a public authority acts in a way which interferes with an individual's right to respect for their private and family life, that interference will violate Article 8 **unless...**

(a) it is in accordance with the law **and** (b) it is necessary (and proportionate) in a democratic society because of one or more of the interests then listed. So, the interests - the **only** times at which it is permissible for a public authority to interfere with Article 8 - are as follows:

> In the interests of national security
>
> To protect public safety
>
> For the economic well-being of the country
>
> For the prevention of disorder or crime
>
> For the protection of health or morals
>
> For the protection of the rights and freedoms of others.

RIPA covers the following surveillance activities;
- Covert Human Intelligence Source (CHIS)
- Intercepting communications
- Directed surveillance
- Property Interference (Obtaining communicated Information).

For the purposes of this guide we shall mostly concentrate on the first and third of these; Covert Human Intelligence Sources and Directed Surveillance (Chapter 10 - Practical Application of RIPA 2000). It is almost inconceivable (never say never!) that a Local Authority officer would be in a position to intercept communications or be involved in property interference. These are the preserve of the security forces and high level police operations and do not need to be discussed in detail here. Suffice to say, if you ever find yourself in a position to use these powers, you will have had extensive and detailed training beforehand!

6.4 Data Protection Act (DPA)

The Data Protection Act applies to the public and private sector, it places liability on individuals to protect all individuals. The act governs obtaining, recording and holding data. For the act to be applicable to data it must;
- Be private information
- The subject must be living
- The individual must be the focus of the data
- The information must be biographical
- The Data must be recorded – However Under the Freedom of Information Act public authorities are expected to, for the purposes of this act, include any unstructured documents or e-mails (private organisations don't have to reveal any unstructured documents). Therefore you will need to keep tidy notes, and don't write anything on them that you wouldn't want others to see as you may have to disclose them, at some stage! However you don't have to disclose any information that is relevant to an investigation or court case.

For data to be protected under the DPA The questions to ask are:

- is the data personal?
- if yes, is it recorded on a computer or other automated equipment; or in
- a relevant filing system; or in an accessible record?
- if yes, is it to be processed?
- if yes, one of the 'pre-conditions' for fairly and lawfully processing the
- personal data must be satisfied

In order for anyone to hold data on anyone else, the collection and storage of such data must have been consented to, and it must be necessary. If data is of a sensitive and personal nature, there must have been explicit consent from the person who's data it is, as well as it being necessary.

The Data Protection Act also places a duty on the collector to process the information properly. Processing data includes doing nothing with it. Therefore all notes made as part of an investigation, whether later used or not, must be kept safe/stored appropriately (see Chapters 9 and 10 on evidence collection and storage).

It is an offence (strict liability) to process personal data without notification unless one of the following exemptions applies:

a. processing for personal, family and household purposes including
b. recreational
c. processing for "core" business purposes of personnel administration,
d. advertising and marketing and PR, and accounts and record keeping
e. processing for certain not-for-profit bodies
f. processing for the maintenance of public registers
g. national security.

For every request the following questions should be asked:

1. Am I sure the person is who they say they are? (For this reason particular care should be taken if the request is made over the telephone.)
2. Is the person asking for this information doing so to prevent or detect a crime or catch or prosecute an offender?
3. If I do not release the personal information, will this significantly harm any attempt by the police to prevent crime or catch a suspect? (The risk must be that the investigation may very well be impeded.)
4. If I do decide to release personal information to the police, what is the minimum I should release for them to be able to do their job?
5. What else (if anything) do I need to know to be sure that the exemption applies? Eg why is it necessary to provide the personal information, or how will it assist in the prevention or detection of crime?
6. Even if it is decided the exemption applies the personal data does not have to be released

7. If in doubt, for example a duty of confidentiality may be breached by the release, the requesting organisation can be asked to obtain a court order for release
8. Release of the personal information in obeying the court order will not be a breach of DPA

For further information consult the Office of the Information Commissioner.

Principles of Data Collection

When carrying out data collection it should be proportionate and relevant to its purpose.

There are 8 principals that must be applied to data gathering and processing.

1. Data collection should be fair and lawful, therefore it must comply with RIPA (see Chapter 10).
2. It must be collected for specified and lawful purposes.
3. Data must be adequate, relevant and not excessive.
4. Data must be accurate and up to date.
5. Data should be kept no longer than necessary.
6. The subjects rights must be respected.
7. The appropriate security measures should be undertaken – the level of security will be dependant on the harm that could be caused if the data fell into the wrong hands and the nature of the data to be protected.
8. The data should not be transferred outside the EEA (as the country may not be secure). Data can be put on the intranet with the subjects consent as long as the appropriate precautions are taken.

Let us look at each in further detail:

1. Information must be gathered fairly and lawfully.

   The data subject must be informed that data is being gathered about them & how the data will be used, the purposes for processing and any other information which the data subject would need to have to make the processing fair (subject to exemptions, for example where to do so would prejudice the prevention or detection of crime), public authorities must have a statutory basis or power for processing personal data – they must act within their powers (*intra vires*) (see DPA Schedule 1 Part II paragraph 1.(2)) & information should not be obtained by deceiving or misleading the subject. Exemptions from the Fair Processing Code where the data was obtained from a third party include, disproportionate effort for the data controller.

   Where investigations are conducted under the Regulation of Investigatory Powers Act 2000 (RIPA) (5.3, above) and these involve the processing of personal data, that must still be processed fairly and lawfully because DPA will apply (see further the Employment Practices Data Protection Code Part 3 from the Information Commissioner).

2. Data must be gathered for specified and lawful purposes.

   Data should only be obtained for lawful purposes, as specified to the individual and where personal data are disclosed to another person, the data controller must consider how the recipient intends to use the data (see further DPA Schedule 1 Part II paragraph 6).

3. Data must be adequate, relevant and not excessive.

4. Data must be accurate and up to date.

   Personal data shall be accurate and where necessary, kept up to date (see DPA Schedule 1 Part I paragraph 4).

5. Data shall not be kept longer than necessary.

6. Subject's rights must be respected.

> Personal data shall be processed in accordance with the rights of the data subject under DPA.

7. Appropriate security measures.

> Appropriate technical and organisational measures shall be taken against unauthorised or unlawful processing of personal data and against accidental loss or destruction of, or damage to, personal data (see DPA Schedule 1 Part I paragraph 7).

8. Restriction on transfer of data outside EEA.

> Personal data shall not be transferred to a country or territory outside the European Economic Area (i.e. the member states of the European Union plus Norway, Iceland and Liechtenstein) unless that country or territory ensures an adequate level of protection for the rights and freedoms of data subjects in relation to the processing of personal data (see DPA Schedule 1 Part I paragraph 8).

Further to 8, *above*, for the performance of such a contract the following must also be satisfied.

1. The transfer is necessary for reasons of substantial public interest. The Secretary of State may specify by order the circumstances in which a transfer is to be taken to be necessary for reasons of substantial public interest.
2. The transfer is necessary for the purpose of, or in connection with, any legal proceedings (including prospective legal proceedings).
3. The transfer is necessary for the purpose of obtaining legal advice, or the transfer is otherwise necessary for the purposes of establishing, exercising or defending legal rights.
4. The transfer is necessary in order to protect the vital interests of the data subject.
5. The transfer is part of the personal data on a public register and any conditions subject to which the register is open to inspection are complied with by any person to whom the data are or may be disclosed after the transfer.
6. The transfer is made on terms which are of a kind approved by the Commissioner as ensuring adequate safeguards for the rights and freedoms of data subjects. It is not the practice of the Commissioner to consider or approve individual draft contracts submitted to her.
7. The transfer has been authorised by the Commissioner as being made in such a manner as to ensure adequate safeguards for the rights and freedoms of data subjects.

Where the eighth principle does not seem to apply:

a) When under a contract with the data processor the data controller transfers personal data from the UK to a data processor outside the EEA, but under the terms of the contract the data controller remains legally responsible for ensuring the information is processed in line with the data protection principles.
b) Where the personal data physically passes outside the EEA but where no substantive processing operation is performed on the personal data, eg where an email is sent from a sender to a recipient in the UK, but the internet route is outside the EEA.

Exemptions from the Data Protection Principles

As with the Human Rights Act, there are a number of exceptions to the eight data protection principles. These are contained in full in Part IV (sections 28-36) and Schedule 7 and in various Statutory Instruments. In summary the exceptions relate to amongst other categories:

- National security (A certificate of exemption, signed by a Minister of the Crown, is conclusive evidence of the fact that the exemption is required for safeguarding national security. This can be overturned by the Information Tribunal on appeal. For further detail on this exemption see s.28 DPA).
- Crime and taxation

- - the prevention or detection of crime
  - the apprehension or prosecution of offenders; or
  - the assessment or collection of any tax or duty or of any imposition of a similar nature)
- Information available to the public by or under an enactment.
- Disclosures required by law or made in connection with legal proceedings
- Armed forces
- Management forecasts and planning
- Negotiations between the employer and employee
- Legal professional privilege
- Releasing information to prevent or detect crime;
- The Information Commissioner has issued a Data Protection Good Practice
- Note Releasing Information to prevent or detect crime v1.0, 08.08.06. It
- includes the following points:
- DPA does not stop the release of personal information because it is needed
- for a s.29 purpose
- Section 29 is an exemption in DPA that allows the release of personal
- information for a s.29 purpose, but there are limits on what can be released
- It only allows the release personal information for the stated purposes and
- only if not releasing it would be likely to prejudice (that is, significantly
- harm) any attempt by police to prevent crime or catch a suspect

Access

Subjects are allowed access to information about them. Requests must be made in writing so that the identification can be verified, if you need to you can ask for further information or identification before giving out the data requested. You must confirm what data you have about them and if you do have data about them or not. If there are images or details of other people with the requested data, these must be redacted. Responses must be made within 40 days, this period starts from when you receive the fee or any additional information that you have requested. However you do not need to provide information if this will take a disproportionate effort and the person requesting the information should take all reasonable steps to assist you in obtaining the information for them. They must identify themselves, be specific about what information is required and should explain to you for what purpose they required the information. The same rules apply if you are requesting information from another organisation, therefore its best to fill in a data request form.

Enforcement of Breech of DPA

The DPA grants enforcement powers to the Information Commissioner, as well as powers to search premises and seize materials. Enforcement Notices are issued where the Information Commissioner's assessment is that there has been a breach of the principles and it cannot be settled informally. In support of the Information Commissioner's enforcement is the power to serve an information notice requiring the data controller to provide information specified in the notice. If the Information Commissioner considers that breaches of the data protection principles have occurred, enforcement action can be taken against the data controller, who can appeal to the independent Data Protection Tribunal. Where the Tribunal upholds the Commissioner's enforcement action and the data controller continues to break the principles, it becomes a criminal offence for which the Commissioner can prosecute (see s.47(1) DPA).

The data controller must inform the Information Commissioner of certain details about the processing of personal data carried out by that data controller. Those details are used by the Commissioner to make an entry describing the processing in a register which is available to the public for inspection. The principal purpose of having notification and the public register is transparency or openness. The public should know or should be able to find out who is carrying out processing of personal data and other information about the processing, such as, for what purposes the processing is carried out.

We've seen in the previous chapters how the laws in Great Britain have evolved over a great period of time, evolving in an almost organic way to reach the stage we now find them. This evolution of the law has often come at great cost and against a background of civil unrest, uprising and war, and all of these are invariably accompanied by hardship, famine and personal loss. The enforcement of this law has also evolved in the same way. Gone are the days when a feudal Baron would send three or four heavily armed knights to extract tolls or fines from the populace. As modern day enforcement officers, we must never lose sight of the importance of this evolution. The law has grown up with a single aim; that of protecting the population of this country against tyranny and oppression. The law is not personal. It does not make distinction based on religious or sexual preference, or on basis of ethnicity. The law of the country is applicable to every citizen of the country equally. You may hear it said, and quite often, that the law is not equal. That there are those who are treated more equally than others, perhaps based on wealth or influence. If this is the case it is the fault of no one but the citizens of this country for allowing it to be so. We are all of us responsible for allowing or preventing the actions of the society in which we share. Therefore, as enforcement officers, but also as citizens who may one day have to answer questions from the other side of the dock, please remember the time and historical significance of that which you are choosing to serve. Please remember that the law of this nation and the continued goodwill of the people of this nation toward that law, rests in your hands. You are the frontline; the face of the court. Make sure it is a fair face. An open face, and an understanding face.

6.5 Freedom of Information Act 2000 (FOIA)

The FOIA creates a right to access to all recorded information held by public
authorities, this includes any information relating to anyone, as long as it is not private or sensitive information. Under the Act, information such as unstructured personal data held by public authorities for personnel purposes, there is also, a class-based exemption, including investigations and proceedings conducted by public authorities, court records, and trade secrets. Additionally a 'prejudice exemption', that includes the interests of the UK abroad and the prevention and detection of crime.

Anyone wishing to request information must do so, in writing, giving the applicant's name and address, and describing the information sought, they must be specific with their request.

Provided compliance does not exceed the prescribed financial limit, the information should be provided within 20 days of receipt of the request.

Even though there are exemptions and even if the information request may fall into those such a category, the public authority must still consider whether the information must be
released in the public interest, unless an absolute exemption applies (e.g. information supplied by or relating to bodies dealing with security matters).

If the information requested meets the necessary requirements and the information is not supplied within the prescribed time, the information commissioner can serve an enforcement notice requiring disclosure.

It will be a DPA matter where a living person makes a request regarding personal information about them, as the DPA gives individuals rights of access to the information which is held about them. This right is commonly referred to as a "subject access right". If necessary and at the request of an affected individual, a court may order a data controller to comply with an individual's subject access rights (see s.7(9) DPA).

Whether the request is brought under the FOIA or DPA (s.40 FOIA), unstructured personal data (i.e. paper records making reference to individuals) is also covered where a public authority holds it. Private sector organisations are not subject to this extended meaning.

Under the DPA there are exemptions from the need to make information available, as follows;
The data controller is entitled to withhold information in limited circumstances. It is necessary to consider if these exemptions apply, on a case-by-case basis. The exemptions include; if the individual makes repeated requests to access the same or similar information – this would excuse the data controller from responding to vexatious requests (see s.8(3) DPA);
Where the data includes information about another person who has not consented to the disclosure of that information, unless "it is reasonable in all the circumstances to disclose [the information]... without the consent of the other individual" A balancing of the interests of the two individuals is required by the data controller in this situation. If the data includes information which is marked as "confidential" it may be legitimate to withhold the release of that information (see 'third party' information) (sees.7(4) DPA);
Where the information is a reference given in confidence by the data controller to a third party for the purpose of educating, employing or training the data subject or in relation to services provided by the data subject (see

DPA Schedule 7 paragraph 1);
Where the information relates to a management forecast and its release will prejudice the controller's ability to conduct its business or activity (see DPA Schedule 7 paragraph 5);
Where the information relates to negotiations between the data controller and
the data subject, the disclosure of which may prejudice those negotiations(see DPA Schedule 7 paragraph 7)
Where information and to the extent of the release being likely to prejudice the combat effectiveness of any of the armed forces of the Crown (see DPA Schedule 7 paragraph 2);
Where data controllers process personal data in the course of marking
examinations and personal data in examination scripts, subject to conditions
after publication of results (see DPA Schedule 7 paragraph 8);
Where a claim to legal professional privilege could be made in respect of the
information in legal proceedings (see DPA Schedule 7 paragraph 10);
Where disclosure of information would expose a data controller to proceedings for the commission of an offence (other than a DPA offence – e.g. breach of Official Secrets Act) (see DPA Schedule 7 paragraph 11);
For the purposes of safeguarding national security (see above s.28 DPA);
To the extent that the disclosed information would be likely to prejudice the prevention or detection of crime, or the assessment or collection of any tax, duty or imposition of a similar nature (see above s.29 DPA);
Where provision of the information would prejudice the proper discharge of regulatory functions by public authorities regarding malpractice (see s.31 DPA)

Requests under FOIA for personal data that relates to a third party will be treated as a FOIA matter. However, in determining the response to the request FOIA requires consideration of DPA.

6.6 Criminal Procedure and Investigations Act 1996 (CPIA).

The CPIA sets standards and procedures for investigators that:

- regulate the investigation process;
- regulate the recording and retention of material that is found or is generated in the course of an investigation.

The Code of Practice (The Home Office Code) made under Part II of the CPIA governs the regulatory aspects of the CPIA. Although the Home Office Code applies only to police officers, other investigators (including HSE inspectors) are required to "have regard" to any relevant provisions of the Home Office Code

The CPIA requires that "all reasonable lines of enquiry are pursued" in the course of an investigation. Implicit in this phrase is the requirement that investigators should pursue lines of enquiry that could assist the defense. This is clearly a move away from the normal investigation process in which the investigator primarily looks for evidence to support the prosecution case. It requires the investigator to be a "finder of fact".

6.7 - Criminal Justice Act 2003

The Criminal Justice Act 2003 *received Royal Assent on 20th November 2003.* The Act was brought in to bring up to date various areas of the criminal justice system in England and Wales and, to a lesser extent, in Scotland and Northern Ireland. CJA2003 contains a wide range of measures, amending the law relating to police powers, bail, disclosure, allocation of criminal offences, prosecution appeals, *autrefois acquit* ("double jeopardy"), hearsay, bad character evidence, sentencing and release on license. As with the Acts previously mentioned in this Chapter, CJA2003 is an over-arching piece of legislation which will influence most aspects of taking a prosecution to court. As such, an investigator/enforcement officer will need to have a good knowledge of this piece of legislation.

The Act is in fourteen parts. We shall concentrate here on the sections most relevant to the day to day work of an investigator or enforcement officer, but as with all legislation so far discussed, it is always worthwhile reading the full legislation to get a broader view of its impact. For example, although we will not cover it in detail here, the Criminal Justice Act 2003, Part 12, deals with the sentencing of dangerous offenders. Particularly, it covers sentencing in relation to the offence of Murder. Imagine you are interviewing a suspect in relation to such an allegation. Do you think it would help to have some idea of the sentence this person may face if found guilty? To have some idea of what they may be willing to risk in order to escape justice?

The full list of contents of the CJA2003 is as follows:

Part 1 - provisions on the Police and Criminal Evidence Act.

Part 2 - provisions on bail.

Part 3 - provisions on conditional cautions.

Part 4 - provisions on charging.

Part 5 - provisions on disclosure.

Part 6 - provisions on allocation and sending of offences.

Part 7 - provisions on trials on indictment without a jury.

Part 8 - provisions on live links.

Part 9 - provisions on prosecution appeals.

Part 10 - provisions enabling retrial for serious offences following acquittal (double jeopardy).

Part 11 - provisions on evidence of bad character (Chapter 1) and provisions on hearsay evidence (Chapter 2).

Part 12 - provisions on sentencing and is split into a number of Chapters.

> Chapter 1 - general provisions about sentencing.
>
> Chapter 2 - provisions on community orders for offenders aged 16 or over.
>
> Chapter 3 - provisions on prison sentences of less than 12 months.
>
> Chapter 4 - further provisions on orders under Chapters 2 and 3.
>
> Chapter 5 - provisions on dangerous offenders.
>
> Chapter 6 - provisions on release of prisoners on licence.
>
> Chapter 7 deals with the effect of life sentences.
>
> Chapter 8 - other provisions about sentencing.
>
> Chapter 9 - supplementary provisions.

Part 13 - miscellaneous provisions and

Part 14 - general provisions.

Provisions Relevant to Police Officers

Parts 1 to 4, CJA2003 have particular impact on how the policing role is carried out.

Part 1 of the Act makes fundamental changes to the process for establishing and amending codes of practice under the Police and Criminal Evidence Act 1984 (See Chapter 14 for further details of PACE). At present, PACE codes cover stop and search, searching of premises, detention, identification, and the recording of interviews. Issuing a new code or revising an existing one requires extensive public consultation and an active process of parliamentary consideration. The amendments made by CJA 2003 provide for a targeted consultation process and for a level of parliamentary scrutiny proportionate to the amendments proposed, thus speeding up the whole process.

As a result, CJA2003 has given the police extra power in regards to stop and search, allowing officers to perform searches on those suspected of criminal damage. Furthermore, any person accompanying a constable on a search of premises may now take an active part in the search, as long as they remain accompanied at all times. This is particularly useful in cases where a substantial volume of evidence or raw data may need to be collected and sifted at the scene of a crime. In the case of computer, forensic or financial evidence, this may require expert help provided by a person who is not a constable, but who may be an *Expert Witness* (see 11.13 and 18.8)

In Part 2, CJA2003 amends the prisoners right to apply for bail. The right of a prisoner to make an application to the High Court is abolished. Previously an application could be made to the Crown Court and the High Court as of right. The right to make a bail application by way of judicial review remains, although only if its more stringent tests applicable are satisfied. The Crown Court is now effectively the final arbiter of bail in criminal cases. Prosecution appeals against Magistrates' Courts decisions to grant bail are extended to all criminal offences which could lead to imprisonment.

Part 3, introduces conditional cautions. Alongside the common practice of issuing a caution (see also 16.7) which are unconditional, police now have the option to issue a conditional caution. As with any caution, conditional or otherwise, guilt must be accepted by the offender for the caution to be issued. Conditional cautions must be issued in accordance with a Code of Practice, issued by the Home Secretary. They will impose conditions upon the offender. If these conditions are later breached, the offender may then be prosecuted for the offence.

Note: The Criminal Justice and Immigration Act 2008 extends the adult conditional caution scheme to young offenders.

Part 4 of CJA 2003 contains a number of provisions relating to the charging and holding of offenders. The Act extends to persons who are aged 14 and above the provisions in the Police and Criminal Evidence Act 1984 enabling officers to detain a person after charge to test for specified class A drugs, subject to conditions in section 63B of PACE (as introduced by Section 57 of the Criminal Justice and Court Services Act 2000). An appropriate adult is required to be present during the testing procedure for those under the age of 17. The Secretary of State may alter the minimum age by order subject to the affirmative resolution procedure. Particularly useful to know should you be instructed as a private investigator to the defence of such a case.

The Act extended the time for which someone could be detained without charge, under the authority of a superintendent, from 24 to 36 hours for any arrestable offence, rather than for any serious arrestable offence.

The Act extends the powers of the police to enable them to take fingerprints and a DNA sample from a person whilst he is in police detention following his arrest for a recordable offence. Fingerprints can now be taken electronically and the police will be able to confirm in a few minutes the identity of a suspect where that person's fingerprints are already held on the National Fingerprint Database. It will prevent persons who may be wanted for other matters avoiding detection by giving the police a false name and address. Fingerprints taken under this provision will be subject to a speculative search across the crime scene database to see if they are linked to any unsolved crime. The DNA profile of an arrested person will be loaded onto the National DNA Database and will be subject to a speculative search to see whether it matches a crime scene stain already held on the Database. This will assist the police in the detection and prevention of crime.

Provisions Relevant to all Enforcement Officers/Investigators.

Perhaps the part that is most relevant to us in terms of this book as it affects all enforcement officer/investigators, no matter what role you are in, is that of disclosure, (Part 5 of the Act). This is particularly relevant as it affects any officer conducting a prosecution.

CJA2003 makes amendments to the Criminal Procedure and Investigations Act 1996 relating to prosecution and defence disclosure. Following these amendments the prosecution are under a continuous duty to disclose evidence.

The test for disclosure is important to know and remember –

Evidence which undermines the prosecution case or assists the defence case.

Disclosure Officer

The decision as to whether or not unused evidence meets the above requirement rests with a Disclosure Officer.

In some organisations, or on large scale investigations, it is not uncommon to have a team of disclosure officers working on a case. However, there will always be a Lead Disclosure Officer who has overall charge of the team. At other times, on small scale investigations, it is perfectly acceptable for the Investigator to act as Disclosure Officer.

It is the Disclosure Officers role to ensure that disclosure is provided as required by CPIA 1996 and CJA 2003. Failure to disclose evidence may lead to a a wrongful conviction, an successful abuse of process argument, an acquittal or the quashing of a conviction on the grounds of unsafe evidence.

Disclosure of Prosecution Evidence

Firstly, it is worth noting that the defence cannot force a prosecutor to disclose any such evidence until such times as a defence statement has been produced. Guidance issued by the Attorney General also makes it explicitly clear that the defence should not make general and unspecified claims in defence in the hope of advanced disclosure. In other words, a defence statement must clearly state the points on which the defence wish to argue their case. Only after this is received by the prosecutor are the prosecution under an obligation to provide disclosure.

Section 8 application to the court to force the prosecution to disclose an item of evidence.

As previously stated, prior to disclosure, the defence statement must now state each point at which issue is taken with the prosecution and why, and any particular defence or points of law (such as evidential admissibility or abuse of process) upon which the defendant is going to rely. On top of this, the defendant must also provide a list of defence witnesses, along with their names and addresses. The prosecution may then interview those witnesses.

Details of any defence expert witness instructed must also be given to the prosecution, whether or not they are then used in the case. However, the law on legal privilege are not amended by CJA 2003, so the contents of any correspondence or expert report would remain confidential to the same extent as before.

Co-defendants must now also disclose their defence statements to each other as well as to the prosecution. The duty to serve defence statements remains compulsory in the Crown Court and voluntary in the Magistrates' Court.

The defence can seek further disclosure using the method known as a 'Section 8' application.

A Section 8 application may be made in the following circumstances:

"(1) This section applies where the accused has given a defence statement under section 5, 6 or 6B and the prosecutor has complied with section 7A(5) or has purported to comply with it or has failed to comply with it.
(2) If the accused has at any time reasonable cause to believe that there is prosecution material which is required by section 7A to be disclosed to him and has not been, he may apply to the court for an order requiring the prosecutor to disclose it to him."

Section 8 enables the defence to apply to the court for further disclosure of unused prosecution material if certain conditions are met.

Subsection (1) of section 8 provides that the section applies when the defence has given a defence statement under sections 5, 6 or 6 B of CJA2003, as discussed above, and the prosecutor has complied with his continuing duty to disclose or purported to comply with it or has failed to comply with it.

Subsection (2) of section 8 enables the accused to apply to the court for an order requiring the prosecutor to disclose material, to the accused, if the accused has reasonable cause to believe that there is prosecution material that should have been, but has not been, disclosed to the accused pursuant to the prosecutor's continuing duty to disclose.

Other Significant Aspects of CJA 2003 having bearing on Investigations

A "terminating ruling" is one which stops the case, or in the prosecution's view, so damages the prosecution case that the effect would be the same. Adverse evidentiary rulings on prosecution evidence can be appealed for certain serious offences before the start of the defence case. These appeals are "interlocutory", in that they occur during the middle of the trial and stops the trial pending the outcome of the appeal. They differ in this respect from a defendant's appeal which can only be heard after conviction.

Also very relevant to the prosecutor is that CJA 2003 amended the mode of trial provisions to allow the court to be made aware of a defendant's previous convictions at the mode of trial stage (that is, when the Magistrates' Court decides whether certain offences are to be tried summarily before them or before a judge and jury at the Crown Court). The right to commit to the Crown Court for sentence (when the Magistrates' Court regards its own powers as insufficient) is abolished for cases when it has previously accepted jurisdiction. These provisions amend the previous position when a defendant whose bad prior record means that he is tried summarily and then sent elsewhere for sentence; the same type of court deals with both trial and sentence in ordinary cases. The provisions were introduced under section 41 and section 42 of Part 6 of the Criminal Justice Act 2003

As well as previous convictions, CJA 2003 also allows the prosecution to raise matters of bad character. Evidence of the defendant's bad character includes not only previous convictions but also previous misconduct other than misconduct relating to the offence(s) charged. This fundamental change in the law means that under section 101(1) of the Criminal Justice Act 2003 the prosecution is free to adduce evidence of the defendant's bad character subject to it passing through any one of seven gateways, **unless** it would have such an adverse effect on the fairness of the trial that it should not be admitted. Subsection 1 provides: in criminal proceedings evidence of the defendant's bad character is admissible if, but only if—

(a) all parties to the proceedings agree to the evidence being admissible,

(b) the evidence is adduced by the defendant himself or is given in answer to a question asked by him in cross-examination and intended to elicit it,

(c) it is important explanatory evidence,

(d) it is relevant to an important matter in issue between the defendant and the prosecution,

(e) it has substantial probative value in relation to an important matter in issue between the defendant and a co-defendant,

(f) it is evidence to correct a false impression given by the defendant, or

(g) the defendant has made an attack on another person's character.

Further to changing the law regarding the admissibility into evidence of a defendant's convictions, CJA 2003 imposed statutory restrictions, for the first time, on the ability of defence lawyers to cross-examine prosecution witnesses about their own criminal records.

Hearsay Evidence

Section 114 of the CJA 2003 defines hearsay evidence as:

A statement not made in oral evidence in criminal proceedings and admissible as evidence of any matter stated

Notably, the Act made substantial reforms to the admissibility of hearsay evidence, building upon the reforms of the Criminal Justice Act 1988, which regulated use of business documents and absent witnesses. Various categories of the common law were preserved and the remainder abolished. A new power was incorporated to permit hearsay evidence if certain 'interests of justice' tests were met:

- It is in the interests of justice to admit it (see section 114(1)(d))
- The witness cannot attend (see section 116)
- The evidence is in a document (see section 117)
- The evidence is multiple hearsay (see section 121)

The meaning of "statements" and "matter stated" is explained in section 115 of the CJA 2003. "Oral evidence" is defined in section 134(1) of that Act.

Trials and Juries

The Act permits offences to be tried by a judge sitting alone without a jury in cases where there is a danger of jury-tampering. It also expands the circumstances in which defendants can be tried twice for the same offence (double jeopardy), when "new and compelling evidence" is introduced.

The Act expanded the number of people eligible for jury service, a) by removing the various former grounds of ineligibility, and b) by reducing the scope for people to avoid service when called up. Only members of the Armed Forces whose commanding officers certify that their absence would be prejudicial to the efficiency of the Service can be excused jury duty.

This has been controversial, as people now eligible for jury service (who were previously ineligible) include judges, lawyers and police officers. .

A case where a judge was satisfied that there was "evidence of a real and present danger that jury tampering would take place", and "notwithstanding any steps (including the provision of police protection) which might reasonably be taken to prevent jury tampering, the likelihood that it would take place would be so substantial as to make it necessary in the interests of justice for the trial to be conducted without a jury may also be conducted without a jury. This provision came into force on 24 July 2007.

On 18 June 2009, the Court of Appeal in England and Wales made a landmark ruling under the terms of the Act that resulted in the Lord Chief Justice, Lord Judge, allowing the first-ever Crown Court trial to be held without a jury. The case in question involves four men accused of an armed robbery at Heathrow Airport in February 2004. It will be the fourth time the case has been tried, but this time in front of only a single judge. The trial opened on 12 January 2010.

The Act allows for retrial for serious offences and thus creates an exception to the double jeopardy rule, by providing that an acquitted defendant may be tried a second time for a serious offence.

The prosecutor must have the permission of the Director of Public Prosecutions prior to making the application for a second trial. Authority to give permission may not be exercised generally by Crown Prosecutors (typically employed lawyers of the Crown Prosecution Service), but can be delegated. There is a requirement for "new and compelling evidence", not adduced during the original trial, to be found. A "public interest" test must also be satisfied, which includes an assessment of the prospect of a fair trial. The application is made to the Court of Appeal, which is the sole authority for quashing an acquittal and ordering a re-trial. The offence to be re-tried must be one of a list in Schedule 5 of the Act, all of which involve maximum sentences of life imprisonment.

CJA2003 was not the first legislation to affect the double jeopardy rule: an Act in 1996 provided that an acquittal proved beyond reasonable doubt to have been procured through violence or intimidation of a juror or witness could be quashed by the High Court.

The first person to be re-tried under the Criminal Justice Act 2003 for an offence he had been previously been acquitted of was Billy Dunlop. He was acquitted of murdering his former girlfriend Julie Hogg in 1989. The application was brought by the Crown with the consent of the Director of Public Prosecutions, given in writing on 10 November 2005 and heard by The Lord Chief Justice of England And Wales on 16 June 2006.

Sentencing

Included here for the sake of information and completeness, though not necessarily of day to day importance to the investigator, Part 12 of the Criminal Justice Act made substantial amendments to nearly every part of sentencing practice, containing 159 sections and referring to 24 schedules. The regime set out in the Powers of Criminal Courts (Sentencing) Act 2000 was almost wholly replaced, despite having been passed only three years previously and not yet fully in force.

CJA2003 sets out in statute the principles underlying sentencing: punishment, crime reduction, reform and rehabilitation, public protection and reparation. These were previously part of the common law. The Act also created the Sentencing Guidelines Council to give authoritative guidance.

The previous and varied types of community sentence (such as community punishment order, community rehabilitation order, drug treatment and testing order) have been replaced by a single "community order" with particular requirements, such as unpaid work, supervision, activity, curfew, exclusion, residence and others, alone or in combination with each other. The intent was to tailor sentences more closely to the offender.

The previously deprecated "suspended sentence of imprisonment" returns, also allowing elements of a community order to be imposed at the same time. This ensures the offender knows what sentence of imprisonment is facing him or her if he or she fails to comply with the order or commits a further offence during the period of suspension. Provision is made for sentences of intermittent custody, and custodial sentences followed by period of community work and supervision.

CJA2003 replaced the previous law on the mandatory sentencing of defendants convicted of violent or sexual crimes, introducing compulsory life sentences or minimum sentences for over 150 offences (subject to the defendant meeting certain criteria). The Act created a new kind of life sentence, called "imprisonment for public protection" (or "detention for public protection" for those aged under 18), which may even be imposed for offences which would otherwise carry a maximum sentence of ten years.

In response to unprecedented prison overcrowding, Parliament passed sections 13 to 17 of the Criminal Justice and Immigration Act 2008 (with effect from 14 July 2008), which imposed stricter criteria for the imposition of these sentences, and restored judicial discretion by providing that they were no longer compulsory when the criteria were met.

The House of Lords ruled in *Regina v. Home Secretary* that the Home Secretary was not permitted to set minimum terms for life sentences. The reasoning was on the basis that in order to have a fair trial under Article 6 of the European Convention on Human Rights, a defendant should be sentenced by an independent tribunal (that is, a judge) and not a politician who will have extraneous and irrelevant concerns which may affect his or her judgment. The then Home Secretary, David Blunkett MP, responded in a written response to a parliamentary question on 25 November 2002.

The case of Anderson deals with the Home Secretary's power to set the tariff, or minimum period a convicted murderer must remain in custody until he becomes eligible for release. This power has ensured ministerial accountability to Parliament within the criminal justice system for the punishment imposed for the most heinous and serious of crimes. ... This judgment will affect only the issue of who sets the tariff in each case. As is proper in a democracy, Parliament will continue to retain the paramount role of setting a clear framework within which the minimum period to be served will be established. I am determined that there should continue to be accountability to Parliament for these most critical decisions. ... I intend to legislate this Session to establish a clear set of principles within which the courts will fix tariffs in the future. ...in setting a tariff, the judge will be required, in open court, to give reasons if the term being imposed departs from those principles.

Specific plans were announced by Mr Blunkett on 7 May 2003, applying to murders committed on or after 18 December 2003. Schedule 21 of the Act sets out the minimum terms for those convicted of murder. These terms are in the form of "starting points" which the sentencing judge is required to start from, before increasing or decreasing the minimum term according to other circumstance of the offence and offender. A set of aggravating and mitigating circumstances are set out in the schedule, and sentencing judges must give reasons for their choice of starting point and departures from it. The starting points are as follows:

- Whole life - imposed upon offender over the age of 21 at the time of the offence, where the offence involves
    - the murder of two or more persons, where each murder involves any of the following-
        - a substantial degree of premeditation or planning,
        - the abduction of the victim, or
        - sexual or sadistic conduct,
    - the murder of a child if involving the abduction of the child or sexual or sadistic motivation,
    - a murder done for the purpose of advancing a political, religious or ideological cause, or
    - a murder by an offender previously convicted of murder
- 30 year minimum - imposed upon offender over the age of 18 at the time of the offence, where the offence involves
    - the murder of a police officer or prison officer in the course of his duty,
    - a murder involving the use of a firearm or explosive,
    - a murder done for gain (in furtherance of robbery or burglary, done for payment or done in the expectation of gain as a result of the death),
    - a murder intended to obstruct or interfere with the course of justice,
    - a murder involving sexual or sadistic conduct,
    - the murder of two or more persons,
    - a murder that is racially or religiously aggravated or aggravated by sexual orientation, or
    - a murder normally resulting in a whole life tariff committed by someone under 21.
- 15 year minimum - applies to any murder not covered by another category
- 12 year minimum - applies to any murder committed by someone under the age of 18

Since the legislation was passed, many judges have set lower terms than those suggested by the Act. The principles of this legislation did indeed state that judges could set lower terms than those recommended, but if the Attorney General was of the opinion that the minimum term was unduly lenient he could petition the Court of Appeal to have the term increased. The (slightly inaccurately described) "double jeopardy" discount, whereby the Court of Appeal takes into account the uncertainty and distress to the respondent prisoner of being sentenced a second time, was explicitly excluded by the Act in relation to minimum terms for murder.

Chapter 7 - Beginning the Investigation

7.1 - The First Steps

You've already taken them, haven't you?

Consideration of the law? Whether or not any of the statutory legislations mentioned in the previous chapter are applicable or can be interfered with if necessary? Whether there is even a case to be answered…

Well, yes of course, but now we really enter the first stage of the investigation proper; the real business of finding out who committed the crime.

Now, what do your notes say?

What do you mean you haven't got any yet!............

7.2 - Record Keeping/Storage

Accurate records should be kept at all stages of the investigation, including the planning stages, and all of the sources of evidence. It is essential that the evidence is gathered and stored in a way that the reliability, credibility, continuity and the integrity of the evidence is preserved.

Even documentary evidence for a civil case needs to be stored accurately, this is best practise, also it may later become a criminal case and then to be used in the criminal proceedings the investigator will need to show how the evidence has been preserved and not tampered with, in order to do this everything that happens to the evidence needs to be recorded. You will also need to record the source of the evidence (you will not always need to reveal this to the defendant but should have a record of it).

Also all information and evidence must be stored securely, in accordance with the Data Protection Act (DPA). In practice this will usually mean in a safe, secure facility that only you or your colleagues/managers have access to. When storing data electronically, you should ensure you have a dedicated file in which to store information so as to ensure there is no means of unauthorised access. Often, this will be a personal disk drive that only you have access to.

Do you have a desk with locking draws? Is there a storage cabinet within the office? Is it secure enough or can cleaning staff access this area?

7.3 - Telephone Logs

From your very first telephone call, to the moment you seal the prosecution file for delivery to the legal department or solicitors office, you should record everything. This includes all telephone records. It may be possible to prove after the fact that a call has been made - by using an itemised bill, for example, but this is still no substitution for contemporaneous notes of any conversation made at the time.

If the contents of a telephone conversation are particularly sensitive or if any significant statements have been made, then it is essential to make a full note of the conversation in your PACE notebook as per the standard procedure detailed in Chapter 11. If your conversation has been overheard by any third party, be sure to ask them to sign your notes.

7.4 - Equipment

Have you got your notebook when you leave the office. Did you remember your authorisation card to prove you credentials? Have you got a pen - very embarrassing cautioning someone for an offence and then asking to borrow a pen to take notes. All basics but essential. The following is a lengthy, though not necessarily complete, list of other items you may find useful:

Body Armour/Stab vest -

Alarming though this may seem, physical attacks on local authority officers is on the increase. It is considered that an officer is more likely to be struck with a blunt instrument, or body part, rather than being the target of high velocity handguns or purpose made edged weapons, such as knives or swords. If you do decide to purchase Personal Protective Equipment (PPE) then make sure it is fit for purpose. Hard shell armour that can be worn below a shirt of t-shirt (covert) will probably protect you from blunt instruments more effectively than more expensive soft armour designed primarily to be bullet proof. It also tends to be much lighter and therefore more comfortable. As with any specialised product, ask the manufacturer for their advice. Be honest about what you expect to face. Not many sub-machine guns find their way into the hands of disgruntled off-licence proprietors.

Digital Camera -

We shall see later how digital images should be captured and stored (Chapter 15). It is therefore important that you have a camera that is compatible with the average system and does not rely too heavily on specialised software to perform.

Binoculars -

Notwithstanding what we have discussed already in regard to the Human Rights Act and RIPA2000, a pair of binoculars is a handy addition should you need to take down a vehicle registration, or when trying to identify offenders. Again, it is not necessary to spend a fortune on these.

Night Vision Glasses -

Not so much of a specialised requirement as you might think, particularly for those who go on to specialise in detecting and preventing Anti-Social Behaviour. Excellent for covert observations.

Dragon Light -

Or any other high powered torch.

Radio -

We shall discuss radio communications in more detail in Chapter 9. It may be that your employer will provide a radio that connects to a town centre ShopWatch or PubWatch scheme, it may be that the CCTV control centre will also have radio to keep officers up to date with incidents or ongoing operations. However, if you work for a private organisation as part of a team, a radio will be indispensable for maintaining quick and effective communications. There is no security guarding outfit that would operate without some form of radio communication system and should you decide to become a store detective, you will definitely need a radio to stay in touch with the uniformed guards. Make sure it's fully charged! You keep your mobile phone charged up. Treat your radio with the same care.

7.5 - Disclosure

See also Chapter 7. Before beginning an investigation it is a requirement under the Criminal Procedure and Investigation Act 1996 that you record who is the officer in charge of the case (presumably, though not necessarily, you) and who is the Disclosure Officer for the case. It is this officer who will have the job of ensuring that all information relevant under CPIA 1996 is disclosed in accordance with that Act. The disclosure officer can be the investigating officer or you may find it is a senior manager. (see template prosecution files in the appendix section) for an example of the kind of sheet to use at the beginning of an investigation. This sheet should go at the head of the file.

Chapter 8 - Personal safety

As a enforcement officer/investigator personal safety is very important. When you are carrying out enforcement against people they can become emotional. Sometimes they may become angry leading to the potential that you may encounter violent situations. Or they may panic and there is the very real possibility of medical problems becoming exacerbated by overly aggressive investigation techniques.

Always check the lone working procedures for your work place, ensure you are familiar with the latest version and have the correct personal protection equipment. Find out if your workplace has a restricted persons list/potential violent persons list, if they have this, check before you go on visits to ensure that the person you are visiting isn't a risk to you.

8.1 - Respect at all Times

Even when you are enforcing you should still treat people with respect. If you explain to them what is going on and why, and take time to listen to them, they are less likely to become angry. You can always start off going into a situation with a friendly approach and become more assertive if this is not working.

If you go into a situation too aggressively/assertively it is harder to calm the situation down and the other person is more likely to become more aggressive in response to how they are perceiving you to be. There is a danger that you can then get into a 'attitude/aggression cycle' where they perceive you as being aggressive and match this with an aggressive manner, your perception that they are awkward or aggressive is then re-enforced and you respond to them in such a way and the situation can quickly spiral out of control. Especially as it is very natural to mirror peoples behaviour, as well as mirroring other peoples behaviour we often end up feeling, how we perceive that person is feeling by the way they are acting, if you act calmly the other person is likely to calm down.

People will also act differently according to their cultural beliefs and customs, for instance they may look away because in their culture it is disrespectful to stare, which may make you think that they are acting shifty. Be aware of cultural differences and don't make assumptions about people.

It is important to go into a situation with a clear mind and not to make assumptions about how they make act based on pre-conceived ideas.
Although you should use your instinct and if they have previously been aggressive, obviously you need to be more cautious and take greater steps to secure your safety.

You should also look at the situation and any trigger factors that may make someone, act irrationally/ be more likely to be aggressive towards you. i.e. tiredness, if you know a driver has been working late the night before its best not to disturb the driver early the next morning.

You should also remain in control of the situation, you must remain professional and neutral and shouldn't react to anything they say. Often in these situations our body may revert to the 'fight or flight' syndrome which will take the blood away from our brain, thus restricting the ability to think calmly. You will therefore need to take deep breaths in through the nose and out through the mouth to help you keep calm.

> Fight or Flight - So named as this is the bodies natural response to dangerous situations - a response honed over millions of years of evolution and consequently, not easily over-ridden by our conscious thoughts. Physical signs of the beginnings of 'Fight or flight' are:

A brief Note on - FIGHT OR FLIGHT

So named as this is the bodies natural response to dangerous situations - a response honed over millions of years of evolution and consequently, not easily over-ridden by our conscious thoughts. Physical signs of the beginnings of 'Fight or flight' are:

1. Increased heart rate

2. our vision may narrow (sometimes called "tunnel vision")

3. You may notice that your muscles become tense.

4. You may begin to sweat.

5. Your hearing may become more sensitive.

All of these changes are part of the fight or flight syndrome. As the name implies, these changes are preparing you for immediate action. They are preparing you to flee, freeze (kind of like a deer does when caught in someone's headlights), or to fight. All of these are adaptive bodily responses essentially designed to keep us alive, and because these responses are important to our survival, they occur quickly and without thought. They are automatic.

8.2 - Personal Space

It is important to remain alert and to watch the other persons reaction so that you are not caught off guard. If you know a particular driver you may find it easier to recognise when they are showing serious signs off stress. These often vary from person to person but when someone who has been shouting suddenly goes quiet, it can mean they are about to attack. Look for danger signs such as raised voice, direct or indirect threats, excessive repetition, excessive eye control, reddening of the face, pacing, taking an aggressive stance, invading your personal space. A reasonable reactionary gap is between 4-6 feet. Don't get too close to the other person (they will also need more personal space if they are angry and invading this may make them more angry), if possible adopt a stance to protect your personal space and make it easy to protect your body, such as putting your hand under your chin and your arm in front of your body, this also make it look like you are intent on listening to them. If possible you could ask them to take a seat, or divert their attention from their anger momentarily, perhaps by asking them a question. When a person is angry they are less likely to hear what is being said, especially from those not involved. However listening and understanding the other person is very important in conflict resolution, make it clear to them that you are trying to understand what they are saying and try and be un-judgmental and impartial.

8.3 - Risk Management

The greater the threat i.e. how likely it is that you may be in danger and the more vulnerable you are the higher the risk to you is. You should always ensure that you are aware of what the risks are and take measures to reduce the risk. You may not be able to control the threat but you can reduce the risk by making yourself less vulnerable, for instance, by not going out on any enforcement either when its late at night or is you feel that there is a threat i.e. the person you are visiting may have been violent or shown signs of the likelihood to become violent, in the past.

It is important that you take responsibility for your own safety and ensure that someone always knows where you are and what you are doing. Put protocols in place such as a signing in and out board where all staff members detail where they are going, if going on visits, and what time they will be back.

Ensure that you are aware of the risks and prepare and take precautions to minimise them. Do not work alone at night, always tell someone where you are going and how they can contact you. Have a code so that you can phone someone up and discretely alert them.

Check if your organisation has a list of potentially violent people that you can check before going out and dealing with people. If someone is potentially violent, avoid going out and visiting them without backup, ask the police to attend with you. Never put yourself in a situation where you are not in control, don't allow doors to be locked etc.

When you are out and about we come in contact with members of the public, who can often be unpredictable, especially at night if they have been drinking. Always wear personal protection equipment (PPE) that includes; stab vest, high visibility jackets for road side working which also have reflector strips and hard wearing boots to protect your feet and ankles. Also have shoulder bags or utility belts so that our hands are free and to avoid us becoming a target.

If you are injured at work and don't have your PPE equipment on you may not be able to claim.

If you use your own car for work to reduce the risks we have contacted the DVLA to take our number plates off of the public register. It is also a good idea to have a less conspicuous car, so that you blend in and don't have personalized number plates. Always check with your insurance company that you are covered to use your car for work duties.

8.4 - Conflict Management Training

As with surveillance, this book will not attempt to teach comprehensive conflict management technique. The arena of personal safety and defensive combat is well served and the serious investigator would do well to invest some type of conflict management training / self defence / break away techniques. Any of these will give you an increased chance of surviving an attack, but as with any potentially dangerous situation, prevention is better than cure. It is important to be aware of when a situation is escalating and to be aware of how you deal with people so that it doesn't actually escalate in the first place.

8.5 - After Work

Also we don't automatically become safe when we stop working, we also need, as any person does, to take care when travelling home to and from work, especially when its late at night/early in the morning - when taking public transport avoid carriages with only one occupant and If you see your way being blocked by a stranger and another person is very close to you from behind, move away. This can happen in the corridor of the train or on the platform or station. Do not be afraid to alert authorities if you feel threatened in any way. Always sit at the front of a bus on the bottom deck near the driver; the same applies to a train.

8.6 - Other Practical Ways to Reduce Risk

- In car parks, always reverse park. If possible, park under a light and near a CCTV camera.
- When parking on the street alongside other parked cars, always allow enough space between your vehicle and the vehicle in front to prevent someone else trapping you. Even if they park very close to the rear of your vehicle, you should have enough to room to drive straight out.
- If unable to park nearby, note the location of any CCTV cameras or fire call points (alarms) in the car park in case someone does try and follow you and you need to raise the alarm.
- Be aware of your surroundings. If there is someone walking behind you, head for the general area of coverage of the CCTV camera. Employ basic counter-surveillance techniques to give them the opportunity to leave.
- Always keep your car doors locked whilst driving to avoid car jacking.
- If you do ever have an attacker in your car try driving fast to a Police station, or drive to a built up area and crash into another car at low speed to alert attention or beep your horn, they are unlikely to attack you whilst you are still driving for fear of crashing.
- Make sure that your car is in good repair, and always have more than enough fuel.
- Don't leave valuables in the car. If you must carry things with you, keep them out of sight or locked in the boot.

- Check your phone is charged up, ensure you have credit on your phone before you go out.
- Look confident and give eye contact to show that you have seen any one hanging around.
- Try to avoid wearing headphones or having any distractions such as using a mobile.
- Consider carrying a personal alarm, if used in the vicinity of the attackers head it will stun the attacker giving you a few seconds to escape as well as alerting others that you need help.
- Always keep a torch and spare mobile phone in your car.
- Look at your surroundings and understand them. Always note the location of exits, including fire exits, and plan your escape route as you move.
- Don't allow yourself to get blocked in.
- Look at door hinges so you are familiar with where the door handles are and which way the door may open.
- Keep an eye on anything that someone may pick up and use as a weapon.
- Whenever you go anywhere unfamiliar, check the surroundings, and note all potential hazards.
- If you witness an incident, always check for danger before rushing in to assist. Think about yourself first. Never put yourself in danger and before going to deal with an emergency.
- Before going out, especially on night time operations, ensure that you have the correct clothing to keep warm, are not tired, have enough food and drink etc. You will not make correct decisions if you are tired and hungry and bad decisions can make you vulnerable.
- Be aware that someone may seem drunk but may not be so. People sometimes pretend to be drunk and vulnerable so that you won't see them as a threat. Equally, someone may be hurt but may smell of alcohol as they have had a drink or two but due to an illness or injury such as a head wound or diabetes may be stumbling around and/or slurring words. If they genuienly need help, don't just ignore them, even if they may be drunk.
- Have the emergency services phone number programmed into your phones speed dial.
- Be friendly to people but be wary when talking to strangers and never give any personal details away.
- Don't assume someone is who they say they are, always ask for ID If you are driving an unfamiliar car be more vigilant with your controls but also familiarise yourself with the car and the central locking button, how the remotes work, where all the controls are and ensure it is correctly adjusted so you have maximum visibility.
- Check the vehicle before entering it. If unsure check underneath if you are in an area of high terrorist activity.
- If your car has been broken into your attacker may be inside it. Or your car may have been tampered with.
- Keep windows up and doors locked in unfamiliar surroundings but especially whilst stopped i.e. at traffic lights.
- Be vigilant to what other cars & pedestrians are doing.
- When in traffic, always leave a sufficient gap between you and the vehicle in front so that you can pull away quickly.
- Always have your car keys in your hand and don't press to open it until you are near enough to get in.
- If you need to speak to someone in the car only wind down the window slightly.
- Don't be predictable – change your movements daily and avoid predictable times and routes of travel.
- Don't talk about specific investigation or about your work to people who do not need to know.
- Have next of kin contact details on your phone – programme in an ICE (in case of an emergency) number.
- Keep a first aid kit in your car

8.7 - Terrorism

In today's current climate you also have to be aware of possible terrorist attacks;
Be wary of large vehicles parked outside public places, or anyone acting suspiciously, Keep an eye out for suspicious abandoned packages, briefcases or rucksacks and don't touch the package, clear the area and report it to the Police.

Before terrorists attack they will check out the area first – this is known as hostile reconnaissance. If someone looks like they don't fit in and they are paying too much attention to the surroundings, especially of they seem to be looking at security systems, raise the alert.

Terrorists can be anyone; they come in all shapes and sizes. Especially as en enforcement officer it is important to be aware of what you discuss with strangers or what others may overhear.

For further information on personal behaviour see Appendix 7, Personal Behaviours.

Chapter 9 - Surveillance and Counter-Surveillance

The subject of Surveillance is wide ranging and complex. It can take months of practical instruction to even begin to come to terms with the nuances of the various aspects. This guide is will attempt to offer information on basic techniques - but it is worth bearing in mind there are a number of courses available which aim to teach the subject in more detail. They can be found online or at specialist websites such as the Association of British Investigators, www.the-abi.org.

Surveillance is the monitoring of a person or a group of people for the purposes of determining their actions. Surveillance can take place with or without the knowledge of the target.

9.1 - Overt Surveillance

Overt Surveillance is any form of surveillance conducted in such a manner that the target could be reasonably expected to know they are the subject of surveillance. Examples of overt surveillance include retail store CCTV systems and town centre CCTV systems. The reason this is overt is because there are signs displayed in public areas notifying members of the public that they are being monitored. Overt Surveillance is not only performed by CCTV. Enforcement Officers are increasingly using overt surveillance when on patrol as a means of deterring crime, recording any crime that is committed, and protecting themselves. They do this through the use of hand held , or otherwise mounted cameras (headsets, vehicle frames). As long as there is clear direction to any person that recording is taking place, this type of surveillance is considered overt. To ensure evidence collected in this way is admissible in court, it is best practice to verbally inform persons of any filming. In this way, there can be no later claims of confusion!

9.2 - Covert Surveillance

In contrast to 8.1, above, Covert Surveillance is any form of surveillance undertaken without the knowledge of the subject. This is the type of surveillance that most people associate with investigation - the camera taking long range photographs from the building across the street, the pizza delivery van parked for weeks in the same spot with four men camped out in the back with their eves-dropping equipment. In reality, such extreme measures are relatively rare, and you will find most covert surveillance is conducted with nothing more than your own eyes and ears (and, for environmental health officers, your nose!).

9.3 - Pre-Surveillance

Before undertaking any surveillance, please refer to Chapters 6 and 10 which cover the Regulation of Investigatory Powers. Any surveillance should be undertaken with reference to this legislation even if there is no immediate intention to use the evidence for prosecution by a local authority. You never know where a case will eventually end up. Similarly, while we are on the subject, it should be noted that it is usually unacceptable to place any individual, business or groups under surveillance without previous intelligence to support such action. Surveillance is intrusive and should only be used when there is good cause to do so. Not to follow this rule could lead to allegations of undue harassment.

9.4 - Blending In

It is easier than you may think to fit in with your surroundings. Most people are extremely unobservant and will fail to notice the small tell-tale signs that mark you as an interloper in any particular situation. Wigs and false beards are generally out, although a basic cover story may be useful. If resorting to such tactics, the golden rule is to invent a cover that sticks broadly to the truth. Do not over complicate your story. NEVER claim personal connection with anyone you don't genuinely know - imagine the embarrassment when the conversation turns suddenly to mutual acquaintances you know nothing about. Ensure you are comfortable in your surroundings. Do you regularly frequent the tea rooms of the Ritz? Are you au fait with how to order a bacon and egg sandwich at a builders café off the Holloway Road? Do you know ????ETC ETC ETC. If not, don't panic. Simply ensure that you do plenty of research before embarking on the surveillance project. Search the internet, speak to people who do know about these things. Try to experience the venue as a paying customer before you end up on a professional engagement. If you still think you will struggle to carry off the deception, think carefully about taking on the job, or your method of completing the task. It is better to decline and give the appearance of being too busy, than to take on a contract you are unqualified to complete.

Clothing

While it is useful to wear clothes suitable to your surroundings, it is not essential. Never compromise your health (inclement weather) or personal safety (ability to escape quickly) in the interest of surveillance. It is nearly always possible to reach a satisfactory compromise. If in doubt, a pair of jeans will carry you through most situations.

Note: Beware children! They have a heightened sense of incongruity and are not afraid to comment loudly on things that have confused their sense of continuity or otherwise aroused their suspicion.

9.5 - Static Surveillance

This is any surveillance undertaken from a static position whether that be a park bench, a parked vehicle, or an adjoining building. Static surveillance is often proceeded by mobile surveillance. Static surveillance can last for minutes or months. Useful tips include:

Having a prop. Bring a newspaper or a book if you anticipate sitting anywhere alone for a long period of time. Or a laptop if the situation allows. A newspaper is especially useful as any relevant notes can be written on the paper while you pretend to complete the crossword. If you are not sure writing on the newspaper will provide enough space, a separate sheet of paper can be used as this will only look like rough scribbling to any casual observer.

Making sure you have a clear view. Sounds obvious until you try to watch a target from even the relatively short distance of ten feet away. Although it is highly likely your target will not even notice your presence, the mere fact that you know your reasons for being there will make you uneasy. You will consciously try not to look too much, thus potentially missing essential detail. The trick is to pick a position close enough to afford you have a good, clear view, but far away enough to allow you to watch continuously. As with all good surveillance, this ability will develop with practice.

If possible, use mirrors. Beware of the angles of reflection. While you can see the target, it is possible they can see you. It is not always as easy as you might think to watch continuously in this way.

9.6 - Mobile Surveillance, Foot

Foot surveillance is often used around town centres and enclosed areas, for short distances. It is surprisingly easy to follow someone without them noticing as many people simply do not pay attention. However, any person who has a heightened awareness, i.e. someone who has or is about to commit a crime, those with a guilty conscience, or those with some element of training in counter surveillance will notice the things others do not. Useful tips for successful foot surveillance include:

Follow on the opposite side of the road. Most targets will not check all of their immediate area. They may well notice the person behind them but will not often see the person across the road. Remain at a forty five degree angle or greater from the targets line of sight to prevent being spotted in their peripheral vision.

Use reflective surfaces to maintain visual contact. Shop windows, car windows, Without looking straight at the target you can see where they are headed.

Carry a map. Ideal in large cities. Look like a tourist. In this way you can stop suddenly to check your bearings thus helping to negate any basic counter-surveillance methods.

9.7 - Mobile Surveillance, Vehicle

Mobile surveillance, the following of targets by vehicle, is more rarely used, although its use is more prevalent in domestic investigation cases. The main point to remember is that you are not the police, and you are definitely not James Bond. Traffic laws are not to be broken simply because the vehicle in front has to be followed at all costs. If you know your expected route beforehand (targets home to targets office, for example, driver the route and make a note of any roadworks/tricky junctions/ places where you will have to be very close to reduce the chances of losing the target. More tips include:

Follow that car! When foot or static surveillance becomes mobile without warning, a taxi ight be your only option. A cliché, perhaps, but a useful tool nonetheless, the taxi can be the investigators only hope of staying in contact with the target.

Maintain a safe distance In cities it is advisable to follow directly behind the target vehicle. This may seem blatant but there are far too many chances for you to lose your target - traffic lights, sudden junctions, busy roundabouts. Away from cities, on long motorway stretches or quieter country roads, it is enough to follow with two or three vehicles between you and the target.

Park at the earliest convenience. The aim is to stay within visual contact.

9.8 - Use of Cameras

As covered in 8.1, the use of cameras can be overt. For covert use of a camera you will sometimes require specialist equipment - button hole cameras, hidden microphones. However, ordinary digital video recorders can be easily adapted for use in a covert fashion. Again, there are courses describing in detail the many methods an investigator can adopt, but for now it is enough for us to consider the basic options:

1. Camera in a handbag. For ladies, or confident men. Place the camera in the handbag and cover with a other contents.
2. The mobile telephone camera - perfect for unobtrusive recording. Pretend to be texting or even speaking on the phone when in reality you are filming. IMPORTANT - you will need to ensure you can download any images to a secure server (Detailed in Chapter 10). Not all mobile telephones will allow you to do this.
3. Headcams - can often be worn underneath a hat, obscuring all but the lens. Has the added advantage of filming whatever you happen to be looking at.

9.9 - Electronic Surveillance

Using electronic equipment to listen in the private conversations is not allowed and can only be authorised under extreme circumstances by the Secretary of State. This also covers mail intercept and any other form of highly intrusive action. For this reason, we will not cover the use of covert electronic surveillance., However, there is no reason that telephone call cannot be recorded providing fair warning is given beforehand. This is exactly the type of notice given regularly by insurance companies/utilities companies etc. Another method of warning is an audible beep on the line. This does not have to be accompanied with any further explanation and it is worth remembering this in case you ever hear it.

9.10 - Multiple Teams

In a word - Practice! Aside from any other information, this is the one key instruction. It is hard enough to follow a moving vehicle through a crowded city without losing your target, let alone manoeuvring other vehicles to intercept and take over the observations at the same time.

Multiple team members need to be willing to speak quickly, act decisively and all need to know they have the full backing and understanding of fellow team members. This kind of co-ordinated operation can only be achieved after many months not to say years of practice. It is as well, should you be considering a specialisation in surveillance, to organise regular training sessions with work colleagues in order that this kind of speed and accuracy become second nature.

9.11 Contact between Team Members

Basic radio procedure is shared by most emergency services and you would do well to learn the protocol. Not only will this help you to follow conversations, it will hep you to become a trusted part of any multi-agency team. Some basic rules are as follows:

> 1. Make individual messages brief but talk often - in other words, tell each other where you are at all times but do it using short sentences.
> 2. make sure you have back up communication devices such as mobile telephones or landline numbers.
> 3. ALWAYS assume a third party is listening in on your call. Radios are least secure, mobile telephones slightly more secure and Landlines most secure. However, nothing is 100% safe. NEVER divulge sensitive or confidential information over the airwaves.

See Appendix 5, Phonetic   Alphabet and Common Radio Procedure.

9.12- Planned Withdrawal

As with any type of operation, the key to the success of surveillance is knowing when to withdraw. It is imperative that surveillance activity stops at the point you have enough evidence to build a strong case, and before the subject becomes aware of your presence. If your target becomes aware of your presence it not only risks the operation , but also your personal safety. Never exceed your authorisation - it is not only dangerous, it is pointless as any evidence gathered in an unlawful manner will not be admissible at court. Not only that, you could find yourself being charged with harassment or worst.

9.13 - Spontaneous, or Unplanned, Withdrawal

Always have an emergency fall back for surveillance in areas of high risk. This should be a well populated, well lit area with multiple exits. You should try to ensure that this fall back position is located close to any form of transport you may be using, be that private vehicle or public transport. If you have time it is advisable to reconnoitre areas of particularly high risk, and plan for routes of escape, including obtaining information on local transport availability. Take note of road works, of temporary traffic lights, of barriers which are locked after certain times. Imagine withdrawing to your car only to find the exit to the car park locked until morning - not good!

8.14 - Counter-Surveillance

Counter-Surveillance is the art of reducing a surveillance operatives chances of obtaining information about you, your actions and your motives. If you suspect you have become the target of surveillance, you should take appropriate steps. The main thing is to stay alert, to note even the smallest details of your surroundings whenever possible and to be alert for any unusual changes in those details. Other methods of counter surveillance include but are not restricted to the following:

9.15 Static Surveillance

Do not sit close to windows.
Watch for those taking notes, or whose camera or mobile phone is pointed towards you (this can include when rested on a table - it only takes a second to press the button)
When possible, sit facing the entrance to a premises, or at least, looking out into the room.
Beware the positions of private CCTV systems.
If appropriate, engage suspicious persons in conversations. Casually enquire as to their business. Ask for directions, a light. If they are following you, they will be nervous and will react awkwardly unless very well trained (in which case, you might want to ask yourself how you made such powerful enemies)

Foot Surveillance

Entering a nearby building and leaving immediately by a different exit.
Stopping after turning a corner
Hailing a taxi
Entering a bus or a train just as it stops or starts
Varying your pace repeatedly
Stopping to look in shop windows.
Dropping a scrap of paper to see if anybody picks it up

Vehicle Surveillance

U-Turn
Parking in a busy a street
Circling the block
Turning left or right at a busy junction
Stopping just beyond a curve or just after the brow of a hill

9.16 Electronic Surveillance

Equipment for the de-bugging of rooms, protection against eavesdropping devices and computer viruses are all available commercially.

As can be seen with all of the above methods, counter-surveillance is generally about performing out-of-place actions and watching closely for the results.

Chapter 10 - Applying for Authorisation under RIPA 2000

10.1 - A Necessary Tool

Having determined that your investigation is sufficiently urgent enough to warrant an interference of Article 8 of the Human Rights Act for any one of the legitimate reasons (*in the interests of national security, public safety or the economic well-being of the country, for the prevention of disorder or crime, for the protection of health or morals, or for the protection of the rights and freedoms of others)*, you must now obtain authorisation to undertake covert surveillance.

Investigators may lawfully carry out covert direct surveillance, with the relevant authorisation providing that the surveillance is done in a lawful, necessary and proportionate way.

So…

10.2 - Directed Surveillance

If you are carrying out direct surveillance you don't need a warrant, just RIPA clearance. Direct surveillance is if someone is not expecting to be watched, i.e. if you have CCTV signs you can watch someone who is on CCTV (this is overt surveillance) but if you start to follow them with the CCTV cameras, they will not be reasonably expecting this and therefore it then becomes direct (covert) surveillance, this is okay if it is spontaneous i.e. you see them commit a crime and use the cameras to direct the Police to them, however if you know someone is going to be at a place at a certain time and you specifically set up an operation to watch them you will need RIPA clearance. When deciding the question to ask yourself is – What level of privacy is reasonable to expect. Even though someone maybe in a public place it is still reasonable to expect a certain level of privacy, anything that interferences with this will be classed as direct surveillance and you will need RIPA authorisation for this.

Directed Surveillance - is surveillance that is:

1. Covert but not intrusive
2. Carried out for the purposes of a specific investigation
3. Conducted in a way likely to provide 'private information' about any person (not just the subject of the surveillance)
4. Is NOT an immediate response to events or circumstances, the nature of which means it would not be reasonably practicable to get an authorisation under RIPA for carrying out the surveillance

5. 'Private information' must not be interpreted too restrictively. It comprises the right to establish and develop relations with others. It should be taken to include activities of a professional or business nature.

6. For the sake of clarity, covert surveillance is not considered to occur when using binoculars or cameras to reinforce normal sensory perception and does not involve the systematic surveillance of an individual. (See *Covert Surveillance Draft Code of Practice*, Home Office, 2000).

7. Situations where RIPA will apply and authorisation will be required will include:

    Recording telephone calls
    Sitting in cars carrying out observations and taking notes
    Use of Dictaphones etc when not on private premises as surveillance aids to make covert recordings of the subject
    Use of hidden CCTV to obtain evidence against a specific individual, eg to obtain evidence against anti-social tenants.

Investigators must consider in each case whether authorisation will be required for noise nuisance monitoring. The Council's standard letters addressed to the suspected source of the noise complaint warn that covert surveillance will take place and therefore where a statutory notice has been served on the person believed to be the source of the noise RIPA is unlikely to apply because the suspected source would then be aware they are likely to be subject to surveillance. However, if the notice is merely served on the owner/occupier of the premises and the source of the noise is believed to be a third party, authorisation under RIPA may be required as the investigation may (i) be covert in relation to that third party and (ii) may reveal private information about them.

10.3 - Closed Circuit Television Cameras

RIPA does not apply in situations involving the general monitoring and use of overt cameras, such as town centre cameras.

However, there may be occasions when CCTV is utilised to provide evidence about specific individuals in pre-planned operations. In such circumstances, the CCTV system must not be utilised unless the CCTV operators are satisfied, and have seen, that authorisation has been granted for that surveillance to take place. Except in exceptional circumstances (such as emergencies or at weekends).
To decide if you need a RIPA authorisation for your surveillance, ask yourself the following questions;

Are my investigation actions covert, i.e. does the **target** know I am watching?
Is it surveillance? (Did I just happen to be in the right place at the right time and notice the offence being committed?)
Is it relating to a specific investigation/operation? (Similar to above)
Am I likely to obtain private information?*
Is it planned?

Note - We must be extremely careful here. Many actions by persons could be deemed to be private. Private does not only relate to surveillance directed within a home. GIVE EXAMPLE HERE

If the answers to all of these questions are yes then you will need RIPA authorisation.

In practice, most covert directed surveillance will require RIPA authorisation. This is because it is likely you will answer yes to four our of the five above questions in most cases. The only question which provides for any level of ambiguity is that concerning private information. However, as we have seen in the above example, this can be a difficult decision to make. The rule of thumb should always be - If in doubt, seek authorisation.

Why do we not need authorisation for town centre CCTV?

The cameras are not hidden. There are within view of the public and there are notices advertising their use. Therefore, they are not covert.

A BRIEF NOTE on the scope of RIPA application   -

RIPA applies only to public bodies and not private companies, unless the private companies are acting on behalf of the public body. However, if a private company will, in the future, pass its investigation over to a public body i.e. a company investigating a staff member of theft may pass the investigation details over to the Police, then RIPA authorisation may need to be granted for any surveillance undertaken. If authorisation is not sought, when in court, the evidence not obtained in accordance with RIPA may not be taken into consideration. Therefore, obtaining the correct authorisation under RIPA, will ensure that the action is carried out in accordance with the law and will therefore make the activity less vulnerable to challenge under the Human Rights Act 1998. The action must still be lawful, necessary and proportionate.

Where does authorisation come from?

Each Authority or Public body that may have reason to employ directed surveillance will have appointed a number of Authorising Officers. These officers will not necessarily have any particular background in surveillance but they will almost certainly be among the most senior officers in the organisation.

Authorising officers must not grant authorisation unless they believe it *necessary*:

- In the interest of national security
- For the purpose of preventing of detecting crime or preventing disorder
- In the interests of the economic well-being of the UK
- In the interests of public safety
- For the purpose of protecting public health
- For the purpose of assessing or collecting any tax or duty etc payable to a government department
- For any other purpose specified by the Secretary of State by Order,

and *proportionate* in that the evidence to be gained by surveillance **cannot be gained by other means.**

This last point, that of proportionality, is a very important consideration. There must be serious thought as to whether there is any other means of obtaining the information and whether there is likely to be any collateral intrusion or interference with the privacy of third parties. Surveillance should, in most cases, be looked upon as the option of last resort.

What can be authorised?

- The directed surveillance or covert human intelligence source specified in the authorisation
- The authorisation must specify:

    - the conduct or use of the source or type of surveillance
    - the circumstances
    - the person against whom the source is used (if appropriate)
    - the purpose of the investigation or the operation involved

(See Appendix 6: example of form to be used for authorisation of covert directed surveillance)

10.4- Urgent Authorisation

What if I find myself in a position where there is no time to seek authorisation?

For an immediate response it is recognised that you may have to just react to circumstances and, given time constraints, may be unable to obtain RIPA authorisation.

Additional rules apply for authorising the use of covert human intelligence sources. Sufficient arrangements for all covert human intelligence sources must be in place to ensure:

- An officer has day-to-day responsibility for dealing with the source and for their security and welfare ("the handler"). This should be the officer responsible for the management of the investigation
- Another person has the general oversight of the use made of the source ("controller"). This should be the handler's line manager
- Someone must have responsibility for maintaining a record of the use made of the source. This must be the officer responsible for the management of the investigation
- The records must comply with the *Regulation of Investigatory Powers (Source Records) Regulations 2000*
- Authorisations must always be in writing, except in urgent cases where the grant or renewal of an authorisation can be given orally.

10.5 - Expiry and renewal of authorisations

The following time limits apply to an authorisation:

Type of authorisation	Expiry periods
Urgent oral authorisation	A maximum of 72 hours
Covert directed surveillance	A maximum of 3 months but must be regularly reviewed and cancelled when appropriate
Covert Human Intelligence Sources	A minimum of 12 months (1 month if source is under 18) but must be regularly reviewed and cancelled when appropriate

Renewal of an authorisation can occur at any time before it expires by an officer who could grant a new authorisation in the same terms. The authorising officer must also ensure time-limits are kept under strict review. However, before renewing an authorisation for the use of a covert human intelligence source the officer must consider:

- The use of the source since the grant or last renewal of the authorisation
- The tasks given to the source and the information supplied by him or her.

Renewals of authorisations must be recorded on the appropriate forms.

If you are planning to watch somewhere for a long period of time, for instance sitting outside a shop to see if they serve to someone who is underage, it is worth getting RIPA authorisation to cover yourself.

Whatever you do must be lawful, necessary and proportionate. In order to get RIPA authorisation you must carry out a pre-investigation to show that it is necessary and you must keep notes of any decisions that you make at all stages of the investigation.
If you decide that you don't need RIPA authorisation, record in your investigation notes that you have recognised RIPA and made a decision that it is not necessary, this is important if you need to justify it later on, especially if someone else takes over your case and needs to account for your decisions.

You can only undertake surveillance to gain information that you would not be able to gain by any other means and it must be done only to prevent and detect crime or to prevent disorder.

If you are using a RIPA authorisation you must also carry out a risk assessment in order to minimise collateral intrusion, i.e. so that you don't accidentally gain personal information on someone else who is not under investigation but from conducting the surveillance you may obtain information on, such as a neighbour. If you were to then come across information that on a third party suggesting that they were involved in a crime, about to commit a crime, or connected to your current, or for that matter any other investigation, you could conduct surveillance as immediately necessary but at the first reasonable opportunity you would need to apply for RIPA authorisation, as the regulations on RIPA state that;
- Authorisation must be given in writing except in urgent cases where life is endangered or the investigation or operation is in jeopardy.

The authorisation can't be ongoing and needs to be formally cancelled, you need to regularly review the authorisation and cancel or re-new it as appropriate, once you have obtained enough evidence you should stop the surveillance, you can't just carry on in case you gather more evidence. Once you have gathered the evidence you were authorised to gather, if you need to gather more information using a difference source, or you need to gather information about another topic you will need to either amend the current authorisation and resubmit it for approval or submit another authorisation.

10.6 - Cancellation of authorisation

The officer with responsibility for granting or renewing an authorisation must cancel it if it is no longer necessary and proportionate, and the legislative requirements in relation to covert human intelligence sources are no longer satisfied. Officers who have granted or renewed authorisations should therefore renew such authorisations on a regular basis, e.g. at least fortnightly.

If a deputy grants or renews an authorisation, both separately have a duty to cancel if satisfied the conditions are met. If the original officer who authorised the surveillance is no longer available, then it must be cancelled by their replacement or an equivalent, providing they are of the same or more senior management level than the officer who is no longer available.

10.7 - Scope of RIPA Authorisation

If you are planning to watch somewhere for a long period of time, for instance sitting outside a shop to see if they serve to someone who is underage, it is worth getting RIPA authorisation to cover yourself.

Whatever you do must be lawful, necessary and proportionate. In order to get RIPA authorisation you must carry out a pre-investigation to show that it is necessary and you must keep notes of any decisions that you make at all stages of the investigation.
If you decide that you don't need RIPA authorisation, record in your investigation notes that you have recognised RIPA and made a decision that it is not necessary, this is important if you need to justify it later on, especially if someone else takes over your case and needs to account for your decisions.

You can only undertake surveillance to gain information that you would not be able to gain by any other means and it must be done only to prevent and detect crime or to prevent disorder.

If you are using a RIPA authorisation you must also carry out a risk assessment in order to minimise collateral intrusion, i.e. so that you don't accidentally gain personal information on someone else who is not under investigation but from conducting the surveillance you may obtain information on, such as a neighbour. If you were to then come across information that on a third party suggesting that they were involved in a crime, about to commit a crime, or connected to your current, or for that matter any other investigation, you could conduct surveillance as immediately necessary but at the first reasonable opportunity you would need to apply for RIPA authorisation, as the regulations on RIPA state that;

- Authorisation must be given in writing except in urgent cases where life is endangered or the investigation or operation is in jeopardy.

The Police can carry out intrusive surveillance (this is surveillance that is a covert listening device that can either hear both ends of a conversation or is as clear as being in the room with the person that is having the conversation), they have to meet certain criteria, and under more extreme circumstances the Police and Government Security Services can carry out property interference surveillance under the Police Act 1997, this is usually in extreme cases such as that of National security, serious crime or the economic well being of the country, the Local Authority haven't got the power to do this but can carry out under consent, i.e. if they have permission from 1 side to listen into a 2 sided conversation, (for more information, please refer to the Home Office interception Codes of Practice), additionally if a listening device has been placed, with authorisation, in a room to listen to something specific in that room, and whilst their it accidentally picks up on another conversation with a third party, which there is no authorisation to listen into, there would be no breach, as this was incidental, however if it was placed in there, specifically knowing that it would hear that conversation, it would be a breach of RIPA.

Details of intercepted calls are not admissible on court but can be used to gather evidence to help with further investigations.

A telephone company can intercept calls to record or establish fact i.e. a call took place and at what time, however they can't make records for the content of the call (as per article 5 of the Telecommunications Data Protection & Privacy Directive), the content of calls can be recorded for business purposes if the person on the phone is informed and also for issues of National Security.

CHIS – Material obtained via a CHIS can be used in court. A person becomes a CHIS if you ask them to covertly investigate something for you, however if they are giving facts as per there normal course of business they are not a CHIS.

10.8 - Covert Human Intelligence Sources (CHIS)

Defined as establishing a personal or other relationship with a third person for the covert purpose of obtaining information and/or disclosing it covertly. Once authorisation is obtained to conduct directed surveillance against an individual however, further authorisation to act as a CHIS is not required. The authority must not use sources under the age of 18 without following additional safeguards, some of which are listed below.

If test purchases are made and the investigator has a verbal exchange beyond merely requesting and paying for the goods/services they are trying to purchase, they could be acting as a CHIS

A person who merely provides information about possible offences in their civic duty would not amount to a CHIS. However, a person who provides regular information, which is acted upon (and is not directed, by the investigating body) can be classed as a *confidential contact*. In that case, a CHIS authorisation will not be needed, but it would be strongly advisable to securely record all communication with a *confidential contact* in a secure register.

Sources under 16 cannot be used to obtain information about their parents or anyone with parental responsibility for them.

Where a CHIS is under 16, an appropriate adult (such as a parent, guardian, social working or anyone over 18 who does not work for the investigating body) must be present at meetings to discuss the use and welfare of the source.

Where a CHIS is under 18, a risk assessment must also be conducted by the officer in charge of the investigation covering the likelihood of physical and psychological harm arising from the covert activities, and is satisfied the risks are justified and have been properly explained and understood by the source.

Confidential material – At the time of writing - RIPA does not provide any special protection for confidential material, however, the following rules apply where it is likely to be obtained:
The retention or dissemination of such information should be accompanied by a clear warning of its confidential nature. It should be safeguarded by taking reasonable steps to ensure that there is no possibility of it becoming available, or its content being known, to any person whose possession of it might prejudice any criminal or civil proceedings relating to the information, it is also advisable that authorisations relating to investigations where confidential material has been found are be retained.

Additional rules apply for authorising the use of covert human intelligence sources. Sufficient arrangements for all covert human intelligence sources must be in place to ensure:

- An officer has day-to-day responsibility for dealing with the source and for their security and welfare ("the handler"). This should be the officer responsible for the management of the investigation
- Another person has the general oversight of the use made of the source ("controller"). This should be the handler's line manager
- Someone must have responsibility for maintaining a record of the use made of the source. This must be the officer responsible for the management of the investigation
- The records must comply with the *Regulation of Investigatory Powers (Source Records) Regulations 2000*
- Authorisations must always be in writing, except in urgent cases where the grant or renewal of an authorisation can be given orally.

10.9 - Handling and Disclosure of Product/Data Protection

Any product obtained during an investigation must be securely retained where it might be relevant to that investigation or to another investigation or to pending or future criminal or civil proceedings. The officers responsible for the management of an investigation must ensure that product is guarded against unlawful disclosure and potential breaches of the *Data Protection Act 1998*.

Material or product which is not believed to have any use in future investigations or legal proceedings (because it is unrelated or irrelevant) must not be destroyed. The officer responsible for the management of the investigation is responsible for securing its safe custody until such time as either the time limits under CIPA of for potential civil action has expired (whichever is later).

It is not good practice to use material obtained in one investigation, for another investigation particularly by public authorities other than the one that obtained the material. This should be authorised only in the most exceptional circumstances.

Chapter 11 - Principals of Note Taking and Statement Writing

11.1 - Making Notes

Best practice in investigation is to approach each case as if it will eventually end up in the highest court in the land. If this is done, you should never find yourself in the embarrassing position of having to withdraw a summons because the evidence has been gathered in such a way that it is inadmissible.

This applies as much to your initial notes as it does to the final statements submitted. This is because it will be your notes, made at the time of questioning or initial investigation, that will be closely examined by the opposition and their legal team. A statement can often be written at leisure, the detail checked and double checked. But how did you come to know this detail? And can you prove that pertinent details of the case and investigation were noted at the beginning of the investigation and not merely added, whether truthfully or otherwise, for convenience at a later date?

11.2 - Contemporaneous Notes

Obviously it is not practicable to always write up a full and comprehensive statement, therefore you will need to make accurate contemporaneous notes, which you will later use to form your witness statements.

Contemporaneous Notes are those made at the time of, or immediately after any particular incident has occurred. This incident may be the crime itself, or it may be any stage of the investigation from initial questioning of a suspect or witness, to discovery of an important piece of evidence, to seizure of any piece of evidence, right through to the moment at which the case is finally, if ever, declared closed. Best practice dictates that notes made after any incident, if not made immediately, should be made within an hour at the most. You may find that any notes made later than this will be scrutinised closely by the opposing legal team and doubts may be cast over both their accuracy and your ability to the accurately recall facts after more than this length of time has passed.

In practice, your notes should contain a far greater degree of broad factual detail than your statement. This is because your statement will be written to contain the facts pertinent to a particular offence, whereas your notes will contain detail on all actions that occurred at the time of an offence. This is discussed in further detail in Chapter 11.

Notes will also be used to provide an audit/continuity of evidence trail, and to show how any specific decision relating to the investigation was made. You should use a notebook to state why opinions were formed. You may later need to record this evidence in a Decision Log for your court bundle (see Chapter 15). An evidence decision log is needed in the court file to show reasoning for decision making, you will need to record key facts/evidence, in order to show why you made that decision, should you need to justify decision at a later stage, this is especially important if your investigation is serious and turns into a prosecution. At the start of your investigation you may not know if the matter is serious enough for a prosecution and therefore you should treat all investigations as if they may end up in a prosecution, especially as you never know, even something that may seem minor may be linked to or develop into a more serious case.

11.3 - Structure of Notes

Your notes, as well as being used to refresh your memory to write your statement, may also be used in court to refresh your memory. Therefore, your notes must be clear, legible and accurate. Notes should be made at all stages of the investigative process, on numbered pages and in permanent ink so that they cannot be tampered with. However, it is not essential to have such a notebook and any pad or piece of paper can be substituted in an emergency. Indeed, as mentioned in Chapter 9, Static Surveillance, a newspaper can often double as both prop and method of taking notes. In fact, it could be said that the type of notebook is secondary in importance to the structure of any written notes.

The date and time should be recorded (the date and time of the event as well as the date and time that the notes are being written), the location, who was present, what happened in great detail (what has been heard and by whom, what has been done by whom, what has been said by whom, what the scene and location were like, what the weather conditions were like, descriptions of suspects and what they were wearing, how they were behaving, anything seen, touched or smelt). In addition you must record any events leading up to the incident & anything following it, record any subsequent phone calls, any evidence gathered, any interviews taken etc. anything no matter how small must be recorded as all the small seemingly irrelevant details may fit together to make something relevant.

The following should also be observed:

- There are a minimum of seven headings which MUST be completed before any further notes are made. An error and/or omission of any one of these could render the notes inadmissible so extra care must be taken to ensure complete accuracy.
- No ELBOW – no erasures, leaves torn out, blank spaces, no over writing, writing in margins (except dates, times or initials). Dates, times, locations and persons present should be included for each incident. The fuller the notes the better and interviews should be written out word for word.
- Notes are made to refresh the memory and help with the preparation of witness statements, to provide a record and help to maintain the continuity of evidence and they can be referred to in court if made contemporaneously, (Criminal Justices Act 2003).
- You should always sign your notes at the bottom, including the time and the date, and where possible get the defendant to sign them too. It is a defendant or suspects right to refuse to sign your notes. If this occurs simply make a note of this alongside your signature. If any other officers have been present at the questioning, you should ask them to counter-sign your notes. This is particularly helpful when the suspect has refused.

Note - If you check something, record it. Even if there is so no offence to record, just record that a check has been carried out and no offence was taking place.

- Any notebook which is to be used as a PACE notebook should have numbered pages and preferably a serial number to aid with identification. It is good practice to record this serial number before the notebook is used and to keep this record of previously used notebooks in a safe place. Remember - any notebook remains a form of evidence, even after it has been filled and safely filed. An audit trail is essential.
- Always use permanent ink. Separate notes should be made for separate interviews/incidents. Put a line through errors and initial them and put a line through blank spaces so that nothing can be added later, always sign and date the bottom of each page and get anyone else present to also sign and print their name, including suspects, witnesses and colleagues. Do not make assumptions, only record facts, include exhibit numbers of any evidence that has been taken, record time notes began and ended, do not use arrows, dashes or short hand and never go back to notes and amend them.
- When making notes collect as much information as possible to help you ensure you have gathered all the evidence. Do not allow yourself to be hurried no matter how anxious your witness seems to appear to leave.
- Have recorded all the information so that nothing is missed and you can write a fully accurate statement as you may be quizzed on your statement at court, and if you have overlooked something it will get picked up on and may result in you losing the case. Even if you think the offence is relatively minor or may not end up in court its always best to adopt best practise procedures and assume you are going to court with the evidence as the case may develop or the minor offence may be linked to/lead onto something much more serious and those minor details that you didn't think were important may become crucial. Always make notes and write your own statements up asap whilst events are clear in your mind.
- Identify possible witnesses, and obtain evidence from them as soon as possible, after the event (section 139 Criminal Justice Act 2003).

WARNING - A note or record (which may be written or recorded electronically, digitally, or audio recorded), is a primary source of evidence. Therefore you should not write anything in your note book or next to those notes that may embarrass you in court.

All notes should be kept and stored appropriately (see Chapter 7). This includes anything written about the case, even your own scribbles when you are on the phone to a suspect or anyone linked to the case and when you are planning the interview or scribbling key points in the interview, even if your notes are covered in doodles or seem illegible and you have now typed/written them up you MUST keep the originals (if you don't a lawyer will pick up on how you couldn't have made such neat detailed notes so where were the originals). Your notes are evidence, and as such MUST be stored appropriately and securely, if you fail to do this not only do you jeopardise the case but you will also be in breach of the Data Protection Act. You must have an appropriate filing system for notes and exhibits so that they can be found quickly, this includes keeping them long after the case has been concluded in case of any subsequent appeals. Any electronic records must be tamperproof.

11.4 - Statements

Whilst writing your statement, where as changes in legislation mean that you are allowed to refer to a colleagues notes it is sometimes best to avoid doing so and stick to your own version of events, although this will obviously depend upon the situation. It is crucial that your statements are your own, your own thoughts and memories, it is an offence to fabricate the truth.

When writing your statement, think about the issues that you need to address i.e. what are the important facts that are imperative to the case, not all of your notes have to go into the statement i.e. your opinions but you must not omit any facts, the statement is a legal document stating all the facts that will help the court to make up their mind (even if something weakens your case it must be included) anything you saw, did or heard must be included, you may also want to include details of location and environmental issues i.e. if it was daylight, sunny or cloudy and raining. If you add anything into your statement that is not in your notes you can include it but you must explain why it isn't in your notes.

Back up any information you put in i.e. The time was 10am, I know this from looking at the Town Hall clock. Think about it from the other sides point of view, what will they be looking for, get your story across and insulate yourself from cross examination, i.e. if it was dark and in the description of the suspect you have put his/her eye colour – how could you be sure to see this in the dark? Is this accurate or had you remembered it from a previous encounter with them? Think of yourself as the judge, what have you understood, and how could you improve your statement to make it clearer. Perhaps split each stage of the incident down into separate paragraphs to make it easier to read.

Your statement should preferably be typed, with double-spacing, events written out in the order that they happened and the paragraphs numbered so that it can be easily followed, referred to and read out in court.

Your statement must be signed and dated on all pages, as soon as it has been written and printed out and you must state how many pages at the bottom of the page i.e. page 1 of 1 any gaps ruled out, and it must be written on an appropriate form as in accordance with The Criminal & Justice Act 2003 (section 9) – Often referred to as a S9 form or, for police, an M111 form.

The date should be written in full (Americans write the numerical date the opposite way to us and it can get confusing), exhibits must be numbered and referred to in the statement, and ideally put in bold (you may also need to mention where exhibits were found, by whom, who is producing them, were they copied, where they have been stored. Surnames should be in always write it in your own words, include witness details on the back of the statement to retain immunity, don't leave anything out *(It may leave doubt if you take the detail out).*, if there are gaps such as breaks, record the breaks, avoid approximations. Ensure you write in chronological order, don't overwrite, tear out pages or erase anything. Record all questions/comments/answers in full and don't paraphrase, if it's a long interview, transcribe it in full and exhibit it separately. As well as recording the date, time, place, people present, all key times, all relevant facts, record time notes/statement began and ended, where written, sign and date bottom of each page.

If you are going to use abbreviations, write in full first and then put in brackets afterwards, avoid using lots of abbreviations and if there are lots of technical terms you may decide to include a glossary at the back of your statement (this maybe necessary of expert witnesses who may have to explain lots of technical information).

Previous convictions can now be disclosed as 'bad character disclosure' but must be put in a separate document not a witness statement.

Additional statements are allowed, for instance if you need to add something or something else comes to light after you have written the statement you may write an additional statement, you may need to explain why you have done this, it is best to try and avoid lots of additional statements, it maybe necessary to re-write a statement, in which case you must disclose your pervious statements.

11.5 - Writing Statements for Others

If writing a statement for someone else as well as them signing it you must sign it and specify that you have written it on their behalf. When writing a statement for someone else write it in their language and not yours, you can seek clarification from them but must you mustn't coach them.

Remember, unless in a civil case, hearsay can not be used and must be avoided, (see below for rules on hearsay).

11.6 - Expert Witness

Don't give opinion or make inferences unless you are an expert witness, in which case you can make opinions but only in your field of expertise and you must make it clear that this is an opinion and not a fact and you must explain how & why you have come to that opinion.
An expert witness statement, must also include;
- Substance of all instructions received (whether written or oral).
- Questions upon which an opinion is sought.
- Materials provided and covered.
- Documents, statements, evidence, information or assumptions which are material to the opinions expressed or upon which those opinions are based.
- Information relating to who has carried out measurements, examinations, tests etc.(and if they were carried out under the experts supervision).
- Methodology used.
- Any material facts or matter which detracts from the expert's opinions.
- Any points which should fairly be made against any opinions expressed.
- Crossings out initialled by the maker.
- No writing in margins except dates, times or initials.
- Records from the time the instructions were received & for the whole of the time that they are involved.
- Express updates, alterations or comments with clarity.
- It should be sufficiently detailed so that other experts in the field can follow the nature of the work undertaken, scrutinise it and recognise any assumptions made and inferences drawn.
- Again all rules as per standard statements should be observed, i.e. it should be written chronologically, and signed and dated etc.

Some tips if you get writers block, try producing a spider diagram and witting the issues/points to prove in the middle and then remember key facts to list. Put together a chronology/time line and then fill in the details, put something down on paper, a blank page remains a blank page (but remember to exhibit all notes). If you write something down to do its more likely to get done.

11.7 - Hearsay

Section 114 The Criminal Justice Act 2003 (CJA 2003) defines hearsay evidence as any 'statement not made in oral evidence in the proceedings.' Reliance on a statement made otherwise than while giving evidence to prove the truth of a fact asserted remains hearsay.

The general rule is that such a statement is inadmissible as evidence of the truth of the facts stated.
The rule applies:
- to both examination in chief and cross-examination;
- whether the statement was made by the witness personally or by some other person;
- to any `out of court' statement, whether oral, written or otherwise;
- to statements given as evidence of the truth of its contents - if the statement is given for any purpose which is relevant to the facts in issue in the case, it is admissible, for example, evidence given as to a person's state of mind, rather than what was actually said.

Reasons for the Rule

The rule was originally intended to ensure that evidence that might be no more than rumour and gossip, and therefore be regarded as unreliable, was kept from consideration in determining innocence or guilt in the trial process.

Exceptions to the hearsay rule

There are many exceptions to the rule against hearsay, allowing hearsay evidence to be admitted at trial. The range of these exceptions and the flexible interpretation of the exceptions have contributed to the difficulties in applying the rule. However, the Criminal Justice Act 2003 (CJA 2003) simplifies and relaxes certain aspects of the rule and the exceptions to it.

The new provisions of the CJA 2003 came into force on 4 April 2005. They set out when hearsay evidence will be admissible and when it can be excluded.

The new provisions will apply only to trials begun on or after the date of commencement

The CJA 2003 clarifies the position by making sketches, photofits etc. hearsay The Act seeks to retain the distinction at common law between real evidence and hearsay. Evidence that is purely mechanically produced, such as a photograph or CCTV footage of an offence, is not subject to the hearsay rule. If evidence is produced by a computer or machine, but relays information that has been supplied by individuals, the hearsay rule will apply if the party seeks to rely on the printout to prove that what the person (supplier) said was true.

Section 129 CJA 2003 provides a further safeguard where a representation of any fact –
  a. is made otherwise than by a person, but
  b. depends for its accuracy on information supplied (directly or indirectly) by a person,
  the representation is not admissible in criminal proceedings as evidence of the fact unless it is proved that the information was accurate.

Statements adduced pursuant to, and satisfying, section 129 are not hearsay. Because the document produced by mechanical means is not hearsay, there is no infringement of the rule against multiple hearsay (i.e. information passing through many hands in the course of business). If the information is accurate, there is nothing to prevent the accuracy of the data being proved by any admissible means.

Under section 114(1), evidence amounting to hearsay will be admitted by the court (subject to its general discretion to exclude evidence if:
- there are statutory provisions allowing it to be;
- it falls within a common law exception preserved by section 118 CJA 2003;
- the parties agree to it being admissible; or
- the court is satisfied that it is in the interests of justice for it to be admissible (see below).

The new statutory exceptions introduced by the Act are replacements for sections 23 and 24 CJA 1988.

In deciding whether it is in the interests of justice for hearsay to be admitted (see above), the court must have regard to the factors set out in section 114(2) and any others it considers relevant

These exceptions overlap and hearsay may well be capable of being admitted under a new statutory provision, an old common law exception or the 'interests of justice' discretion.

Statutory provisions

Cases where a witness is unavailable

Under section 116 CJA 2003, first hand (as opposed to multiple) hearsay evidence, whether oral or documentary, is admissible (subject to the court's general discretion to exclude it – see para 48 below) provided:
- Oral evidence in the proceedings would be admissible of that matter;
- The witness is identified to the court's satisfaction;
- Any of the following five conditions is satisfied:

The person is dead:
S/he is unfit to be a witness because of a physical or mental condition;
S/he is outside of the UK and it is not reasonably practicable to secure his/her attendance;
S/he cannot be found despite reasonably practicable steps having been taken;
S/he does not give oral evidence through fear and the court gives leave for the statement to be given in evidence.

Article 6(3)(d) of the European Convention on Human Rights specifies the right of the accused "to examine or have examined witnesses against him and to obtain the attendance and examination of witnesses on his behalf under the same conditions as witnesses against him". This right is not absolute, and whether reliance on section 116 is challenged on Article 6 grounds may depend on whether the defence has the opportunity to challenge, at some stage, the evidence of the missing witness and/or whether the prosecution case is based solely on the evidence of the absent witness – would there be a case to answer without it?

11.8 - Business documents

Section 117 CJA 2003 closely replicates section 24 CJA 1988. The distinction between business documents prepared for criminal proceedings and business documents that have not been prepared for criminal proceedings is retained, and in order for documents prepared for criminal proceedings to be admissible, either the witness must be unavailable - in accordance with the provisions of section 116 CJA 2003 – or the person making the statement cannot reasonably be expected to have any recollection of the matters dealt with in the statement.

The section applies only to documents. In some cases, a document may record what somebody else has said (e.g. works manager's accident report book may contain statements by workers).

There is a three stage admissibility test:
- The document must have been created or received by a person in the course of a trade, business, profession or other occupation or as the holder of an office;
- The supplier of the information must have had, or be reasonably supposed to have had, personal knowledge;
- Where information has passed through a number of hands, each person must have received it in the course of trade, business etc.

A court may exclude a document if its reliability is doubtful in view of the source of the information, or the manner in which it was created or received. Care should accordingly be taken when reviewing such statements.

The rule permits multiple hearsay, and avoids difficulties where it is not clear who supplied the information, provided there is every reason to assume that it is reliable and provided oral evidence could be given by somebody of the matter; the fact that that might be a person other than the maker of the statement is irrelevant.

11.9 - Statements admitted under sections 9 or 10 Criminal Justice Act 1967

The Criminal Justice Act 1967 (CJA 1967) provides for the admissibility of written statements in criminal proceedings, other than committal proceedings, to the same extent that oral evidence to the like effect by that person would be admissible. The statement must be signed. It must also contain a declaration of truth.

If you intend to rely on the statement in evidence, you should serve a copy of it on the other parties. If a party, within seven days thereafter, objects to the statement going in as evidence, then the statement cannot be used and the witness will need to be called to give oral evidence to the court. Therefore, section 9 statements are only admissible if all parties agree.

Section 9 CJA 1967 is preserved by the CJA 2003.

Under section 133 CJA 2003, where a statement in a document is admissible as evidence in criminal proceedings, the statement may be proved by producing either the document or a copy of it or the material part of it, authenticated in whatever way the court may approve.

Section 10 CJA 1967 provides that any fact of which oral evidence may be given in criminal proceedings may be formally admitted, for the purposes of those proceedings, by either the prosecution or the defence. Formal admissions are discussed in the Rules of Evidence section.

Common law exceptions

Section 118 CJA 2003 preserves certain common law categories of admissibility:
1. public records;
2. common law rules on reputation and tradition;
3. statements forming part of the res gestae;
4. confessions by an accused;
5. admissions by an agent, e.g. a company director;
6. common enterprises
7. experts' reference to the works of others within their field

11.10 - Res Gestae

The phrase "res gestae", which means "a transaction", is used to describe an out of court statement which relates to and is closely associated in time and place with a state of affairs or event so that it can be said that they form part of the "same transaction". An example is spontaneous statements made by onlookers in response and at the same time as the commission of the offence in question.

A commonly used example is a statement made by witness A, the victim of an attack, in the presence of witness B, made just after the attack, indicating the identity of the attacker. Under the "res gestae" exception witness B may be able to give admissible evidence of what was said by witness A. The rationale is that there is thought to be less danger of concoction or fabrication of the evidence in circumstances where the events in question are likely to monopolise the thoughts of the witness.

Where the statement relates to a specific event, the question for the court is whether the possibility of concoction or distortion can be disregarded. The court will consider the circumstances in which the statement was made to decide whether the event was so unusual or startling or dramatic as to dominate the thoughts of the person such that the words spoken were an instinctive reaction to the event

Where the statement relates to the maker's state of mind, emotional or physical state, the statement is admissible to prove the state of the maker of the statement at the time when the statement was made. It is not admissible to prove the cause of this state.

This exception should not be used as a substitute for calling an available witness, but may be relevant where a fatally injured person has made a statement immediately after an accident, to a work colleague or other person. Careful consideration will need to be given to the use of such statements, to ensure that the defendant has the right to challenge such evidence. This again takes account of the requirements of Article 6 ECHR.

11.12 - Confessions; Confessions by an agent e.g. company director

A confession of an accused includes a statement that is wholly or partly contrary to the person who made it. It is not necessary for the statement to be made to a person in authority.

Confessions obtained without a caution are likely to be found inadmissible. See chapter 14 - The Importance of the Caution.

The confession of the accused, made in the presence of a third party (who may also be a co-accused) is admissible as an exception to the hearsay rule as part of the evidence given by that third party, provided it complies with section 76 of the Police and Criminal Evidence Act 1984.

Such confessions amount to informal admissions and are statements that are, or turn out to be, adverse to the case of the person who makes it. Such statements are generally admissible to prove the truth of the facts they contain, so long as the statement was originally made by a defendant.

In the case of an `officer' or `agent' of the company, they are in effect the embodiment of the company. A confession made by him or her will amount to an informal admission, and will be admissible under PACE. You must ensure that the agent or officer of the company making the confession is authorised to do so by the board of directors, or equivalent, for the body corporate.

The existing rule that evidence of verbal statements or confessions given by a third party (i.e. someone other than an accused) is inadmissible hearsay is retained. First-hand hearsay (a statement made by a person in a document) is admissible, subject to sections 116 and 117.

New provisions relating to confessions by a co-accused are set out in section 128 of the CJA 2003, which inserts a new section 76A in the Police and Criminal Evidence Act 1984.

The effect of this new section is that, subject to certain safeguards, a confession made by a co-accused may be given in evidence for another person charged in the same proceedings. The confession must be relevant to any matter in issue in the proceedings.

For example, in a joint trial of two defendants, a confession made out of court by Defendant A may now be put in evidence by Defendant B as evidence of the facts stated, as long as the confession is relevant to Defendant B's defence, provided that the confession meets the provisions set down in 76A. However, the court must be satisfied on the balance of probabilities that the confession was not obtained by oppression or in consequence of anything likely to render the confession unreliable, and in doing so should ensure that the suspects rights to a fair trial under Article 6 are respected.

The fact that a confession has been wholly or partly excluded as a consequence of these provisions does not affect the admissibility in evidence of any facts discovered as a result of the confession. For example, as a result of information gained from a confession some documentary evidence was found in a storage facility of a factory. In these circumstances that material would be admissible (provided that it could be properly introduced on its own merit), even if the confession was ruled inadmissible.

In addition, if the nature of the confession is such as to show that the accused speaks, writes or expresses himself in a particular way, then as much of the confession as is necessary to show this point will be admissible. Evidence of how such facts were discovered will be inadmissible unless this evidence is given by the defendant or on his behalf. Such evidence must be introduced as an exhibit to a witness statement.

11.13 - Expert evidence and reference to the works of others in their field

Once the primary facts on which the expert's opinion is based are proved, the expert can rely upon things written or said by other experts. The expert should specifically refer to this other work. This is confirmed by section 118 CJA 2003. You should refer to the 'Expert Evidence' section for further details.
Physical Evidence in Court – Expert Reports.
To the extent that expert evidence relies upon an earlier report, the report will be hearsay. However, as per section 127, it may be admissible, but only if the person who provided the original information can reasonably be supposed to have had personal knowledge of the matters stated. When expert evidence relies on such a statement, notice must be given to the defence, who must be given the name and address of the person whose statement is relied upon. The defence will then have an opportunity to object and where this occurs, the court must decide whether it is in the interests of justice to permit the expert to base his or her conclusion on the hearsay statement, or whether the supplier of the original information should also be called as a witness.

11.14 – Credibility

Previous inconsistent statements

Section 119 CJA 2003 changes the law. Whereas a previous inconsistent statement went only to weaken or cancel out the credibility of a witness, the statement as proved will now be evidence of any fact of which direct oral evidence by the statement maker would be admissible. The judge will direct the jury as to the appropriate weight to be attached to the statement, taking into account Article 6 ECHR considerations.

11.15 - Previous consistent statements

The previous consistent statements of a witness have not as a general rule been admissible prior to the CJA 2003. They were allowed to be used for certain specific circumstances, including for refreshing the memory, to rebut allegations of recent fabrication, for previous consistent identification and the reaction of the accused when the accusation was first put to him or her.

Under section 120 of the CJA 2003, if a statement is admitted, it will only go to the consistency of the witness, not to the truth of its contents. A previous consistent statement made by a witness called to give oral evidence will be admissible in one of three ways:
- to rebut a suggestion that his or her oral evidence had been fabricated;
- to refresh a witness's memory, on which he has been cross-examined; or
- as an out of court statement falling within section 120(4)-(7), viz:

- the statement identifies or describes a person, object or place or
- the statement was made when the matters stated were fresh in the witness's memory but he does not remember them and cannot reasonably be expected to do so well enough to give oral evidence in proceedings; or
  a. the witness claims to be a person against whom the offence was committed; and
  b. the offence is one to which the proceedings relate;
  c. the statement consists of a complaint made by the witness (whether to a person in authority or not) about conduct which would, if proved, constitute the offence or part of the offence; and
  d. the complaint was made as soon as could be reasonably expected after the alleged conduct; and
  e. the complaint was not made as a result of a threat or a promise; and
  f. before the statement is adduced the witness gives oral evidence in connection with its subject matter.

11.16 - Capability

Under section 123 of the CJA 2003, a statement will not be admissible as evidence under sections 116, 117, 119 or 120 if it was made by a person who did not have the required capability at the time when he or she made the statement. 'The required capability' means that the witness should be capable of understanding questions put to him about the matters stated and giving answers to those questions that can be understood.

Section 124 CJA 2003

Under section 124 of the CJA 2003, if, in criminal proceedings, a written statement is admitted as evidence and the statement maker does not give oral evidence, then:
- any evidence relevant to the witness's credibility is admissible; and
- evidence which could otherwise be put in cross-examination as relevant to his credibility as a witness can be given with the court's leave; and
- evidence that he or she made any other inconsistent statement is admissible for the purpose of showing that the witness contradicted himself.

The maker of the statement for these purposes and for the purposes of section 117 is each person who supplied or received the information, or created or received the document. If evidence is admitted under section 124, and an allegation is subsequently made against the maker of the statement, the court may permit the party to lead additional evidence of such description as may be specified by the court for the purpose of meeting the allegation.

11.17 - Section 124 CJA 2003

Under section 125 CJA 2003, in a Crown Court trial, if the court is satisfied – following the close of the case for the prosecution – that the case against the defendant is based either wholly or partly on a statement not made in oral evidence in the proceedings and the evidence in the statement is so unconvincing that, considering its importance to the case against the defendant, his or her conviction of the offence would be unsafe, the court must either direct the jury to acquit the defendant of the offence or – if it considers that there ought to be a retrial – the court must discharge the jury.

Section 126 CJA 2003 sets out the court's general discretion to exclude evidence. Under this provision, the court may refuse to admit a written statement as evidence if the statement was made otherwise than in oral evidence. The court will need to be satisfied that the case for excluding the statement (taking account of the danger that to admit it would result in an undue waste of time) substantially outweighs the case for admitting it, whilst considering the value of the evidence. This does not restrict the court's general powers to exclude evidence, either under section 78 of the Police and Criminal Evidence Act 1984 (exclusion of unfair evidence) or generally at common law (see Collecting witness evidence – Admissibility of confessions).

11.18 - Additional requirement for admissibility of multiple hearsay

Under section 121 of the CJA 2003, a hearsay statement is not admissible to prove the fact that an earlier hearsay statement was made unless:
- either of the statements is admissible under sections 117, 119 or 120; or
- all the parties to the proceedings agree; or
- the court is satisfied that the value of the evidence in question, taking into account how reliable the statements appear to be, is so high that the interests of justice require the later statement to be admissible for that purpose.

For the purposes of this section, 'hearsay statement' means a statement, not made in oral evidence, that is relied on as evidence of a matter stated in it.

11.19 - Evidence given at retrial

Section 131 CJA 2003 replaces paragraphs 1 and 1A of schedule 2 of the Criminal Appeal Act 1968. The section deals with evidence given at retrial and states that evidence that was given orally at the original trial must be given orally at the retrial unless all parties to the retrial agree otherwise or section 116 CJA 2003 applies or the witness is otherwise unavailable but the court decides it is in the interests of justice for the statement to be admitted.

11.20 - Memory refreshing

A witness giving oral evidence in court may use a document to refresh his or her memory, provided that the document was made (or verified) by him at an earlier time, and provided:
- he states that the document records his recollections of the matter at that earlier time and
- his recollection of the matter is likely to have been significantly better at the time the document was made, than at the time of his oral evidence

Where a witness is giving oral evidence about matters to which he has already given a recorded oral account, and he states that the account represents his recollection of the matter at the time, and his recollection of the matter is likely to have been significantly better at the time of the previous account and a transcript of the recording has been made, then the witness may use the transcript to refresh his memory

11.21 - Video recording

For offences trial-able on indictment or for prescribed trial-able either way offences, the court can authorise the video recording of an interview with a witness to replace evidence in chief for that witness (see Physical Evidence in Court - Sound and Videotape Recording).

A brief note on - COMMON LAW ADJUDICATION

We saw in Chapter 3 the way in which common law is created and potentially how flexible its evolution is. And whilst it is this flexibility that makes common law such an adaptable tool, it can offer considerable complication when applied for enforcement purposes…

In a common law jurisdiction several stages of research and analysis are required to determine what "the law is" in a given situation. First, one must ascertain the facts. Then, one must locate any relevant statutes and cases. Then one must extract the principles, analogies and statements by various courts of what they consider important to determine how the next court is likely to rule on the facts of the present case. Later decisions, and decisions of higher courts or legislatures carry more weight than earlier cases and those of lower courts. Finally, one integrates all the lines drawn and reasons given, and determines what "the law is". Then, one applies that law to the facts.

Chapter 12 - Photographic and CCTV Evidence

This section deals with the procedures that must be followed to ensure admissibility of photographic and CCTV evidence. At this point it must be stressed that we are not talking solely of evidence gathered under RIPA authorisation, and the following procedures and protocols should be adopted in all cases regardless of whether RIPA authorisation is needed. You are advised to consult the Home Office publication, Digital Imaging Procedure v2.0 November 2007.

Gathering electronic information – If this surveillance is covert, you will need to consider RIPA clearance. However if conducting overt recordings in order to ensure they are overt enough not to need RIPA clearance you will need to ensure CCTV signs are clearly displayed and if you are recording audio as well as visual you will also need to specify audio recordings. The standard CCTV symbol with text to say audio and visual recording should be sufficient. If you are using a body warn recording device such as a head camera, or a camera on your vest or bike a high visability vests that states you have CCTV recording and displaying the CCTV sign on this, would be sufficient. It is also advisable to inform the subject that they are being recorded in order that there is no confusion.

When using CCTV evidence you should adhere to the Information Commissioner CCTV Code of Practice July 2000, (See appendix 8)

12.1 - CCTV from Private Business.

Often you will need to seize CCTV evidence from private businesses for further study in a controlled environment. The CCTV should be provided by the business operator but often in the case of small business this is easier said than done. Many small businesses do not have CCTV systems or else they will have no idea of how to provide footage from often poorly maintained systems. Be prepared to receive CCTV footage in all formats from VHS to memory stick. If the CCTV is provided in a rare format, you may need to contact the makers of the equipment to arrange for the correct program to be able to view and exhibit the footage.

12.2 CCTV from Town Centre Control Rooms

Provided with evidence bags and statement detailing the accuracy and veracity of the cameras used.

12.3 Storage of Hardcopy

Dependent on Protective Marking as listed below, 11.11.

12.4 Taking Photographic Evidence

Firstly you must ensure the photos are taken legally. If the photos are taken covertly you will need RIPA authorisation, if the photos are taken with the overt use of video in a public place in this context is outside the scope of the requirements for covert surveillance as within the provisions of part 2 of the Regulation of Investigatory Powers Act 2000. However, the overt collection and retention of images in a public place falls within the provisions of the Data Protection Act 1998. Prima facie there is no requirement to comply with the codes to the Data Protection Act but, in order to meet with the requirements of the Act, it will be necessary to follow the codes with the exception of the requirement to place public notices.

The disclosure requirements of the Criminal Procedure and Investigations Act 1996 and the Attorney General's code will cover recovery and disclosure of the existence of the images in any trial thereto.

The provisions of the Human Rights Act 1998 overlay all such activity. In particular:

Article 6. The right to a fair trial may be affected if disclosure of images does not occur. If images are withheld that are material to any criminal trial then clearly there is a risk of breaching Article 6, thus rendering the criminal trial unfair. Any decision made not to disclose certain images should be in consultation with the Crown Prosecution Service and upon their advice.

Article 8. The right to respect for private/family life. The definition of this convention right has been the subject of much discussion through stated cases over recent years.

P.G. and J.H. v United Kingdom European Court App. No. 44787/98
Private life is a broad term not susceptible to exhaustive definition. Aspects of gender identification, name, sexual orientation and sexual life are important elements of the *personal sphere* protected by Article 8. The Article also protects a right to identity and personal development, and the right to establish and develop relationships with other human beings and the outside world and it may include activities of a professional or business nature. There is. Therefore, "a zone of interaction of a person with others, *even in a public context,* which may fall within the scope of "private life"....[Para. 56]
Private-life considerations may arise, however, once any systematic or permanent record comes into existence of such material from the public domain.
Perry v United Kingdom (2004) 39 EHRR 3.
The monitoring of the actions of an individual in a public place by the use of photographic equipment which does *not* record the visual data does not, as such, give rise to an interference with the individual's private life (at para .38)

The right to respect for private/family life may be infringed if there is no proper and established rationale on which the taking of the images is based.

Article 10. The right to freedom of expression should be considered carefully when dealing with lawful public protest at which no disorder or crime is anticipated. The sensible use of overt video at such events will be justified where the legitimate aims include:

Preventing disorder or crime

The protection of rights and freedoms of others; and

The protection of health or morals

Secondly you must ensure continuity of evidence;

The photos must be downloaded and stored securely, in a way that they can't be tampered with stills should be printed and given an exhibit number, a log of all exhibits must be made.

All used film/tape must be placed into the protective sleeves and sealed in an exhibit bag. It is good practise that the label on the exhibit bag will show the tape/film register number, the investigator's details, signature and the investigator's exhibit number. The investigator will be responsible for the retention of all used tapes until they are forwarded to the designated exhibit officer. The investigator will record the tape reference number and exhibit number of any types of film used in their pocket book. A log should be kept of where the exhibits are stored and when they are passed from the investigator to the exhibiting officer.

12.5 Evidence Logs

All evidence should be logged on an evidence log.

12.6 Date and Time

In the same way as notes must contain date and time, so must photographs and CCTV evidence.

12.7 Seizing Photographic evidence from other sources

It is important, for continuity of evidence to document, evidence gathered and where it is sourced from, especially for evidence taken from other sources, a statement will be necessary.

12.8 Storage of Images

Images collected and presented in hard copy must be stored in a secure environment in just the same way as other seized evidence and CCTV hardcopy.

12.9 Electronic Storage

Storage systems should comply with Protective Marking requirements as described below, 11.11.

12.10 Protective Marking of Images

Previously known as classification, the Protective Marking of images falls into the same category as used for marking any other documents of a sensitive nature. The Government Protective Marking Scheme can be adapted for private use and there is no reason why documents and images gathered as part of a private investigation should not be marked as would those collected by the Police or Government Agencies. There are five categories of marking:

>Not Protectively Marked
>Restricted
>Confidential
>Secret
>Top Secret

It is extremely unlikely that you will ever use the Top Secret marking and highly unlikely that you will use the Secret marking. However, you may occasionally have access to documents or images marked Secret.

95% of documents will fall into the first three categories, broadly broken down as 30% Not Protectively Marked, 50% Restricted and 15% Confidential.

Restricted documents are those that, if compromised, could lead to:

>Substantial distress to individuals
>Lack of effectiveness in operational capacity or security
>Investigations being prejudice
>Commission of crime being easier
>A statutory restriction on disclosure of material
>A breach in any undertakings to maintain the confidence of material provided by third parties
>A disadvantage in policy or commercial negotiations

Chapter 13 - Seizing Evidence, to include Computer based Electronic Evidence

From time to time it will be necessary to seize physical evidence which will help to prove the facts of the case under investigation. As with photographic and CCTV evidence procedure in Chapter 12, there are strict guidelines to how this must be done in order for the evidence to be admissible in court. Computer based Electronic Evidence is even more delicate as one wrong move could destroy the evidence. You are strongly advised to seek expert advice on accessing computer based evidence. Only the basics of seizure of computer based electronic evidence are outlined below.

13.1 - Record Everything

Once again, this goes back to the most basic of rules - keeping accurate records. In the same way as telephone calls and photographs are logged, any evidence found should be logged separately to ensure complete accuracy when compiling the prosecution file. At the point of seizure you should allocate an exhibit number to the object. This exhibit number can then remain with the object throughout the case providing a clearly defined audit trail from initial investigation through to final action.

13.2 - Photographing Physical Evidence

It is best practice, though not always feasible, to photograph physical evidence in situ. This provides evidence not only that the object or objects are genuinely connected to the investigation, but also that they originated in the exact location you say they did. Location could be vital to the evidences value. Photographing of objects should proceed as detailed in Chapter 12.

13.3 - Seizure without Camera

If no camera is available, a note detailing time, place and date of the seizure should be made in your pocket notebook as per chapter 11 The person you have taken the evidence from should sign and date your PACE notebook, it is also good practise to get your co-investigator to also sign to say that they have witnessed this is a true version of events, if this person is a suspect or refuses to sign it is especially important to get a colleague to witness and sign, to validate the procedure.

Evidence should be bagged, labelled and logged in the usual way to ensure continuity of evidence.

13.4 - Evidence Bags

Once the evidence has been recorded, the object can be placed inside an evidence bag. You will see that the front of the bag shows a serial number. This number should be entered onto the evidence log. All other details should be completed at the time of seizure and the bag sealed. Evidence bags can be re-opened at a later date providing the original bag is kept and exhibited. This process can occur several times so that you eventually end up with two or three evidence bags inside a sealed fourth along with the original exhibit. A separate note should be made each time you open a sealed evidence bag, although, when preparing a case file, one statement will often be enough to cover all exhibits. Examples of typical evidence bags and completed evidence bags are shown at Appendix 12.4.1, 12.4.2 and 12.4.3

13.5 - Seizing Computer Based Evidence

Electronic evidence capture for the investigation and solving of crime is ever-increasing in importance and frequency. Many crimes are now facilitated by the use of electronic devices such as mobile telephones, personal organisers and laptops. Seizing these items could be vital to the success of an investigation. But how to go about it without altering or destroying any potential evidence? And how to prove the evidence is genuine?

There are four principles laid down by the ACPO (Association of Chief Police Officers) in regard to the seizure and access of electronic information:

Principle 1 - No action taken by enforcement agencies or their agents should change data held on a computer or storage media which may subsequently be relied upon in court.

Principle 2 - In exceptional circumstances, where a person finds it necessary to access original data held on a computer or on storage media, that person must be competent to do so and be able to give evidence explaining the relevance and implications of their actions.

Principle 3 - An audit trail or other record of all processes applied to computer based electronic evidence should be created and preserved. An independent third party should be able to examine those processes and achieve the same results.

Principle 4 - The person on charge of the investigation (the case officer) has overall responsibility for ensuring that the law and these principles are adhered to.

Taken from Good Practice Guide for Computer Based Electronic Evidence, ACPO and NHTCU, National Hi-Tech Crime Unit.

Really, the above can be summarised as follows:

If in doubt, do not touch anything!

Computer based evidence requires expert knowledge. If any action is liable to alter or change data held, as in Principal 1, then the only course of action is to so nothing. However, if you are confident that the electronic data can be seized without damaging the data, then seizure should be conducted as per the processes outlined in 12.1 -12.4

Alongside these principles, further precaution must be taken when dealing with electronic evidence.

13.6 - Computer Evidence

Actions on Seizing Computer

Do not let anyone touch the electronic device after you have decided to seize it.
Allow any printers to complete printing tasks
Photograph the device in situ as per Chapter 12. If no camera or video camera is available, draw a sketch of the system.
Record what is shown on the screen at the time of seizure
Record what is shown on the screen if the screensaver is halted. **The Case Officer must decide if this is a necessary action.**
If the computer is switched on, unplug the power cable from the computer hard drive, **not the wall socket**
If the computer is switched off then leave it off. **Do not, under any circumstances, switch the computer on.**
Label all ports/cables and external parts so that the system may be re-constructed at a later date
Carefully remove the equipment labelling each part as a separate entry on your evidence log.
If present, ask the user if there are any passwords or codes for the system.
Search the area thoroughly for any passwords or documents related to the system. This can include notebooks, diaries, adhesive notes etc.

Equipment to Take

The real answer is as much as you can manage.

Where computers are concerned you can never tell immediately whether a seemingly innocuous looking piece of equipment is going to be needed. In this case, you should err on the side of caution and take everything. Alongside the basic units and operating equipment this will include any disks, instruction manuals, power supply units, memory cards and the like. Printers should be taken for forensic analysis of connected printouts. Any documents printing at the time of seizure should likewise be taken for the same purpose.

13.7 - Electronic Organisers and Personal Digital Assistants (PDA's)

Electronic Organisers and Personal Digital Assistants usually have a different operating system to laptops and desktops. They do not usually write to a hard drive and for access, they will almost certainly have to be turned on. This effectively nullifies Principle 1 and thus increases the burden on the investigator to ensure principles 2 and 3 are strictly adhered to.

Further problems can occur if batteries are removed or if an external reset button or sequence is available. For this reason, the following precautions should be observed:

> If found switched off, do not switch the device on - this will reduce battery life leading to potential loss of information.

> If found switched on, consideration should be made as to whether the device should be switched off to preserve battery life. Although bearing in mind once you turn it off you may need to key in a password to turn it back on.

WARNING - A device may be accessible if found switched on. If switched off, you may require a password to access the device. Is it better to leave the device switched on? PDA's often enter sleep mode if not used for a period of time. This sleep mode may require the re-entry of a password. Tap the screen periodically if you wish to prevent the machine from entering a secure mode.

> When using evidence bags, first place the device inside an envelope to prevent access through the bag. If available, use a recharging unit and plug this into the device before sealing it in the evidence bag.

> Hand the device to an expert at the earliest opportunity to prevent data loss through battery expiry.

13.8 - Other Electronic Storage Media

A number of electronic devices can store data. These include, but are not limited to, the following:

- Mobile Telephones
- Pagers
- Landline telephones
- Answering Machines
- Facsimile Machines
- Dictating Machines
- Digital Cameras
- Internet Capable Digital TV

It must be considered at all times that any of these devices, if seized, may lose data when switched off or disconnected from a continuous power supply.

WARNING - Mobile phones in particular may enter a secure mode after a period inactivity. Prevent this by occasionally using the keypad or touch screen.

13.9 - Transportation of Seized Evidence.

All seized evidence must be transported with extreme care. You should remember that the items remain the property of the suspect or victim until decided otherwise by a court of law. You may have to return the items and may be held responsible for any damage suffered while the property was in your care. **Treat all seized evidence with the same care and attention you would bestow upon your own belongings.**

Beware of heat sources.

Beware of magnetic fields, particularly when transporting electronic items as these can erase electronic memory. Anti-static bags can help to prevent against electronic data loss from disks, memory sticks, PDA's.

Beware damp or cold as this can damage the structure of evidence, warping some materials and making writing illegible.

Make sure large items are securely fastened before transport.

If in doubt, employ the services of a professional removals firm.

13.10 - Storage of Physical Evidence

All evidence must be kept in a secure, tamper free environment. See Chapter 12 & 13. This can be a locked file, a safe, a secure server (in the case of digital evidence) or a WORM (write once, read many times) media device. This WORM device will itself need to be locked away. We shall discuss secure digital storage further in 12.8. Consider carefully the reliability of your storage. If any doubt can be introduced as to the security of your storage facilities, the evidence may not be admissible in court. Depending on the classification (see 12.1) you may even wish to use a bank deposit box, or a security specialist. However, you must ask yourself the question: how secure are they?

13.11 - Storage of Digital Evidence

See Chapter 12.8

Chapter 14 - Conducting Interviews

14.1 - An Interview is…

"The questioning of a person regarding their involvement or suspected involvement in a criminal offence or offences which, under paragraph 10.1, must be carried out under caution. Whenever a person is interviewed they must be informed of the nature of the offence, or further offence." (As defined in the PACE codes of practice).

It is an interview that will be carried out under caution, because in accordance with the PACE principals anyone being questioned in relation to an offence must be cautioned, in order to inform them of their rights and of the legal implications of the interview, (If someone is not a suspect they will not be cautioned and therefore it will be an ordinary interview and not a PACE one).

Investigators should be aware that where it is possible that a criminal offence has been committed, the interview should be conducted by the prosecuting authority. Section 29 of the Data Protection Act, section 29 says that you can share information with other departments, if for a compatible cause, such as for the detection and prevention of crime, although you must tell the defendant that you are sharing the information and you must also tell the defendant what offences you are investigating.

By the nature of an interview it is a face to face meeting with anyone who is suspected of committing an offence, (it is not appropriate to carry out a telephone interview as, among other reasons, it would be impossible to verify the identification of the person throughout the interview).

The interview is carried out in order to consider the evidence and to hear their side of the story to establish if they did commit the offence or if there are other circumstances, or defences that would prove their innocence, and therefore to ask them questions, in relation to that offence, to get the truth. It is therefore there chance to give their account.

The purpose of the interview is to obtain accurate, and reliable information, in order to get to the truth. It should be entered into with an open mind, information obtained should be investigated against what the interviewer already knows, or what can reasonably be established.

This must be done in a fair and open manner and must therefore follow PACE codes of practise.

Even if you know the answers to the questions, or the defendant has already told you (See significant/provisional statement), you will still need to ask the questions so that the defendants answers are recorded as the defendants own words.

The interviewer is not bound to accept the first answer given, questioning is not unfair if it is persistent, as long as it is done so in a reasonable and fair way.

Remember there are friendly interviewees i.e. witnesses and then there are suspects. The moment a witness becomes a suspect they should be cautioned in accordance with PACE.

It is best to collect as much information as possible before the interview.

Time lines are very useful throughout the investigation they help to summarise and clarify points, they are also very useful during the interview as you can quickly see what events have happened in what order, this will help you with your questions and also to check the validity of what the defendant is saying.
During the interview , you may decide to focus on specific areas of the timeline so that you are in affect dividing up the time line and taking a stage at a time, in order to break it up into smaller more manageable areas, rigorously examine each sub-area in turn, and probe every element so that you can more easily recognise any anomalies in the defendants statements. At the start of every investigation you should plot everything that has happened relevant to the case on a timeline.

From the start of the investigation, from the initial enquiry/complaint, start compiling records of what action has been taken, what evidence is found etc. this will make the investiagation process and recalling facts easier.

14.2 - The interview process

Interviews of suspects/defendants must be done under caution and comply with Code C of PACE, and Code E if it is tape recorded. There are many different ways of conducting interviews, interviews may be conducted using the PEACE model – planning and preparation, engage and explain, account, closure, evaluation.

Under code C a caution must be given when there are grounds to suspect someone of an offence, before any questions are put to them unless the questions are merely to establish their identity. The interviewee must be reminded of the caution after any breaks, and a reason for the break given. A record must also be kept when anyone is cautioned. The interviewing officer should inform the interviewee of the nature of the offence, or further offences. If you further offences become apparent from your questioning, you can investigate them during this interview, however once you start court proceedings you can't add them on, you will have to have another interview so that you can investigate them appropriately and let the defendant have his say.

When conducting interviews if its likely that details of further offences may come up that may be relevant to other departments, such as fraud, you will need to warn the interviewee that further details of further offences may be investigated and/or passed to other departments for investigation, at the start of the interview to satisfy myself that they have been warned of the offences
Furthermore the interview must also tell the interviewee that they are free to go at anytime, as they are not under arrest and that they are entitled to legal representation.

All prearranged interviews are tape recorded. Three copies of the tapes are produced. The interviewee is offered one, the other is the working copy for the investigation and the third tape is sealed in the presence of the interviewee and signed by the interviewee, using a designated seal.

You will also need to ensure that there is a copy of the PACE codes of practise in the interview room, so that they can be referred to at anytime during the interview.

14.3 - Why Conduct an interview?

When carrying out an investigation it is important to Interview the suspect/defendant so that they have chance to have their say and put their reasons or defence across before you decide to prosecute them. In fact, to not do so could be seen as an abuse of power;
In *R v Trustham* 1997 the judgement states that; '*To deprive a suspect of the right to give an explanation at the earliest opportunity despite him having been cautioned that anything he did say would be written down and may be given in evidence, must be a breach of a person's human rights and is clearly an abuse of the process of court.*'

Although there is no legal requirement that the suspect/defendant is interviewed before any decision whether to prosecute is taken, it is always best to as;
  a. To reduce the likelihood of an abuse of power allegation being made.
  b. The interview may provide important information revealing further lines of enquiry, further offences etc.
  c. The interview may provide relevant information to be considered in the prosecution decision.
  d. To be open and fair, allowing them to answer allegations and give their own account.
  e. To satisfy the governments enforcement concordat.

The 'Hampton' report also goes onto discuss that any enforcement action must be proportionate.

Reference should also be made to the crown prosecution service's code of crown prosecutors.

This refers to the evidential stage and the public interest stage, when deciding to proceed with a prosecution. Therefore to bring about a prosecution as well as having the necessary evidence, the prosecution must be in the public interest. It is more likely to be in the public interest to bring about a prosecution if the offence is serious, a conviction is likely and without it the offence may continue or be repeated or if the defendant has relevant previous convictions. Once you have begun your investigation, collected any relevant evidence and taken notes and statements from witnesses, you will be ready to interview any suspects. Of course, if easier you may decide to interview the witnesses in this way, in which case you will not always be
Firstly - important to note that there will not always be a need to conduct the interview under PACE. Different types of interview and we will deal with non-Pace first as this is smaller section.

14.4 - Interviews not conducted using PACE 1984

Generally, this will be the interview of a witness or victim. For this reason it is not necessary to caution the person beforehand. They are unlikely to say anything that will implicate them in a crime and there is no reason for the interviewer to suspect they will. However, it is worth bearing in mind that should they do so, you must immediately caution them at which stage the interview will come under the guidance of PACE 1984. For now, we shall assume this has not happened.

Firstly, you should ensure that the interviewee is comfortable. Do they have drink? Would they prefer to sit somewhere else? Have they any urgent appointments to attend?

Having established that they are happy to continue, take a moment to outline the purpose of the interview. Explain why it is necessary to hear their side of the story. **Remember, you are an independent investigator.** It is all to easy to become quickly sympathetic to any victim or witness but you have no guarantee yet that what they are telling you is the truth. Ask them to explain the facts. Do not allow yourself to be drawn on points of opinion and try to limit any expression of sympathy. In practice, this is extremely hard to do but you will need to be careful. At a future stage of the investigation, you may be asked why you have taken sides.

14.5 - Interviews conducted under PACE 1984

Anyone suspected of committing an offence, that is to be asked any questions in relation to that offence, other than to establish the identity of that person, must be cautioned before any questions can be asked. This includes any type of questioning not just formal interviews. For instance you could carry out a road side interview under caution. For an evidence to be admissible in court, any questioning must be done under caution. If you are interviewing a witness who you don't believe to be a suspect at the time of interviewing, as soon as you have reason to believe that they could be a suspect you must caution them. Alternatively if someone tells you something before you have cautioned them, which implicates them as a suspect, you must caution them and then put what they said to them again to give them the opportunity to confirm or deny it under caution (significant statement).

When investigating a suspect/cautioning them it is important to get all of their details and verify their identity, this is why you can not have an interview under caution over the phone and if someone does tell you something over the phone you will have to stop them and ask them to come in, so you can then caution them, and put what they said to them under caution.

Offenders details;
- Name
- Address & Post code
- Date of birth
- Place of birth
- Nationality
- NINO – National insurance number
- Telephone number
- Physical Description
- Record ID seen (photocopy and certify the document as original seen).

It is always important to certify any photocopies taken, put the date, you name, original seen and sign. Without this there is no proof that the originals have been seen and if the documents were falsified, there will be no evidence to prosecute as they could deny they showed you the original and therefore they you can't show that any documents have been falsified.

Code 10.1

A person whom there are grounds to suspect of an offence must be cautioned before any questions or further questions are put for the purpose of obtaining evidence.

Code 10.2
When a person who is not under arrest is initially cautioned, he must at the same time be told that he/she
(A) Is not under arrest or under any form of detention.
(B) May obtain legal advice if he/she wishes.

Code 10.4
The caution shall be given in the following terms:

"YOU DO NOT HAVE TO SAY ANYTHING, BUT IT MAY HARM YOUR DEFENCE IF YOU DO NOT MENTION WHEN QUESTIONED SOMETHING WHICH YOU LATER RELY ON IN COURT.
ANYTHING YOU DO SAY MAY BE GIVEN IN EVIDENCE."

Minor deviations do not constitute a breach of this requirement provided that the sense of the caution is preserved.

Code 10.5
When there is a break in questioning under caution the interviewing officer must ensure that the person being questioned is aware that he remains under caution. If there is any doubt the caution should be given again before the interview resumes.

14.7 - RECORDS OF INTERVIEW

Code 11.3

An accurate record must be made of each interview with a person suspected of an offence.
The record must state:-

The **place** of the interview

The **date** of the interview

The **time** it begins and ends

Any **breaks** in the interview

Names of **all** persons present

The record must be made during the course of the interview unless in the investigating officer's view this would not be practicable.

It must be a **verbatim** record.

Code 11.4
If an interview record is not made during the course of an interview it must be made as soon as practicable after its completion.

Code 11.5
Written interview records must be timed and signed by the maker.

Code 11.7
Any refusal by a person to sign an interview record when asked to do so in accordance with the provisions of this code must itself be recorded.

14.8 - The Importance of the Caution

The caution gives an interviewee all the necessary information needed to make up his or her mind on whether to participate in an interview. It is ESSENTIAL that the interviewee fully understands the caution before the interview can commence. If there is any doubt cast by the defence on the interviewee's understanding of their rights under PACE 1984, it is possible that the interview will not be admissible as evidence. Disastrous if the interviewee has admitted liability.

The caution, once again, is:

"You do not have to say anything, but it may harm your defence if you do not mention when questioned something which you later rely on in court. Anything you do say may be given in evidence."

Let us break this down into component parts.

This means you don't have to say anything, which means you have the right to remain silent and you don't have to answer my questions but if you go to court and tell them something in court, which you didn't tell me when I questioned you, and it was something that it would have been reasonable for you to have told me when I questioned you, then the court will wonder why you didn't answer my question at the time and they may therefore look negatively on you and this could affect your defence.

If the caution is not understood here is an explanation;

Explanation of the Caution

"What I have just told you is made up of three parts:

The first is "You do not have to say anything unless you wish to do so"

> This means that although I will be asking you questions, you have the right not to answer them.
>
> Do you understand this part?

The section part is "but it may harm your defence if you do not mention when questioned something which you later rely on in court".

> During this interview, I will be asking you questions and I will record your replies, If this case goes to court and you tell the court something which you did not tell me during this interview (and you would have reasonably been expected to tell me) then the court may draw their own conclusions about your reasons for doing this.
>
> Depending on what you failed to mention, it may harm your defence.
>
> Do you understand this part?

The final part is "anything you do say may be given in evidence"

> If this case goes to court, then anything that you say during this interview, which has bearing on your case, may be used as evidence.

> Do you understand this part?

14.9 - A Significant Statement

Is when, a suspect, before being cautioned makes a statement in relation to the offence. It may well be that the person wasn't a suspect at the time and was being questioned as a witness. Or it may be that, having just turned up at a crime scene, and before having a chance to establish a suspect or read a suspect the caution, the suspect says something significant to the investigation, such as admitting they carried out the offence.

When this happens, details of the statement should, where possible, be written in the officers PACE notebook and signed by the defendant as a true representation of what has been said (PACE code ???). At the first opportunity the defendant should then be cautioned, told of the offence being investigated and their statement should be read back to them and then they should be asked if they still want to maintain this statement and if they want to add anything further.

14.10 - A Significant Silence

If questions aren't answered or aren't answered satisfactorily this must be recorded. If someone is exercising their right to silence you should still continue to put any necessary questions to them, in order to give them a chance to answer all of the questions otherwise they could say 'you didn't ask me that, if you did ask me that I would have answered.'

14.11 - Confessions

Much as with a significant silence, a confession should not necessarily mean the end of the interview. You may still need further evidence to secure a prosecution. What if this person has admitted to the crime when they did not actual commit it? It is not as rare as you would think, and should not only be thought of as a device used by those seeking attention. That said, in simple cases, a confession at interview will quite often be enough to complete the case. Often a confession will be offered along with mitigating evidence, "I did it because..." or "I did it but only..." It is important that all of this information is collected. Remember, a PACE interview is an opportunity for a suspect to offer his side of the story. Things are not always as they first appear...

A brief note on - INTERVIEWS AS PART OF JOINT PROSECUTIONS

There is a clear need for good communication. In particular, where the lead authority dealing with the premises identifies the need for a 'case conference', other responsible authorities will support the lead authority to gather all views in preparation for enforcement. The lead authority will be expected to co-ordinate such case conferences.

There may be occasions where a partners' assistance is sought in respect of the investigation of an offence, or future targeted action. By working together on such occasions partners should be able to achieve more wide reaching results.

In the case of joint operations, the following points should be agreed

- Identify the roles and responsibilities of each partner.
- Detail the resources required.
- Explain the objectives and expected outcomes.
- Comment on the timescale to achieve them.
- Identify the central point for coordination.

In undertaking joint operations parties must ensure that they are compliant with current legislation.

Parties understand that there may be other organisations involved in an operation that have not signed this protocol. In these instances the principles of the protocol should be adhered to.

Exchange and Handling of Information

The purpose of this document is to assist the exchange of information whilst not overriding existing legal safeguards on personal information. The manner in which information can be exchanged takes into account the following legislation;

- The Data Protection Act 1998 - for the processing of personal information.
- The Human Rights Act 1998 - for the rights of the individual's privacy.
- The Freedom of Information Act 2000
- The Licensing Act 2003, section 185
- The Common Law Duty of Confidence.

Exchange of information should be conducted in a timely and accurate fashion and confirmed in writing, (written confirmation includes in electronic form).

There are a variety of data types to consider when exchanging information, all have legal implications for the parties. The parties agree to comply with their legal obligations in respect of all disclosures.

14.12 - Interview Technique. The PEACE Method

Planning and preparation

Before conducting the interview you should ensure that you are adequately prepared;

To fail to prepare is to prepare to fail. Planning an interview is very important to ensure that the necessary topics are discussed and the relevant points are proved as well as any defences and mitigating circumstances being explored so that an ambush defence on the court day can be avoided.

Planning is the mental process of getting ready, writing the interview plan – identifying the purpose of the interview and the offences, the points to prove, what is already established and what has to be established etc. what topic areas will form the structure for the interview and what key questions will be asked etc.

Preparation is the physical preparations such as booking the room, choosing a second interviewer, getting the tape and tape seals ready etc.

Template 14.13

PEACE Interview Plan

| **Interviewee** | «ClaimantForename» «ClaimantSurname» | *Date* | |

Purpose of the Interview

Potential Offences

Points To Prove	*Potential Defences / Excuses*
Facts Established	*Facts to Determine*

Prepared by: - «MyFullName»

Engage and explain

The engage and explain stage is the start to the interview, it sets the tone of the interview and should put the interviewee at ease, it includes common courtesies such as asking the interviewee how he/she would like to be addressed and explaining the process of the interview so the interviewee knows the process of what's happening, including covering all legal formalities such as explaining that the interview is in accordance with PACE, explaining what this means and cautioning the suspect (and explaining the caution where necessary), explaining that they are free to leave or stop the interview at any time to seek legal advice, that they can have a break at anytime if they need one, as well as explaining the offences that are being investigated, and any possible further offences etc.

Account

Get the defendants account of what happened - don't spend too much time asking q on facts that are already established (although you need proof – if you already have this then move on, if not you will need to ask Q in order to get this.

Closure

The closure is important to summarise what has been said so that it can be confirmed that what been said has been understood accurately, at this stage the points to prove must be addressed (although this should have already been done at the end of each topic when the suspect may perhaps have been unaware of the significance of the question).

It is also important to give the interviewee the opportunity to clarify anything that they said and to add anything further, including anything they wish to say that wasn't asked of them.

Then there are the legal formalities; giving the suspect formal notice of their right to a copy of the tape (if the interview is tape recoded) and good practice to tell them what happens next, not what action you will take as this may change upon other evidence, but the actual process and what the possible outcomes are.

At this stage you should also give the defendant the opportunity to add anything to his/her account.

Evaluation

After the interview you should look at the following;
1. The information obtained during the interview;
2. The evidence accumulated during the whole investigation;
3. The interviewers reflection on performance during the interview.

14.13 - The funnelling technique

The funnelling technique starts off by asking the interviewee a wide open question, which instructs them to recall their movements and activities in the fullest detail, omitting nothing. This allows you to get a wide overview of what happened, from the interviewees point of view and allows you to understand their agenda, it also gives you an event line to work within which makes it easier for you to structure and keep control of your interview.

The interviewer can the ask more questions and probe for information in a structured manner, to get further details on each topic.

As the interview is more structured it means significant questions are less obvious to the suspect and as the suspect is less likely to notice them, they will be more likely to talk.

- Its an effective way of getting the maximum information from the interviewee (suspect), because it gets the suspect to 'open up'.
- This technique makes it easier to manage the interview, and therefore pick out any discrepancies and challenge them accordingly.
- Because its systematic and logical as the interviewer I will be in control of the interview and able to manage the flow of it from topic to topic, meaning that I will be less likely to miss anything out and will be able to cover all topics in order to cover all of the points to prove and will also be less likely to be distracted/'thrown off of course' by the interviewee or the interviewees solicitor.

14.14 - The conversation management interview model

With this system there are specific roles to play, the lead interviewer and the secondary interviewer. Although both roles are equally important there are some significant difference. Before the interview starts the lead will need to insure that the planning and preparation stages have been carried out and that they have got an appropriate interview plan, before actually starting the interview. Team work is necessary here.

During the interview the lead does what the name suggests and takes the lead throughout the interview, managing it in accordance with his/her plan, starting the interview with the first 'open' question and managing and steering the direction of the conversation and questioning. The lead opens the interview with a wide open question to allow the defendant to give his/her account.

The secondary interviewer is there to support the lead, pick up anything the lead misses and steer the conversation to allow the lead 'thinking time' where necessary. As well as ensuring that adequate probing has been carried out so that all the points to prove were covered.

The lead manages the engage and explain phase including the purpose of the interview, ensures the interview moves from topic to topic in a disciplined way, obtains an accurate and detailed account of what has happened from the interviewee, clarifies points, challenges points, addresses any points to prove where necessary and manages the closure.

The secondary interviewer carries out all the administration items, such as meeting and greeting the interviewee (suspect/witness) and makes them a drink etc. (where applicable) and ensures they are ready to start the interview before going into the interview room, operates the tape machine, makes exhibits ready upon request etc. therefore allowing the lead to focus on the interview and his/her topics and next line of questioning, 'conversation managing'.

The secondary interviewer also takes notes (even if the interview is tape recorded) so that if any points need clarifying at any point during the interview they can be clarified, and carries out summaries, when requested by the lead.

At the end of each topic the lead should check if the secondary interviewer has any questions, to ensure that nothing is missed in order that all points to be proved can be covered during the interview.

If the secondary interviewer has no further questions then he/she should summarise the main points agreed so far, during this summary the lead can look at the next topic on the plan and get ready to ask the next question(s) to cover this topic.

The lead starts the probing questions and the secondary interviewer will support the lead and ask probing questions, where appropriate and support the lead in his/her challenges, once the lead has raised them. The secondary interviewers role during probing is crucial, as it is the secondary interviewers responsibility to ensure all the necessary probing questions have been asked.

To summarise the roles, the process requires effective team work between the lead and secondary interviewer so that the lead can determine the structure, agenda and direction of the interview, whilst the secondary interviewer is responsible for ensuring that each area is rigorously probed and accurately summarised before the lead interview moves onto the next topic and to ensure that nothing has been overlooked.

The way the conversation model works is;
1. Planning & preparation completed (prior to the interview)
2. Engage and explain inc. the nature of the offence & caution if applicable.
3. Explain the purpose of the interview
4. The first focused wide open question to obtain the 'suspects agenda' is asked by the lead interviewer – this will make up the overall structure of the interview. The lead interviewer rigorously probes (5WH questions).
5. The second interviewer rigorously probes (5WH questions).
6. The second interviewer provides an accurate summary.
7. This process is followed for each topic on the suspects agenda
8. The lead officer then moves onto the interviewer's agenda and the above process is repeated.
9. If there any inconsistencies you can move to the challenge phase.
10. You then summarise, draw any conclusions, consolidate the information and close the interview.
11. You then need to carry out an evaluation of the interview.

Remember when doing any interview to keep an open mind and not be distracted by personal attitudes and ideas.

Summaries

It is important that each item is summarised so that the interviewer can go back to a particular point and clarify what was said, they can check anything that was said, at any point throughout the interview and can therefore challenge any contradictions.

It also means that they are recording the suspect, account accurately and have no misunderstood anything that he has said.

It also means that the interviewers can ensure that they have covered all of the points to prove. Therefore a good summary will clarify key statements that Mr Ball has made, it will also cover all statements that answers the points to prove so that the suspect can't back track later on and say that, that wasn't what he said or wasn't what he meant.

A good summary will also ensure that all questions with regards to the points to prove are confirmed without the suspect realising that these are significant questions.

Therefore a good summary will take place at every topic rather than just at the end of the interview.

A good summary will also allow the interviewee to deny/or clarify that was said and to add anything further that they may wish to say (when its relevant to that particular topic).

Challenge area – You will need to pick up on points that 'don't add up', you can probe and ask more questions but you should wait until the end of the interview before challenging them, or wait until after a break, or until a second interview so that you can make any follow up enquiries and prepare your challenges. By challenging the inconsistencies at this stage you can point out all the inconsistencies at once and therefore have the max. impact. Plan out who will say what during the 'challenge' phase of the interview.

The structured agenda

For your interview you must have an agenda, you must know where your questions are heading and anticipate possible answers/alibis from the defendant.

You may want to draw yourself boxes of possible topics that you may ask – this is your agenda.

The things that the interviewee/defendant might want to talk about is their agenda. You may want to start of talking about items that are on their agenda to get them talking and get them to open up.

Additional information required with regards to identification of witnesses;

In R v Turnbull 8 points of recognition were established, when dealing with witnesses to asses how accurate their account may be, these points are as follows;
1. The amount of time the witness had the accused under observation, (obviously the longer the witness observed the incident or person, the greater the confidence that can be placed in their testimony).
2. Distance the witness had from the suspect/incident, (did it remain constant? What is the witnesses judgment of distance like?).
3. Visibility, (weather, lighting, witnesses eye sight).
4. Observation, (did the witness have a clear unobstructed view or was the view obstructed?).
5. Knowledge of suspect (did the witness know the suspect, if the witness did know the suspect it would make it easier for them to recognise and identify the suspect).
6. Were there any special reasons for the witness remembering the suspect, such as any particularly distinctive features etc.?
7. What was the time between the original sighting and subsequent information, were any records made, are they exhibited?
8. Are there any errors in the witnesses account, any reasons for error such as colour blindness etc. or do they have a motive to lie.

14.15 - The Cognitive Interview

Another model of interviewing is the cognitive interview. This is a memory enhancing interview for use with witnesses and victims, rather than suspects.
The stages to this are as follows;
1. Introduce the interview – engage and explain, build rapport and reduce anxiety.
2. First free recall – Ask the interviewee to take themselves back to the scenario and recall everything that happened.
3. Once they have done this ask them to go back through the events in reverse order, when they do this in reverse they will need to think more in depth and concentrate more on the sequence of events and therefore may recall more details that they couldn't before, (this stage isn't appropriate for children or the elderly as they don't have the same ability to sequence things).
4. The third recall stage requires you to wait for them to tell you about certain aspects and then zoom in on these aspects and probe them fully by asking them to think about details such as people, places, objects, actions, times/dates, and revoke senses such as taste, touch, smell, sounds, feelings.
5. Then wait till the end to carry out a accurate summary, unless you need to summaries points at an earlier stage for clarification purposes.
6. Then write up a report on the interview and what was said.

14.16 - Disclosure prior to an interview

There is no requirement to disclose evidence, in advance of the interview. However you will need to inform the defendant or his/her solicitor of the nature of the under investigation. It is good practice to disclose the fullest amount of information so that the defendant can fully understand the offence and the solicitor can do his/her job and advise the client without having to advise him to remain silent, or even adjourning the interview/having long breaks to discuss, which could happen if they didn't fully understand the offences fully due to lack of information, but obviously without giving too much information away so that it may prevent the investigator from getting a full account from the suspect. It would be unfair to conduct an interview without giving the defendant prior notice of the offences that you are investigating.

You will need to decide not only what to disclose before the interview but at what stage to disclose evidence during the interview.

14.17 - Dealing with representatives intervention

The law society guidelines state that the solicitors role is;
- To protect their clients basic and legal rights
- To continue to advice their client throughout the interview
- To request that all times they and their client shall be addressed with appropriate formability.
- They shall not answer for their clients.
- They shall intervene if;
- Their client requests or requires legal advice
- The interviewer questioning is inappropriate
- The interviewer refers to evidence but does not produce it
- The interviewer produces evidence that the solicitor and client have not had chance to examine.
- If anyone attempts to pressurises their client.
- A break is needed.

You may need to remind the solicitor's/representative of their role. A trade union representative, is there to represent employee and may give legal advice relating to employment law, therefore they have the same restrictions as a solicitor.

It is therefore the right of the investigator to put questions to the defendant and it is up to their client if he/she wishes to answer them and the solicitor should give their client the option to answer them as he is not allowed to answer questions on behalf of his client, the questions are necessary as part of the investigation process to find the facts and if he/she needs to take a break to advice his/her client they are welcome to but if not we will carry on with the interview.

Furthermore the Home Office C.I. 22/92 addresses this issue and states in the principals that the interviewer is not bound to accept the first answer given, questioning is not unfair merely because it is persistent. (although be mindful that hammering continuous questions at the interviewee could be seen as oppressive, and would therefore be a breach of PACE).

Additionally the trade union representative is only there as a representative and can offer moral support, and advice on policy matters but other than this should have no further involvement, and therefore should not be interrupting the interview.

It is essential that an accurate record is kept of the interview, either in a pace complaint note book or on specified record paper.

When conducting investigations you also need to be aware of points to prove and possible defences & the burden of proof / standard of proof for that Act.

14.18 - The Interview Procedure

An interview can be a formal planned interviewer under caution or you may find that you are at the scene of a crime and have to ask possible suspects questions, you will therefore need to caution them and will therefore be carrying out an interview, you will therefore need to carry out the following actions;

As soon as an officer suspects that a person has committed an offence, the caution should be administered before putting further questions to the interviewee. Whilst there is nothing wrong in asking further questions before doing so – particularly in order to identify the responsible person in cases of doubt etc – that evidence will not be admissible in court.

Inform the person that you believe they have committed an offence, and that you need to ask them questions about it. Before you do so, you need to caution them. The caution is printed on the front inside cover of PACE notebooks, and is:

"You do not have to say anything but it may harm your defence if you do not mention when questioned anything that you later rely on in court. Anything you do say may be given in evidence".

Record the time, date and place of where you cautioned the interviewee and record their reply. Ask whether they understand the caution, and if they have not repeat it (see below for an explanation of the caution). If they still do not understand then another form of words may be used so that it can be understood. Ensure they understand that they are not under arrest and are free to go but also they understand whether they may be committing any further offences of obstruction or failing to answer questions (if contained in the relevant Act). Record their replies in your notebook.

If you do not need to ask any further questions, obtain the interviewee's signature in your notebook under your notes. If they refuse to sign, make a note of their refusal and if possible have that witnessed by another person.

If you need to ask questions other than those to verify their identify, inform them they do have the right to have a legal adviser present it should be possible to arrange for them to attend a further, more structured interview, for further questioning at a later date, when the interview can be tape recorded..

Sometimes it may be better not to caution the interviewee until you have asked questions to ascertain the culpability or to seek further information. Remember that you cannot use any statements in court once you suspect them of having committed an offence if they are made before being cautioned.

As well as informing them of the offence you suspect they have committed you will need to say that if any evidence of any further offences come to light you may also investigate these or pass such information over to other departments or agencies who may want to investigate these matters.

14.19 - Formal taped interviews

All interviews, except the very briefest, should be tape-recorded.

Before inviting an interviewee in for an interview, book the interview room with the tape recorder in (In CSC), with enough time to set up and spare time in case the interview over-runs, if this is not available you could book another room and the portable tape recorder (you will also need to ensure that you have a personal alarm).

Send the pro-forma appointment letter to interviewee, giving two clear working weeks, and possible a range of a few dates so that they can pick the most convenient, unless (a) the matter involves an imminent or serious risk to health or safety; or (b) the relevant legislation requires notice in another form. The pro-forma appointment letter should state the legislation which it is alleged has been infringed, and details of the alleged offence. You should also indicate whether you require the interviewee to bring any specific information or evidence with them, e.g. maintenance record books. You should also ask them to bring proof of ID, such as a valid passport.

14.20 - Before the interview

(a) arrange to have a colleague present at the interview if required;
(b) ensure you have all the necessary information in the file and prepare your questions, you may want to use the PEACE model (See below), & produce a timeline of the sequence of events leading to the offence, reference can be made to the exhibits on this, this will make the interview flow better (See below).
(c) mark all exhibits to be used during the interview. They should be marked with the initials of the officer who obtained them, followed by a consecutive number. (Exhibits to be produced by John Smith will be marked 'JS1', 'JS2') etc. If you have more than a few exhibits, put them in order with a content page it will make it easier for you to refer to them in the interview.

Ensure you have enough tapes, the tape seal(s) and the PACE code of practice – the latest edition is the August 2007 edition plus the CODE E supplement.

14.21 - Before Starting

(a) the tape-recorder (if not using the interview room with it in).
(b) sufficient tapes (one as a master tape and one as a working copy) for the interview. Tapes last for 90 (they have to be turned over after 45 minutes) and must not be opened before the interview;
(c) one tape seal for each master tape;
(d) the exhibits;
(e) a 'Do Not Disturb – Interview in Progress' sign;
(f) current PACE Code of Practice;
(g) the Formal Notice to Persons Being Interviewed (see below);
(h) Notice to Person Whose Interview Has Been Tape-Recorded (see below);
(i) PACE record of interview (in the event of the tape malfunctioning);
(j) Your PACE notebook.

Complete the relevant parts of the Notice to Person Whose Interview Has Been Tape-Recorded and the tape seal before the interview to avoid forgetting about it afterwards.

14.22 - Legal Advice and Procedure

If an interview takes place at a Police Station, interviewees are entitled to free legal advice during an interview. If an interview takes place anywhere else, this is not the case. Interviewees are still entitled to seek legal advice and to be accompanied at the interview by a legal representative, but they will not be provided this service free of charge. They will have to pay for the legal advice. This is an important distinction when considering joint prosecutions or where separate agencies work together and may conduct interview together. See 14.11.

14.23- Conducting the Interview

At the outset, explain to the interviewee that the interview is a taped interview under caution and that officers have to follow a legal procedure during the interview. Show the interviewee the unopened tapes, which must then be opened in their presence. Explain that one tape will be used as the master copy and the other as a working copy. Give the interviewee a copy of the Formal Notice to Persons Being Interviewed, and offer to read to them if they require.

Place a tape in each of the decks and press record. The tape-recorder will sound an alarm for about ninety seconds before recording begins. When the alarm stops:

(a) state your name, the date, time and place of the interview;
(b) ask everyone else in the room to identify themselves for the purposes of the tape;
(c) inform the interviewee of the purpose of the interview, and formally caution them. Ensure that:

>the caution is understood
>
>they are aware that they are not under arrest
>
>that they are entitled to have a legal advisor or an interpreter present either then or at any point in the interview.

- they are made aware that the interview will be carried out in line with the PACE codes of practice and that they can refer to the codes of practice at any stage throughout the interview.
- Clarify that you had opened the tapes, that were previously sealed in their presence.

Remember that you should try not to ask leading questions, e.g. questions that tend to suggest the answer or should not make any assumptions or any sarcastic comments.

During the interview....

If the tape recorder indicates a short recording time is left – tell the suspect and round off that part of the interview.

If any breaks are taken, including to turn the tapes over you must state that the interview is being stopped and if applicable the reason the tape is being stopped and the time, then the time, date and location tape needs to be stated again when the interview is re-started and who is present, the interviewee must also be reminded that they are still under caution and if it has been a long break they should be re-cautioned.

At the conclusion of the interview………… summarise what has been said and check whether the interviewee has anything else to add to the interview. State the time that the interview has finished and turn off the tape machine. Anything which is said after that point cannot be used in evidence!

Explain what happens next.

Remove both tapes from the machine in front of the interviewee. Label <u>both tapes</u> with the relevant exhibit number for that investigation.

Complete the rest of the details on the tape seal(s), and ask the interviewee to sign the seal in front of you. If the interviewee and his legal representative refuses to sign, ask a senior officer not connected with the interview to witness their refusal and for them to sign instead.

Attach the seal(s) to <u>each</u> master copy of the tape(s) used, and inform the interviewee that it will be locked in the office safe, and will only be opened if a court directs it should be. The other tape will be kept securely with any other evidence relating to the investigation. It will be transcribed and a copy sent to the interviewee, although they may have to pay if they wish to have a copy of the tape as well, depending on your company policy.

Remember that evidence gained in the course of the investigation and recorded on tape can only be used for that specific investigation, and not for other offences investigated by other agencies or departments.

Record the fact that the interview took place in your PACE notebook, and investigation file (once you have the tape transcripts they should go in here) for inclusion in your witness statement. The transcript or tape of the interview must be produced as exhibits in the event of a court case.

Take a photocopy of any exhibits they have brought and their ID shown, certify these as true copies and put these in the investigation file.

At the end of the interview return any equipment, unused tapes and the PACE code of practice books.

14.24 - Post interview evaluation

After the interview it is worth carrying out a post interview evaluation so that you can review the defendants account and see what evidence has been gained, what points have been proved or disproved and what further information/investigation is required and identify any other follow up action that needs to be carried out as a result, for instance you may need to go away and check the suspect account and then hold another interview to carry out any challenges or to clarify anything further, at a later date. You may also need to look at the rest of your evidence for the whole investigation in light of the outcome of the interview and to analyse your own performance, did you do everything correctly and how was your interviewing technique? You may then come up with improvements for next time, you may also want to discuss this with the second interviewer and point out any mannerisms or areas for change/improvement and give praise where things went well.

14.25 - Further offences

If further offences come to light after you have invited the defendant in for an interview, you can raise questions about these further offences in an interview, however if details of these come to light after the interview you will have to re-interview the defendant again to give him chance to have his say in relation to these offences, you can then use these to form part of your prosecution / enforcement action, however once the prosecution process has started you can't just add these on so you will have to take subsequent action.

Chapter 15 - Preparing a File for Prosecution

15.1 - Prosecutions

Prosecutions would in general be suitable for most serious offences in the following circumstances where:

- there is a blatant disregard for the law, particularly where the economic advantages of breaking the law are substantial and the law-abiding are placed at a disadvantage to those who disregard it;
- there appears to be have been a reckless disregard for the health and safety of others. This does not necessarily mean legal recklessness, as many offences are strict liability offences not dependent on proving intent;
- where, in relation to licences and permits for charitable collections, people have been deceived into donating money for fraudulent purposes;
- there have been repeated breaches of legal requirements in an organisation and it appears that, particularly in the field of public entertainments, the management is neither willing nor structured to adequately deal with these;
- a particular offence is prevalent and the authority needs to show firm decisive action to ensure the necessary degree of public protection;
- a serious accident or ill-health has resulted has resulted through a neglect of licensing requirements. In this eventuality, due regard should be paid to enforcement action being undertaken under the Health and Safety at Work etc Act 1974 by the Environmental Health department or action by other enforcement agencies;
- a particular contravention has caused serious public alarm; or
- the criteria for the issue of a caution or formal warning is not established.

Prosecution should not be taken where there is a known defence in law. Proceedings should not be referred to the authority's Solicitor unless sufficient evidence is available to prove the case in line with the appropriate legislation, and that there is a realistic prospect of conviction; a bare prima facie case is not enough. The defence case must be considered and how that is likely to affect that of the Council. The quality of the evidence must itself be considered to ensure that it can be used and is reliable. The Council's policies for complying with the Police and Criminal Evidence Act 1984; Criminal Procedures and Investigations Act 1996; and the Regulation of Investigatory Powers Act 2000 must be followed.

However, where circumstances justify prosecution, it should not be avoided just because of the case is difficult and a conviction may not be completely certain. On occasion, it may be considered not in the public interest to proceed with a prosecution and in such instances further consideration to other forms of disposal should be given. The public interest test is similar to that issued by the Attorney-General in *The Code for Crown Prosecutors*. Some factors in favour of prosecution would include:

- the seriousness of the offence. The more serious it is, the more likely a conviction would be in the public interest;

- where a conviction is likely to result in a significant sentence;
- deliberate obstruction to officers or robust refusals to comply with the law occurred;
- the defendant was an organiser or ringleader of an offence;
- there is evidence to show the offence was premeditated or continued for some considerable time before discovery;
- there is evidence that the offence was carried out by a group of individuals;
- the offence was motivated by any form of discrimination;
- the defendant's previous convictions or cautions are relevant to the present offence;
- there are grounds for believing that the offence is likely to be continued or repeated;
- the offence is widespread within the Borough, such as illegal plying for hire;
- there is widespread concern within the Borough over a particular activity.

Occasions where the public interest factor suggests that prosecutions not be brought include:

- where the court is likely to impose a very small or nominal penalty although this should not preclude prosecution where an example or test case is needed;

- the offence was committed due to a genuine misunderstanding or mistake, weighed against the seriousness of the offence;
- any actual or potential loss or harm was minor and the result of a single incident perhaps caused by misjudgement;
- there has been a long delay between the offence being committed and the date for trial, unless the offence is serious (not based on mode of trial but the consequences); the delay has been caused by the defendant; the offence has only recently come to light (note that the majority of licensing offences are summary offences and therefore have a limitation period of six months); or the complexity of the offence has required a long investigation;
- a prosecution is likely to have an extremely adverse effect on the victim's mental or physical health unless they consent to being able to give evidence when required;
- the defendant was elderly or suffering from some significant mental or physical ill health at the time the offence was committed;
- the defendant has put right the loss or harm that was caused but defendants must not avoid prosecution simply because they can pay compensation.

15.2 - Prosecution with warning

If the steps in this policy were observed, an individual or organisation would generally be the subject of some formal enforcement action before a prosecution is considered. However, it is recognised that in some circumstances it may be appropriate to issue a summons without giving such prior warning. This may occur where the contravention is a particularly serious one and the risk to public safety has been correspondingly high. Failure to observe the requirements of formal warnings or those inherent in a caution, or repeated failures to observe informal warnings, should normally result in prosecution.

Although not a specified statutory requirement, this authority will issue a Notice of Intended Prosecution to all offenders prior to the issue of the summons or indictment against them. This Notice should state:

- those against the prosecution is to be directed;
- the nature of the allegation and the precise legislation alleged to have been breached;
- that the offender need not do anything at that stage, but may seek legal advice if they should wish.

15.3 - Prosecution following an accident

The primary consideration in this event should be the seriousness of the contravention (and whether intent or recklessness is required as an evidential factor), and the severity of the accident may only be a subsidiary consideration. The extent the defendants were responsible for the circumstances leading to the accident, and whether previous warnings had been given, are also to be taken into account. Officers should ask themselves what action would have been appropriate if the contravention had come to light in the absence of the accident. Accidents may contribute to the strength of evidence, and thus the chances of a conviction. In all cases where there is a possibility of manslaughter being made the matter must be referred to the Crown Prosecution Service.

15.4 - Prosecutions arising from other criminal acts

Enforcement action may sometimes be required as a result of enforcement action being undertaken by another agency. In the event that a prosecution should be initiated from circumstances arising from the same set of facts, it will generally be advisable for any such prosecution to proceed on the basis of the most serious charge where the penalty is the greater.

Depending on the type of offence will affect what level you have to prove, this is known as standard of proof / burden of proof. If you are prosecuting for a criminal offence you have to prove that the offence was committed 'beyond reasonable doubt', where as civil cases are decided on a balance of probability.

Legislation is graded on its seriousness, this will determine the punishment i.e. the fines set or minimum prison sentence, this will then determine in which court the trial of any offenders breaching that legislation will be tried.

For instance lesser offences will be heard in the magistrates court, where as more serious offences will be heard in the Crown Court, where the defendant will be judged by a jury.

The standard scale for fines for summary only offences is;

Level 1 £200
Level 2 £500
Level 3 £1,000
Level 4 £2,500
Level 5 £5,000

Note; The legislation may specify different fines, applicable for specific offences under that legislation only, therefore it is important to check the legislation and specify accurately the specific maximum fine, in the prosecution bundle (in the case disposal records).

15.5 - Preparing a file for court

Constructing a prosecution file

The Police use the standard MG11 forms, where as most local authorities use their own forms. It doesn't matter what form you use as long as the essential information is there.

The prosecution file, must consist of;

1. **A covering letter/memo to the solicitor – instructing them.**

2. **Content page – this will make it easier to follow (every page in the file should be numbered).**

3. **The case disposal record and summary outlining the case and surmising the main points.**

    Case disposal Record
    (1) please check that the mode of trial is correctly inserted, by checking with the correct legislation.

    (2) Part of the officers decision in cosidering the crown prosecutors code is to consider whether there is a realistic prospect of conviction and whether it is in the public interest to prosecute the case. This invovles having investigated any previous convictions of the defendant, this includes any previous cautions/reprimands/warnings, be they an individual or a company.

    (3) Searches should be made with the Office of Fair Trading and the Police National Computer beforehand, so that the file is prepared with a list of whether the defendant has an antecedent history or not. It is a relevant factor in the officer's decision on whether it is in the public interest to prosecute or whether to consider a caution or warning, please also check with the DVLA for a driver's printout, as this will be relevant for some offences, including licencing matters and a DVLA printout should have been obtained for the file. It is also relevant to the likely sentence.

    (4) Officers should be aware of the possibility that the defence have the right to ask if the officer in the case, including any witnesses for the Council will be relying upon, will have any previous convictions/cautions/disciplinary record, it is important therefore that we notify all witnesses at the outset that the defence do have the right to request disclosure if they have any previous convictions.

    (5) An investigating officer should ensure that they have all the relevant information available to them to be able to make such checks if required in the investigation process, this includes the date of birth, the full correct spelling of the name. This information can then be easily obtained throughout proceedings if requested.

15.6 - Evidence Log

This is a catalogue of all the evidence that you have.

15.7 - Decision Log

An decision log is needed in the court file to show reasoning for decision making. When making decisions record key facts/evidence in case need to justify decision. Therfore need to make good notes throughout the case to help you prepare this.

15.8 - Schedule of Sensitive Material

(1) In accordance with the Criminal Procedure and
Investigations Act 1996. Disclosure officer should
Have an up to date copy available to them for officers use.

(2) Tabulise the description of the item, and the Reason for
Non disclosure

(3) If there is no material that is considered as sensitive,
then the table must still indicate this and be signed off by
the disclosure officer

Any sensitive material must be listed on a separate schedule and the disclosure officer must certify that is the case. Sensitive material is that which the disclosure officer believes it would not be in the public interest to disclose. For Council purposes these may include material given in confidence; material whose disclosure might facilitate the commission of other offences or hinder the prevention and detection of crime; material generated by a financial regulator such as the Financial Services Authority; or material supplied to an investigator relating to a child or young person generated by a third party contacted by the investigator during the investigation.

<u>Way in which material is to be listed on the schedule</u>
a) Each item must be listed separately on the schedule, and consecutively numbered. The description on each item should make clear the nature of the item and be sufficiently clear to allow the prosecutor to decide whether he needs to inspect the material before deciding whether or not it should be disclosed.

b) Items of a similar or repetitive quantity (eg multiple food samples) need not be separately described but can be described by quantity and generic title providing any material which might undermine the case against the accused (the "primary disclosure test") are listed and described individually.

15.9 - Schedule of Non-sensitive Material

(1) To be completed in accordance with the Criminal Procedure and Investigations Act 1996,

(2) If there is no such material, the table
must be signed accordingly by the disclosure officer.

15.10 - Witness Statements

(1) ensure that the name of the person is marked
(2) the s.9 CJA 1976…pre-amble is at the top of the statement
(3) Age of witness: over 18, if under 18 please state age only
(4) Occupation
(5) Address: please **do not** insert this at the top of the statement,
it is confidential and sensitive information, it can be inserted at the
back of the original, along with contact details, home/work, mobile,
also dates to avoid, and date of birth
(6) Statement must be signed and witnessed by an officer and dated
(7) Any further statements with changes or new additional evidence taken at
a different time will require a new statement to be completed in the same way

15.11 - Exhibits

(1) these must be properly labelled and exhibited
in the officers statement, and where he found them.

(2) if photographed, these need to be properly exhibited

(3) if the exhibits are placed in any safe place, a

statement of continuation regarding to whom if was passed
to and where is located should be provided. Continuity of evidence
is important.

(4) any important exhibits e.g such as registration numbers

written down by a witness on papers/or any document at the time
of witnessing the offence should be safeguarded for proceedings and
properly exhibited, this then provides a contemporaneous account
of what was seen, the witness should be able to exhibit this in
her/his statement, any person seizing the document must complete
a statement to that effect, the original documents to be kept
in safe storage for court proceedings. Loss of vital evidence
can mean we lose a case.

(5) Photographs : these should be colour photographs,
at least 4 copies of each, these will be for the
defendant, /solicitor/court clerk/bench /Council's counsel

15.12 - Record of Interview

(1) ensure these are conducted in accordance with PACE provisions
a copy of the recent PACE code shoud be with each officer before
going into the interview. The defendant has the right to access them.

(2) Each officer should be familiar with the PACE provisions before
Interview. Ensure provisions are complied with.

(3) paragraph C: 11: gives specific guidelines on interviews in general.

(4) PACE Code C: gives the code for the Detention, Treatment

and Questioning of Persons by Police officers.

(5) any interview tapes, if given to the defendant, must be signed off as

a copy given to the defendant. File copy showing receipt of this must be kept.

15.13 - Costs

Prosecution file needs to inc. a comprehensive break down of costs

15.14 - Impact Report

It may also be worth doing an impact report for standard cases, especially if its something that the court might view as quite minor, for instance if it's a littering offence whereby someone has dropped a cigarette you may want to write about the impact of people dropping cigarettes, the affect this has on the environment and therefore why it is important to prosecute people for doing this and deter others from committing such offences, as seemingly minor offences can all add up and have a big negative impact on the community, small offences lead onto bigger offences and small amounts of litter will make other litter and will cause a big problem, if the public can think they can drop litter then they will soon start fly tipping larger items and the community will go downhill etc.

- You will also want to put your investigation and prosecution file in chronological order as it will make things easier to find and give you a more logical approach to your working.

- You may also want to bullet point key facts for each witness statement, before court you may want to give witnesses a list of bullet points – facts to be emphasised in their witness statements, questions they may be asked, and points to get across etc. (similar to preparing a case summary listing the main points for counsel).

15.15 - Conducting a Case Analysis

Once you have undertaken the investigation and reviewed all your evidence and once you have started to put it all together, it is useful to undertake a case analysis, to go over everything again and ensure that the file is complete and that you haven't missed anything. To look at the case from the point of view of the defence so that you can anticipate what questions they may ask you, so that you can be prepared.

Case analysis assessment stage;
A – Identify the legal framework i.e. what are the offences/breaches.
B – Point to prove (actus reus / mens rea etc.). Have you proved all the points to prove, is there sufficient evidence and have you highlighted this in the file?
C – Analysis of the facts to prove (identify fact from inferences, look for gaps in the facts, identify strengths & weaknesses in the evidence you are gathering and consider where you need more info and where to get it from, consider what further evidence is needed etc.) Follow up & gather evidence.
Stage D – Decide what action to take, is there sufficient evidence for a prosecution?
What are the possible weaknesses in the case?
Stage E – What are the likely questions that will be asked in court, in the examination in chief.
What are the questions that I would most like my counsel to ask, of me as the investigator in, in examination in chief are;
Of the other witnesses;
Stage F – What are the likely questions that will be asked in court, in cross examination.
Stage G – With reference to the evidence, I would answer the questions as follows............ (this would be my preparation – the counsel would be unable to coach me, or lead me in my answers).

15.16 - Disclosure

See also Chapters 6 and 7.

The disclosure officer *must* also the prosecutor any material below (unless it already comprises a part of the prosecution evidence):

- Records of the first description of a suspect given by a potential witness, regardless of whether that differs from that of the alleged offender;
- Information provided by an accused person which indicates an explanation for the offence with which he has been charged;
- Any material casting doubt on the reliability of a confession;
- Any material casting doubt on the reliability of a witness (including age, infirmity or other physical characteristics);
- Any other material which the disclosure officer believes may fall within the test for primary disclosure.

Continuing duty of disclosure;
There is a continuing duty on all officers to disclose to the prosecutor all material gathered in the course of an investigation - whether or not it is to be used in the prosecution - which meets the test for disclosure. This duty extends throughout the whole duration of any criminal proceedings. This is to allow the prosecutor to comply with its duties of primary and secondary disclosure.

Subsequent action by disclosure officer;
Once the disclosure officer is aware of which material will form the case against the accused, the prosecutor must be supplied with an amended schedule of unused material showing additional material that:

- May not be relevant to the investigation;
- Does not form part of the case against the accused;
- Is not already listed on the schedule; and
- Is not sensitive material.

This need not be disclosed if informed in writing by the prosecutor that he intends to disclose the material to the defence.

The disclosure officer must also review any retained material if a defence statement is given. The prosecutor must then be made aware of any material which might reasonably be expected to assist the defence disclosed by the accused. Apart from the requirement for the disclosure officer to certify that all retained evidence has been revealed to the prosecutor, he must also certify when retained material is reconsidered under this paragraph.

Disclosure of material to the accused;
Where material is requested by the prosecutor to be disclosed to the accused, it will normally be the responsibility of the disclosure officer to ensure that this takes place, either by giving the accused a copy of the material or allowing him to inspect it. Copies must be given unless it is not practicable (e.g. because the object cannot be copied or the volume of material is too great) or undesirable. The latter case will be rare in terms of Council prosecutions and advice must always be sought from the prosecutor before a decision is made to refuse to allow copies to be given. Taped material may be transcribed at the discretion of the disclosure officer.

The disclosure officer will ensure that a schedule of non-sensitive material is provided, where:

- The offence is one triable only on indictment
- The offence is triable either-way and is likely to be tried on indictment or the accused is likely to plead not guilty at a summary trial
- The offence is a summary one and it is considered the accused is likely to plead not guilty.

15.17 - Disclosure of un-used material

Evidence is information which may be presented to a court to help it weigh up the probability of what the truth is, evidence that is relevant and admissible may be used as part of the prosecution case. The Criminal Procedures Investigations Act 1996 (as amended by the criminal justice act 2003), defines that the prosecution must serve or furnish any evidence which they seek to rely on, anything not used which is relevant, is known as unused material and must be disclosed by the prosecutor to the defence.

When disclosing unused material the prosecution does not have to disclose the evidence, merely the information about what evidence they have. The defence can then request to see this if they feel that it is relevant to their defence case. Therefore there is a requirement on the prosecutor to keep all relevant information, even if they are not using it as part of the prosecution case. It is good practise to keep all records, as even if they don't seem relevant at the time they may become relevant later on and this will then prevent any claims of injustice. Therefore information must be recorded in a durable or retrievable form. If you use your notebook in the witness box the defendants solicitor can ask to see it. Therefore it is important to think carefully about what you write in it.

In the attorney-generals guidelines on disclosure he refers to article 6 of the European convention on human rights, stating that a fair trial consists of an examination on not just of all the evidence the parties wish to rely on but also all other relevant subject matter. He then goes onto say, that such disclosure, under The Criminal Procedures Investigations Act 1996 (as amended by the criminal justice act 2003), should assist the accused in the timely preparation and presentation of their case and assist the court to focus on all the relevant issues in the trial and disclosure which does not meet these objectives risks preventing a fair trail taking place.

Furthermore in conducting an investigation, the investigator should peruse all reasonable lines of enquiry, whether these point towards or away the suspect and the duty is on the prosecutor to disclose material in his possession which might reasonably be considered capable of undermining the case for the prosecution.

Before a summary only (magistrates court) trial all evidence on which the prosecution intends to rely on, should automatically be served to the defence. Where as before the trial of an either way offence, the accused is entitled to be furnished with copies of statements or a summary of the case (under the Criminal Procedure Rules Part 21 Advanced Information) and before the trial of an indictable only offence, the accused is entitled to copies of the documents containing the evidence on which the charge is based (under the Crime and Disorder Act 1998 – Service of prosecution evidence – regulations 2005).

15.18 - Disclosure of Sensitive Material

You can apply for sensitive material not to be disclosed, if it is in the public interest that it is not disclosed, in this case you must seek an order for PII – Public interest immunity. A judge would balance the defendants rights against the public interest issue and decide whether this should be granted or not.

15.19 - Continuing Disclosure

Furthermore in addition to the initial duty of the prosecutor to disclose relevant unused material, the duty to disclose is a continuing one. This duty applies both before and after the service of the defence statements. This is set out in section 7A of the CPIA (as amended) / The code 8.2

15.20 - Admission of Fact

When an admission of fact is appropriate

1. You may wish to agree certain facts with the defence, so that these facts will not need to be proved at court. This procedure is known as making admissions of fact, or formal admissions (as distinct from the confession, or informal admission, of a defendant).
2. Making a formal admission is particularly appropriate if it narrows down the issues in contention at trial. It is suitable for evidence that is unlikely to be disputed by the defence. The following facts may be suitable for formal admission:
    - the fact that an accident happened:
    - the fact that an injured person was employed by the defendant:
    - the fact that the defendant was the occupier of premises.

Procedure

3. You should write to the defence, setting out the fact(s) that the prosecution wishes to formally agree as an admission under section 10 CJA 1967. To be admitted under s 10, the admission must be:
    - made before or at the time of the proceedings;
    - in writing, unless it is made in court.
4. If made in writing:
    - by an individual it must be signed by the person making the admission;
    - by a company it must be signed by a director, secretary or some other similar officer of the body corporate.
8. If made, whether orally or in writing, on behalf of a defendant who is an individual, it must be made by the defendant's counsel or solicitor.
9. You may also admit facts at the request of the defence, where you are sure that these are not in contention. Any admission should be in writing and signed by you.

15.21 - Summary of the Investigation Process from Investigation to laying information at Court

The Criminal Procedures Rules 2005 (criminal procedures and investigations act 1996) & The Criminal Procedure (Amendment) Rules 2007 forms part of a statutory framework together with the Police and Criminal Evidence Act 1984 (PACE) to regulate how criminal investigations should be conducted. *For more information, on these rules see* **http://www.opsi.gov.uk**, *where you can download the legislation.*

Between them they cover the whole process of investigation from the initial identification of an offender, the questioning of the offender, the gathering of evidence and the disclosure of the evidence to the offender and the prosecutor.

The best format for carrying out investigations is as follows;

1. Understand the context; the problems, events, situations, history etc. It is important to get as much information as possible, including the complainants details so that we can go back to them at a later date if we have more information, and if appropriate, keep them updated as to what the outcome is.

2. What are the offences and what is the legal framework and points to prove.

3. Ask yourself do you have the authority or resources to deal with it, or do we need to refer it onto other partners, or call upon the resources of other departments to assist? It may well be that an offence has been committed but you may not have the jurisdiction to deal with it, for instance the offence of illegally plying for hire takes place where the journey commences, therefore if you stop an unlicensed driver with passengers that have been picked up from another borough, the Police can deal with this, but to get a Local Authority prosecution for illegally plying for hire you will need to pass it to the borough where the journey took place, obviously if they decide to prosecute you can assist them but you will not be able to bring about a prosecution yourself.

4. Conduct investigation and collect facts – investigate, research, inspection, interview etc. (Get RIPA clearance where applicable & carry out investigation accordance to PACE). Who is the responsible person and do they have the 'ACTUS REUS' and the 'MENS REA' (or is it a strict liability case). As a licensing enforcement officer, it is usually clear who the responsible/guilty person if dealing with offences in relation to a driver, however if the offence relates to an unlicensed premises who have been selling alcohol without a licence it may not be so clear cut as the rates may be paid by one person, someone may own the premises but rent it to someone else, who may have employed another person to manage the business.

NB.

The investigator, the officer in charge of the investigation and the disclosure officer should generally be separate. This need not arise in very simple cases where no detailed investigation is required, for example reporting an individual for a street trading offence directly observed by the investigator and where there is no other material evidence.

In conducting investigations, investigators must pursue all reasonable lines of enquiry, whether these point towards or away from the alleged offender. What is reasonable in each case will depend on the particular circumstances.

All material/exhibits should be carefully labelled with the initials of the witness who may be required to produce them in court, and sequentially numbered in the order they will be produced where there is more than one.

The investigator is responsible for maintaining the security of all material at all times, including up to and during any trial, even where files and material are passed to other officers.

5. Analyse facts/evidence gathered and see if there is enough evidence to prove the case; what are the facts to prove? What facts do you have and what are assumptions or inferences, are their any gaps or ambiguity in the facts? Is there a defence? Is the case worth pursuing? What are the strengths and weaknesses in your evidence? Do you need more information? If so what information do you need?

6. Gather more information investigate, research, inspection, interview etc. / get statements etc. you may at this stage want to re-clarify who to prosecute (take action against), depending on the complexity of the case. (Get RIPA clearance where applicable & carry out investigation accordance to PACE).

Evidence;
All information that is relevant to an investigation must be recorded in a durable and retrievable form. Officers must ensure that all relevant information is recorded on complaint sheets, inspection records, notebooks, or on computer and must form part of the complete prosecution file eventually given to the disclosure officer. The general rules applicable to note-taking apply in that they should be made at the time the information was obtained or as soon as practicable thereafter.

Investigators must retain all relevant material, including material that comes into their possession (such as food samples) as well as material generated by them (such as interview records). Material can be photographed or copied if the original is perishable or supplied to the investigator and is to be returned to it's owner.

The evidence must be retained

- until a decision is made to bring proceedings or to formally caution an individual;
- once proceedings have been started, until either the alleged offender is acquitted, the prosecutor decides not to proceed with the case, or there is a conviction;
- for six months from the date of the conviction or until any subsequent appeal is determined.

Duplicate copies of reports etc which are purely ancillary do not need to be kept.

If material previously thought to be relevant later becomes relevant to an investigation but has not been retained, reasonable steps should be taken to obtain it or ensure it is retained for future inspection or for production in court.

7. Decide what action to take – informal advice, formal advice note, warning, formal final warning, penalty points, formal caution, licence review – suspend or revoke, or prosecution. / Other partners may be involved at this stage (if not before) and action may be taken under their powers. This will mean looking at the strengths and weaknesses in your evidence to decide if there is enough evidence for a prosecution.

8. You will then either need to write up a file note so that details of the offence, evidence and details of action taken, copies of notices/letters can be placed on file or you will need to prepare a prosecution case file of you wish to issue a formal caution or instigate prosecution proceedings.

9. If applicable – Prepare the prosecution case file and pass to the legal team with instructions and details of costs. Take a photocopy of the file and keep a log book to record file movement. Obtain dates to avoid for all witnesses where possible for the next 4 months at least, unless this is a significant matter whereby it is anticipated a trial may take several days, in which case obtain dates for the next 6 – 8 months. If an interpreter will be required, notification will be needed of the language service we will be using, as legal can serve documents, however the defendant may not be able to understand the notice served upon them, please include in your file the language service that is to be used if an interpreter is required for service of documents. Once proceedings have been issued and the matter is before the court, the court will provide an interpreter for all court proceedings.

10. SUMMONS: Is to be laid in Court before the limitation date. The limitation is usually 6 months in the magistrates court, from the start of the investigation to laying the information at court, unless the legislation specifies a limitation period, for instance the Licensing Act 2003 specifies a limitation period of 12 months.

11. SERVICE OF SUMMONS: Must be effected seven clear days before the hearing, this is when all the statements and evidence to hand needs to be served on the Defendant & the Court. Once a summons has been served you will need to notify witnesses and prepare for court, this will include briefing lawyers on the main facts to be drawn from the case, re-reading your statement and be clear about what questions you will be expecting from your lawyer, and possible questions you will be asked in cross examination and how you will answer them.

The legal team will then disclose information to the defendant/defendants solicitors as appropriate. You should have already passed all the relevant disclosure material to the legal team/solicitor. Summary only = no obligation to provide advanced info to defendants. Either way = must serve advanced information including statements. Hear say and bad character evidence can now be used but a notice must be served to let the defence know if it is going to be used. A schedule of material not used must also be disclosed to the defendant when the evidence is served to them.

You must also ensure the summons is served within the correct time limit, this is usually 6 months for a summary only offence and 12 months for an either way offence, although certain legislation actually specifies the limitations and may be different to this i.e. The licensing Act 2003 specifies 12 months.

12. Briefing counsel – If you haven't done so already you will need to brief councel.

13. ENTERING A PLEA: This is an option for the Defendant, who can do this by post or in the alternative opt to come to Court in person. If he enters a plea by post we tend to be informed when we arrive in Court by the Clerk.

GUILTY PLEAS: Means that we are allowed to read out a statement of facts which is essentially factual information of the offence, what we did to confirm the breach, the evidence we acquired to satisfy the charge, history of convictions, and lastly the costs we seek, but witnesses don't give evidence.

NOT GUILTY PLEA: This is seen as a defended case. The Magistrates will determine if they are competent to hear the case, and then seek the parties agreement. Thereafter appropriate directions for the conduct of the case are given, with the number of witnesses required, and how long we believe the case may take. Then a trial date is given.

The Prosecutor will prepare the letter outlining the Rights and Duties of Accused Persons under.
The Prosecutor will ensure that the Notice of Primary Prosecution Disclosure is provided to the accused following a guilty plea for a summary trial.
The Prosecutor will ensure that the Notice of Secondary Prosecution Disclosure is supplied to the accused following the submission of a defence statement, where this is appropriate.

Duty of Accused Persons;
The accused may make a defence statement appearing for summary trial, and must make a defence statement for trials on indictment. Material disclosed to the accused by the Council can only be used for the purposes of those proceedings (and any subsequent appeal). Leave of the court is required to use them for any other purpose, and the accused must also notify the prosecutor they intend to apply for leave. Use without the court's permission may amount to contempt of court.

14. FIRST HEARING DATE: Normally the Court fixes this, but we have an arrangement for all the Non CPS dates.

15. HEARING: The Clerk reads out the charge, takes a note of the parties and or their representatives, confirms that the Defendant is aware of the charge, confirms defendants id, and then hears his plea.

At court you will need to ensure all witnesses arrive on time, issue everyone with a copy of the statement, brief the lawyer and give evidence etc.

This is essentially the way in which matters work in the Magistrates Court. Of course the only thing to add is that if the Magistrates do not deem themselves competent to hand the case, it is committed up to the Crown, and the matter becomes an indictment, with tougher more complex penalties and costs to be incurred by the Defendant.

16. After court - Recording convictions – What offences are recordable and what ones aren't (recordable are held at CRB, others are held locally at the own arrangement of the local authority. There is a need for a national database to hold none police/none recordable convictions (so that other LA may view them as certain things such as fraud and plying may be applicable to them).

Monitoring;
After prosecution you may want to monitor the defendant, to ensure conditions are being stuck to and no further offences are taking place.

Duty of Accused Persons - The accused may make a defence statement appearing for summary trial, and must make a defence statement for trials on indictment. Material disclosed to the accused by the Council can only be used for the purposes of those proceedings (and any subsequent appeal). Leave of the court is required to use them for any other purpose, and the accused must also notify the prosecutor they intend to apply for leave. Use without the court's permission may amount to contempt of court.

CHECK-LIST

Start of Investigation
- Are the initial telephone messages, complaint sheets etc retained?
- Are the appropriate officers authorised?
- Is RIPA authorised necessary?
- Has RIPA authorisation been obtained?
- Are all copies of letters, notices, file notes kept on file?
- Is all material properly numbered/labelled and kept securely?

Investigation
- Are draft witness statements kept?
- Are PACE interviews conducted according to Code of Practice E of PACE and tape-recorded?
- Has the PACE interview been transcribed and checked?
- Are witness statements checked for consistency?
- Is all relevant material passed to the disclosure officer?
- Has the investigator completed a prosecution pro-forma as to disposal of the case?

Referral to the prosecutor
- Has the disclosure officer completed the schedules of used, un-used and sensitive material?
- Has the prosecutor been given any material likely to undermine the case against the accused?
- Has any new material been disclosed that has come to light during the investigation or proceedings?
- Has the disclosure officer reviewed any unused material after submission of a defence statement?
- Are there arrangements for allowing the accused to make copies or see material?

Issue of Summons
- Has the schedule of non-sensitive material and letter outlining the Rights and Duties of Accused Persons been served with the summons?
- Has the Notice of Primary Prosecution Disclosure been served after a guilty plea for summary offences?
- Has the Notice of Secondary Prosecution Disclosure been served after submission of a defence statement?

N.B.
Please note that whilst you are processing prosecution proceedings you can not generate any press, as this may influence the jury and affect the outcome, leading to an unfair trail (mis trail). Also you are innocent until proven guilty and therefore you don't want to say something negative about the defendant until it has been proven. For instance if council ABC catch a rogue trader and prosecute them, they can not name them in the press, until they have been successfully prosecuted (found guilty).

Determining the level of enforcement action to take.

Chapter 16 - Alternatives to Prosecution in Court

16.1 - Summary of Factors to Consider

Once you have carried out your investigation you will decide need to decide, what enforcement action (if any) to take.

Enforcement action will be based on several primary considerations in all instances:

- the views of the victim/complainant where appropriate;
- the consequences for public safety of the alleged offence; and
- mitigating factors on the part of the alleged offender.
- If you work for a local authority do they have an enforcement policy and what does it say – it was stated in the case of R v Adaway (2004) EWCA Crim. 2831 – Rose LJ stated that – "We can not emphasise too strongly that before criminal proceedings are instituted by a local authority, they must consider with care the terms of their own prosecution policy. If they fail to do so…it is unlikely that the courts will be sympathetic.
- The seriousness of the offence.
- The outcome/result of the offence i.e. was someone hurt.
- The history – Has the defender offended before or is this a first offence?
- What is the attitude of the defender/has the defender shown remorse?
- Deterrents?
- Alternatives?
- Is it likely the defender will re-offend, what affect is the action taken likely to have on the future?
- What are the personal circumstances of the defender?

whether racial motivation was an aggravating factor in the offence;

- Confidence (where a commercial organisation) of remedial action being effectively
- You will also need to consider the evidential test (Is there enough evidence for a prosecution) & the public interest test (Is a prosecution in the public interest).

16.2 - Evidential test & Public interest

This refers to the evidential stage and the public interest stage, when deciding to proceed with a prosecution. Therefore to bring about a prosecution as well as having the necessary evidence, the prosecution must be in the public interest. It is more likely to be in the public interest to bring about a prosecution if the offence is serious, a conviction is likely and without it the offence may continue or be repeated or if the defendant has relevant previous convictions.

- Was the offence witnessed by a reliable person a relevant officer, such as a Police officer? Is there CCTV evidence?

It is good practise to produce a written document to explain why/how a decision has been made, this should be in line with the enforcement policy, (all decisions made are usually recorded and entered onto a decision log which forms part of the prosecution file).

Enforcement should not be seen as a punitive response to minor technical contraventions of legislation unless such breaches are of a repeated or long-running nature.

Enforcement action should adhere to the Enforcement Concordat, which is a nationally recognised standard in promoting best practice in enforcement.

Enforcement actions Should always be;

- consistent

- balanced
- fair
- relate to common standards in order to achieve the highest degrees of public protection.

In coming to any decision it is important to consider many criteria, including:

- implemented and monitored;

- the consequences of non-compliance and the likelihood of repeated contraventions;
- the prevalence of the offence and the need by the Council to show decisive action in dealing with the consequences;
- other enforcement action to be undertaken by the authority in order to achieve satisfactory standards of safety; and

- the likely effectiveness of the various enforcement options. This is also dependent on the options available to the authority in certain cases, for example the inability to revoke a public entertainments licence unless the licensee has first been convicted of a breach of the licence conditions.

16.3 - Enforcement Models

If the offence is minor, sometimes it is worth exercising some discretion and giving a warning first. If you do give a warning, then if this is breached you are more justified coming down heavier and you won't be seen as being heavy handed if you have given a warning, however it is important to be consistent and fair and treat everyone the same. Therefore it is useful to have a policy to say what is a minor breach and in what instances you will give a warning first and what offences are sufficiently serious and will warrant an immediate prosecution.

The following model may help you to decide what, if any, action to take (Such models can e written in to become part of you're policy).;

Enforcement responses

| | FREQUENCY OF INCIDENT OVER 12 MONTH PERIOD |||||
Severity	ONCE	TWICE	THREE TIMES	FOUR TIMES	FIVE TIMES
1 – minor breach	ADVICE	ADVICE	FORMAL WARNINGS	FORMAL ACTION (CAUTION OR PROSECUTION	MULTI-AGENCY CASE CONFERENCE
2 – breach of condition or administrative offence	ADVICE	FORMAL WARNINGS	FORMAL ACTION (CAUTION OR PROSECUTION)	MULTI-AGENCY CASE CONFERENCE	MULTI-AGENCY CASE CONFERENCE
3 – breach undermining licensing objective	FORMAL WARNINGS	FORMAL ACTION (CAUTION OR PROSECUTION)	MULTI-AGENCY CASE CONFERENCE	MULTI-AGENCY CASE CONFERENCE	MULTI-AGENCY CASE CONFERENCE

NOTES:
•Each response is cumulative, (ie do not generally issue a formal warning and then subsequently issue advice)

Enforcement tool – David McBain

16.4 - Enforcement options

Having considered all of the relevant information and evidence, the options for action are generally:

- to take no action;
- to increase the frequency of inspections/spot checks;
- to take informal action / issue advice or warning;
- Voluntary rectification
- Mediation
- Administrative penalties / penalty points
- to suspend, revoke or refuse to renew a licence/permit or amend licence conditions;
- Statutory notices (i.e. improvement abatement notices)
- to issue a formal warning;
- to issue a fixed penalty notice / fine;
- to issue a formal caution;
- Diversion tactics
- Formal caution
- Acceptable Behaviour Contract
- Anti-Social Behaviour Order
- Injunction
- to prosecute; or
- a combination of these.

Other enforcement tools include;

- Early Intervention Scheme
- ABCs - ASBOS
- Parenting Contracts/Orders
- Fixed penalty notices
- Section 222 Local Government Act 1972
- Anti-social behaviour injunctions
- Premises closure
- Dispersal areas
- Designated public place orders
- S27 VCRA
- Crack house closure
- Responsible Retailers Agreements
- Criminal prosecutions
- Individual support orders
- Intervention orders
- Tenancy enforcement (injunctions, possession, demoted tenancies)
- Environmental health enforcement
- Educational welfare enforcement
- Partnership working
- Community Involvement
- Youth Diversion (Kickz, PAYP etc)
- CCTV- Mosquitoes etc

Informal action is intended to secure compliance with legislation, particularly where of a technical nature such as that arising from inadequate documentation or of a minor nature such as a single breach of a minor licence condition. Informal action includes offering advice; verbal warnings; and requests for action through the use of letters and notes on files.

It will be used when the act or omission is not a serious one and there has been no prior acts or omission and it is believed that the informal action will be enough to secure compliance.

It is important that advice of informal action is given in writing so that there is an audit trail, should this informal action be escalated to more formal action in the future. When giving advice it is important to give the offender all the facts so that they know what they did wrong and what they need to do to correct their action. If they need to take compliance action they must be informed of what action they are required to take and by when.

Note; All actions should be recorded, including verbal advice, which should be recorded in the officers PACE notebook at the time the advice was given (or as near to it as possible), it is also good practice to get the person advised to sign the entry in the officers PACE notebook.

16.5 - Formal warnings (now sometimes called a Simple Warning)

In some cases a formal warning can be issued, providing no other warnings have been recorded on file in relation to that individual or organisation, it may be sufficient to merely issue a formal warning to the offender. This warning should;

- be in writing;
- clearly state that it is a formal warning that proceedings will be instituted for future breaches;
- clearly specify the precise nature of the offence and how it should be avoided in future;
- state the penalty for non-compliance;
- be addressed to the individuals responsible in the organisation where appropriate, as well as to the Company Secretary; and
- should allow the offender the opportunity to reply to the allegations if they think that the warning is unjustified.

16.6 - Formal action

Licence suspensions and revocations is serious and may have wider implications on families etc.

Hackney carriage suspension should in the vast majority of cases be considered as a temporary measure (broadly equivalent to the issue of a Prohibition Notice under the Health and Safety at Work etc Act 1974), where either;

- further investigation into a specific allegation is required, and the allegation is in itself one of sufficient seriousness;
- a hazard can be easily rectified by the licensee and there is an unwillingness to do so; or

- a prosecution is pending.

Suspension should not be considered as a punitive measure due to the undesirability of the authority being seen as judge, jury and executioner.

The grounds for revoking a Hackney Carriage or Private Hire licence are laid down by statute: ss 60-61, Local Government (Miscellaneous Provisions) Act 1976. A vehicle licence may be suspended, revoked or not be renewed if:

- the vehicle is unfit for its intended use;
- any offence under or non-compliance with any part of the Town Police Clauses Act 1847 or the Local Government (Miscellaneous Provisions) Act 1976, Part II has been committed by the driver or operator; or
- any other reasonable cause.

The grounds for suspending, revoking or not renewing a driver's licence are:

- since being granted the licence the holder has been convicted of an offence involving dishonesty, violence or indecency;
- been convicted of an offence under or has failed to comply with a provision of the 1847 or the 1976 Act; or

- any other reasonable cause.

Grounds for suspending, revoking or refusing to renew a private hire operators' licence are:

- any offence under or non-compliance with the provisions of Local Government (Miscellaneous Provisions) Act 1976, Part II;

- any conduct on the part of the operator which appears to render him unfit to hold an operator's licence;
- any material change since the grant of the licence in any of the circumstances of the operator on the basis of which the licence was granted; or
- any reasonable cause.

In all cases, written notice of the grounds on which the action has been taken must be given to the driver. Situations where a reasonable cause may exist to justify suspension or revocation may include:

- where there has been, or may be, an obvious and serious risk to public safety;
- where there has been a total disregard for the conditions of the licence;
- where a prosecution is pending or has been completed by another prosecuting authority for an offence

which would have the effect of making a new applicant ineligible for a licence; and

- where the contravention is or is likely to be repeated.

Where it is proposed to suspend or revoke any licence, the licence should be given an opportunity for mitigating circumstances to be considered by officers. In determining reasonableness, due regard must be given to the Wednesbury principles of administrative fairness in that all decisions must be ones which any reasonable authority, properly directing itself, would reach.
Associated Provincial Picture Houses Ltd v Wednesbury Corporation [1948] 1 KB 223

Unlicensed activities continuing once a licence has been suspended will always result in a prosecution unless the licensee can show a genuine and reasonable excuse that they did not know of the suspension.

If it is an alcohol licence, before looking to remove the licence at a licensing review, look at what conditions could be placed on the licences, if the issues could be resolved by additional licence conditions this course of action should be taken in the first instance, if after this the conditions are breached then revocation of the licence should be sought.

Legislation relating to the majority of other licences do not contain provisions allowing for the suspension or revocation of licences except under specified statutory grounds. The circumstances under which these occur are detailed below:

	Suspension	**Revocation**	**Refusal to renew**
Cinema	Not possible	Only after conviction	On any reasonable grounds
Theatre	Not possible	Only after conviction	On any reasonable grounds
Music and Dance	Not possible	Only after conviction	On any reasonable grounds
Street Trading	Not possible	At any time	On any reasonable grounds
Amusement with Prizes	Not possible	Not possible*	
House to House Collections	Not possible**	**	X
Street Collections	Not possible	Not possible	On any reasonable grounds°
Scrap Metal Dealers	Not possible	Not possible	Not possible
Game Dealers	Not possible	Not possible	Not possible

Notes

°   decision to refuse or grant licence/permit *may* be open to judicial review
*   If authority has passed resolution to not issue further permits, or where facilities to inspect premises have been denied
**   see section 2(3), House to House Collections Act 1939 for specified statutory grounds available
***   see section 2(3), Nurses Agencies Act 1957

16.7 - Formal Caution (now sometimes referred to as a Simple Caution)

A formal caution is a criminal conviction, excepting a formal caution is an admission of guilt, and will be on the offenders record, it will effect the outcome of a conviction for further offences and may effect their employment rights as they will have a criminal record, however it is not a serious as a prosecution as the offender will not need to attend court and will not be issued a fine or sentencing. Upon conviction at court they may receive a fine, or even be given a custodial sentence, depending on the offence, but they will also be given chance to have their say and depending on the evidence may or may not be convicted. When issuing a caution, the implications of excepting and not accepting a caution must be made clear to the offender, in order that the offender can make a fair and informed decision as to whether to accept a caution or not.

Home Officer Circular 18/1994 "The Cautioning of Offenders" states that "properly used, cautioning continues to regarded as an effective form of disposal, and one which may in appropriate circumstances be used for offenders of any age". The aim of the caution is to deal quickly and simply with less serious offences; divert such cases from the courts; and to reduce the chances of recidivism. Cautions are not alternative sentences and additional punishment cannot be set with them.

Formal cautions may only be issued where a full investigation has concluded with clear culpability established on the part of the individual or organisation. In recording a caution, serious consideration must be given to the matter as it may influence any future decision as to whether or not to institute proceedings should the offender be prosecuted at a later date for another contravention. Cautions may also be cited in court proceedings and are applicable to all criminal offences, including traffic offences. In order to issue a caution you must have the same level of evidence that you would have to bring about a prosecution. If a caution is offered and not accepted you will have to take the case to prosecution.

Who may be cautioned

Due to the potentially serious consequences involved, the offenders' interests should be safeguarded by following these conditions:

- there must be evidence of the offenders' guilt, sufficient to give a realistic prospect of conviction;
- the offender must admit the offence;
- the offender (or, if in the unlikely event in licensing terms, a juvenile, his parents or guardians), must understand the significance of a caution and give informed consent to receiving it.

Cautions will therefore be inappropriate where a person does not make a clear and reliable admission of guilt eg if there are doubts about intent where intent is required to prove the offence; or there are doubts about mental health or intellectual capacity. Prosecutions do not necessarily need to follow in these cases as other assistance to the offender may be more appropriate such as referral to another agency.

In the event a juvenile under the age of 14 is being considered for cautioning, it is essential to provide that they know what they did was seriously wrong, and that where applicable the necessary intent was present.

Consent to the cautioning process should not be sought from the offender until it has been decided a caution will be used in place of other action. The offender must have explained, both verbally and in writing, the significance of the caution, in terms of it affecting future possible prosecutions and that it may be cited in court.

16.8 - When cautions are in the public interest

Factors to be taken into account are:

- the nature of the offence. Where the offence is one involving or had the potential to involve injury to a large number of people, cautions may generally be inappropriate;
- the likely penalty if the offender was convicted by a court;
- the offenders' age and state of health;
- offenders' previous criminal history (including formal warnings issued by the Council and other cautions);
- attitude towards the offence, including practical expressions of regret.

As most licensing offences are triable either summarily or triable either way, nearly all would be appropriate to be considered for cautioning. Where an offence has been shown to be of sufficient seriousness that it is likely a trial on indictment would result, a caution would be inappropriate. A caution would also be inappropriate where the victim has suffered significant harm or loss, such significance being related to the victim's circumstances. Where there has been no victim, the potential harm or loss that may have resulted from the breach should be considered.

Where a racial motivation for an offence is an aggravating factor in determining the seriousness of the offence, a caution may still be the most appropriate form for disposal of the case.

In determining whether to proceed by way of caution, attention may be directed as to the likely penalty to be imposed should the offender be convicted in court. However, the possibility of an absolute or conditional discharge being obtained should not necessarily preclude proceeding with a prosecution.

Special characteristics of the offender should be considered when deciding whether to offer a caution as an alternative to other means. Cautioning should therefore be the presumed disposal route where the offender suffers from a mental illness, physical impairment or serious physical illness. Youth and inexperience (particularly where this may be combined with over-enthusiasm) may also be relevant factors to be taken into account.

Although not in itself decisive, the offenders' previous record (including recent cautions) is an important factor. Previous convictions or cautions may only be relevant if there has been a short period of time between offences; whether the offence pattern indicates a similarity in character and seriousness; and the effects of previous cautions.

The subsequent attitude of an offender should always be considered, together with the wilfulness with which it was committed. Over-enthusiasm or naiveness may be mitigating factors in leading towards cautioning rather than other enforcement options.

An offenders' attitude towards the commission of the offence should be considered. This should include an examination

of the wilfulness with which it was committed and his subsequent attitude. Practical remorse such as an apology or

reparation to any victim should be positive issues that would lend itself towards use of a caution.

Experience and the circumstances of offenders involved in group offences are important. This is particularly the case with offences apart from those concerning licensed drivers, as the majority of offenders in these other cases are likely to be organisations. Despite consistency and equity being important themes of this policy document and behind a decision to prosecute or not, each offender should be considered separately and different disposals may be justified. Therefore it may be appropriate that where an organisation is involved, individuals within it receive a caution although the organisation itself is the subject of criminal proceedings.

Where a caution is being considered, the views of the victim should be obtained. This statement does of course recognise that many licensing contraventions may be victimless, in that they relate to a failure to obtain a licence or to fulfil certain record-keeping conditions. Unless there are clear grounds for not doing so (eg the length of time a licence has been held by the offender or the extent of the failure to comply with record-keeping) a caution is these circumstances should be considered as the favoured disposal route.

If a victim has been identified then they should be contacted to establish:

- their views about the offence;
- the extent of any loss or damage;
- the nature of any continuing threat from the offender;
- whether the offender has made any form of reparation or offer of amends. However, the Council should not become involved in negotiating or awarding reparations or compensation, although it may act as an independent medium through which such offers can be discussed.

Although the victim's consent to a caution is useful, it is not an essential consideration.

16.9 - Administration of the caution

Formal cautions must always be administered in person and, whenever possible, at the Town Hall. Juveniles must always be cautioned in the presence of parents, guardians or other appropriate adults; similar rules apply for members of other vulnerable groups such as those who may not speak English as their first language.

All formal cautions must be recorded in the form prescribed by the Secretary of State. Monitoring of such cautions should also be undertaken. Formal cautions may be cited in court if they are relevant to the offence under consideration. In presenting antecedents, the tribunal should be made fully aware of the difference between a caution and a conviction; offences inviting informal action should not be cited in this manner.

Evidence should be put together for a formal caution, as you would for a prosecution.

Chapter 17 - Tracking offenders & serving summons.

17.1 - The Purpose of a Summons

A summons is issued to demand an attendance at court.

The court generate the summons, after a case has been put to the court. The prosecutor then has to collect the summons from the court and ensure it is served to the defendant. The prosecutor will also have to prove at court, if necessary, (for example, if the defendant doesn't show up) that the summons has been served effectively. Without this proof the case will be adjourned. Therefore it is important that summons are served correctly and that a certificate of service is completed by whomever has served the summons.

The certificate of service must include the date, time and location that the summons was issued to, along with the details and signature of who served it and the name of who it was served to. If you can get the recipient of the summons to sign to say they received it, then even better, but don't put your safety in jeopardy to do this.

17.2 - Types of Summons

Defendant
Witness

17.3 - Delivery by Hand

The most effective type of delivery as you can be sure that delivery has been effected.

17.4 - Delivery by Post

Open to accusation that Summons has not been effectively served. However, in most cases this type of service is acceptable providing some basic precautions are taken. Details are required to provide the most accurate picture of how exactly you came to the conclusion that this type of service would be effective. Ultimately though, you have no guarantee that this has been the case and it will rest with the Magistrate or Judge to decide on the validity of your chosen method. Never forget that your notebook can serve as an impromptu record of service.

17.5 - Signing an Affidavit

For those who are employed as independent investigators, it may be worth signing an affidavit. An affidavit is a sworn testimony, signed in the presence of a Notary Public, that the service has been effected. A Notary Public will usually also be a solicitor but not all solicitors are Notary Publics. The cost is between £10 and £15 per visit. For this reason, if possible you may wish to save up a number of certificates for one visit. Providing, of course, that they all take place within 24 - 48 hours of one another.

17.6 - Tracing Missing Persons

Ways of tracking people;
- Use an enquiry agents / private detective
- Council tax records
- Benefits records
- In land revenue/ NI no / Employee records
- Electoral role – elections dept. council
- Financial databases – expiren – credit history.
- Mobile phone bills
- Council tax
- Store loyalty cards
- Bank records
- PNC (Police National Computer) / court and law enforcement records
- Register marriage/divorce/name change
- DVLA
- Car insurance
- Health records
- Dept work and pensions
- Electoral register – Complied in October and published the following February.
- Employer

- Friends

The Cabinet Officer's 2002 Privacy and Data Sharing report, added data sharing gateway clauses to a number of pieces of UK legislation, data, is now available for various agencies to share.

When people move they tend not to move further than 15 miles, therefore check on electoral register and council tax with other councils in this radius.

Check with utilities – There is a legal obligation for people to tell utility services where they have moved address to.

The council fraud department can check their bank details.

You can also check to see if their last known telephone number has been transferred to a new address (check with BT – This will only be the case if they have been moved into the same telephone code area).

When checking who owns the business;
Ask – Who takes the money? What is the share of the business? Check the business accounts for names and signatories. Check rates, insurance, who's name is on the lease, on planning permission, building regulations, ask to see employee contracts, PAYE, NI employee hours, earnings, tax and insurance – who is paying employer contributions, employee p46 – record at the tax office.

Once there has been a conviction, if it's a notifable conviction it will need to be recorded, therefore when investigating a suspect, or trying to track a suspect it is worth checking various records, if you have access to them (depending on your level of authority), such as HSE database, Local authority database, PNC etc. you may want to check with other boroughs and forces to also see what information they have on local records.

Chapter 18 - At Court

In Chapter 5 we looked at the role of Solicitors or Barristers, the structure of the various types of court, and the types of cases that might be heard in each court. In this chapter we shall look in more detail at how each court works and what exactly you should expect as an enforcement officer/private investigator when attending court to give evidence.

18.1 - Which Court will I be attending?

Let us assume the person or persons summonsed have arrived on time. What next?

Well, the type of offence, and whether it is criminal or civil case, will dictate what court the case is heard at. As discussed in Chapter 4 cases will be heard in different courts depending on the seriousness or special nature of the case. For ease, we shall summarise here briefly:

A. **Criminal Cases**

In criminal cases, offences are split into the following categories:

Indictable

This includes more serious offences (such as murder, rape and robbery). Indictable offences can only be tried at the Crown Court.

Triable Either Way

These offences (such as wounding, burglary, thefts) can be heard at either the crown or magistrates court.

Summary Offences

These are less serious offences and can only be tried in a magistrates court. As an enforcement officer, particularly if working for a Local Authority, summary offences are the type of offences you will be dealing with most regularly.

B. **Civil Cases**

Civil cases will usually be heard at the County Court (civil claims), or, in the case of smaller civil cases, the small claims court, or in a tribunal, for employee tribunal.

A brief note on   - LOCATION

As a rule, cases tend to be heard in the county where the offence took place. However, indictable and either way offences can be heard anywhere in England and Wales.

In the UK we have an adversarial system, which means both sides present their story, or version of events (via solicitors or barristers) often, though not always, calling witnesses to give evidence on their behalf. These witnesses must remain objective, presenting only the facts of the case to the court.

An interesting exception to this general rule is seen in the Coroner's Court. Since 1066, a Coroners Court has operated as an inquisitorial court - the coroner asking probing questions in order to discover the facts of the case. The Coroner's Court cannot attach blame on any party but can based on the findings of the Coroner, request a prosecution. This is most likely to occur in cases where death has occurred through deliberate negligence. In this event, the case will be referred to the crown court.

18.2 - Taking the Case to Court

The first step in bringing any case to court is to lay the information at the relevant court. Remember! – we have seen that a case should only go to court if there is enough evidence to provide a reasonable chance of securing a prosecution, and furthermore, only if a prosecution is *in the public interest*.

IMPORTANT - Some offences have time limits; that is, a limit on how long after an offence is committed when it is still permissible to prosecute. In the main, it is only summary offences that have a time limit, usually of 6 months. So for example, if an offence is committed on September 1st, you only have until March 1st to lay the information before the relevant court. It is best practice to check for time limits each time you begin to investigate a offence you have never dealt with before. It can be very embarrassing to spend a long time preparing a file, detailing months of hard won evidence, only to find out that too much time has elapsed for the prosecution to proceed at court. Your boss will almost certainly not be best pleased!

Having ensured you are within the required time period, the full process for proceeding through court is as follows.

1. The information is laid at the court. This will usually be handled by your Legal Department (in the case of Local Authorities) or your clients Solicitor or Barrister (in the case of Private Investigations). The court will draw up a summons based on this information. The information laid consist of:

- The nature of the offence

- The date and place of the committed offence

- Conduct and statute.

2. The summons is served on the defendant; a proof of service will be required by the Court to show that the defendant has been correctly notified of the case.
(See Chapter 17 Tracking Offenders & Serving summons)

3. Advanced information is served on the defendant. The defence should be supplied with a summary of the prosecution case and/or copies of the statements of proposed prosecution witnesses. It is good practise to serve advanced information to the defence as soon as possible. This ensures a fair trial and also protects you against allegations of attempting to influence the Court. All un-used information/material which is relevant to the case must also be disclosed.

4. First hearing / first appearance – At this stage a plea of guilty or not guilty is entered. If it is an either way offence it is decided where this will be heard and a date is set for the trial.

5. Trial

- Witnesses – are impartial, apart from expert witnesses and are giving evidence based on their witness statement, witnesses can refer to their statements to refresh their memory as long as they were written at a time to make this reasonable, i.e. if written the day before court when the event was 6 months ago they may not be allowed to refer to them.

- A trial starts with the prosecution lawyer calling their witnesses to take the oath, they then question their witness – this is called the examination in chief, the defence then cross examine the witness and the prosecution can then re-examine that witness if necessary. The judge may ask questions and the jury may also pass questions to the judge.

- The defence then calls their witnesses etc.

- Bad character & Hearsay evidence may be allowed under certain circumstances.

- Sometimes the trial may be adjourned or part heard and another trial date fixed.

6. If convicted the judge will set a fine or sentence, and costs will be awarded (costs are means tested). This process may be adjourned for a later date depending on the circumstances of the case.

7. Either party have a right of appeal.

18.3 - What if they don't turn up to court?

It is entirely possible that even having gone to the trouble of locating an offender and serving due process, they will still fail to show up at the correct court on the correct day at the correct time. So what happens now?

If a defendant fails to turn up to court, as long as the court don't believe that the summon was not served correctly (in the case of the court believing that the summons was not served correctly the case will be adjourned and it will be requested that the summons re-served). However if it is established that the summons was served correctly then the Police can issue a warrant for the defendants arrest, the defendant will then be held in custody until the next trial (the court will usually set the next trial date, there and then, by adjourning the case, or they may indeed ask the solicitors to come back to the court to arrange a suitable date, if there are issues with witness availability etc), alternatively the case may go ahead without the defendant, it all depends on the case and the severity of the offence, reason for the defendants absence etc. etc.

18.4 - The Role of the Investigator in Court

It is one thing to understand the various types of court and case, quite another to enter this stilted, ancient, often intimidating arena, for the first time, evidence in hand, not knowing who or what to look at. In this section we shall look at the practical issues of how to address the magistrates or judge, where to sit, what, if any, reference to notes you are entitled to make, and how to make sure your evidence is presented in the most credible way possible.

The investigator will need to investigate all avenues that point towards both guilt or innocence for the defendant, in order that they can make a valid judgement before taking any case to court. All of this evidence they need to disclose, as well as continuing to disclose evidence, even if it may impede the case for the prosecution. As well as looking at the evidence before brining a case to court, the investigator/prosecutor should also be sure that it is in the public interest to do so.

The investigator will need to ensure that the case is ready for court, that all the preparations have been made and insure that all witnesses are given notice and know when to attend (its best to get everyone their early). In court the investigator will need to meet the lawyer and witnesses and ensure all the witnesses have attended and have a copy of their statements, and that they know what to do, where necessary the investigator may also need to help them fill in a claim for expenses. If a witness has not given evidence before the investigator can show them around the court and talk them through the process and reassure them. The investigator will also need to inform the clerk of their arrival so that the clerk knows they are ready to proceed. The investigator will also need to bring along all original evidence and ensure that the lawyer has this when required, and ensure that the lawyer is fully briefed on the case.

As well as dealing with the overall running of the day and ensuring that everyone is where they should be and know what they are doing the investigator will also need to give evidence in court as a witness (when they do this they need to be impartial and only give details of fact, i.e. what they have seen/done etc.).

Pre court preparations – Before hand check everyone has their statements, witnesses have transport for court, know what to wear etc

The investigator also needs to insure that he/she knows the case and their evidence in great detail and are well prepared so that they are confident when they are in court.

18.5 - Giving Evidence

When giving evidence in court the skills that are required by any witness, including the investigator, are as follows:

The witness should be prepared and know their evidence and be confident with it. Confidence will come with practise and experience but also with knowing what will be said – an exercise to help with this is, before court, to think of possible questions that may be asked and prepare accordingly. Statements should be laid out so they are easy to read and find information from, the PACE notebook could have sticky page markers on the relevant pages and all documentary evidence should be in a ring binder with an index. This will make the job of the witness who is presenting the evidence easier as they will be able to find the right information quickly, to avoid getting flustered in the court room.

The witness should be familiar with your evidence and know the difference between inferences, opinion and fact. The witness needs to be impartial when giving evidence in court, they should be objective and not give their opinion (they are only allowed to give their opinion if they are an expert witness and are asked for it).

They are there to help the court by informing them of the facts, and not there to get a certain outcome, and therefore they must be objective, honest, clear, and helpful.

The witness needs to speak clearly and slowly, avoiding jargon. If giving evidence in the magistrates court, it is best to talk at the speed that the clerk is writing, in order to speak at the right pace.

The witness will need to listen clearly to ensure they understand the questions put to them and answer the questions to the best of their ability, and acknowledge if they don't know something, they mustn't speculate.

They should correct any incorrect assertions and must be polite and not argumentative.

They need to have an even temper so as not to be irritated by the lawyer, when being cross examined, they need to be confident and not flustered and have good communication skills, presenting themselves in a positive light. They should also be smartly dressed. Especially if they are the investigator or a professional witness they need to have good note taking and statement writing skills so that they have included everything that they may need to discuss in court and can get across the whole truth (if something is not included in notes or statements you will not be able to discuss it in court as your job as the witness is to give oral evidence based on your statement).

18.6 - Specific Addresses to Court Persons

Courts are funny places. They are seats of ancient learning and discourse and judges can become understandably irate if addressed in the wrong manner.

A witness should also know the court procedure, and always aim their answers to the questions at the judge/magistrates, not the lawyer, addressing them appropriately as follows;

- Magistrates Court – Sir/Madam
- County Court – Your Honour

- Crown Court – My Lord/My Lady or Your Honour (depending on what judge is present)
- Court of Appeal– My Lord/My Lady or Your Honour (depending on what judge is present)
- House of Lords– My Lord/My Lady

If a witness has died their statement may be read out at court, but as they can't be cross examined it's a legal argument between lawyers to prove or disprove that it can be allowed.

18.7 - Witnesses/Dealing with witnesses

Cross examination – Inconsistencies in witness statements can become evidence – a witness may be cross examined as to previous statements made by him in writing, relative to the subject matter of the indictment or proceedings. In civil proceedings, the previous statements of a witness may be admitted, both as evidence of the facts contained in them, and also of evidence as consistency, under Civil Evidence Act 1995, s.6(2). In criminal proceedings, if a witness gives evidence inconsistent with a previous statement which it is proved they made then, by virtue of s.119(1) CJA 2003, the jury can conclude that the original statement represents the facts.

Witnesses can only give fact, the only witnesses that can give opinions are expert witnesses and they can only give opinions on their area of expertise.

18.8 - Professional Witnesses

(See also 11.13 - Expert evidence and reference to the works of others in their field)

18.9 - Court running order in a Criminal Case

First the prosecution barrister/solicitor, (depending on the court you may have a barrister or solicitor – in a magistrates court you may have a solicitor and in a crown court you are more likely to have a barrister, although now both have rights of audience in both courts), will outline his case to the jury (or magistrates depending on the court). He will then tell them what he intends to prove and how he intends to prove it.
Next he will call witnesses favourable to his case and cross examine them. The defence barrister/solicitor is then given the option to cross examine the witnesses. The defence barrister/solicitor then puts his case forward to disprove the prosecutions case, he will put his own witnesses forward and after he has cross examined them the prosecution solicitor gets an opportunity to cross examine them.
After all the witnesses have been in the witness box, the prosecution barrister/solicitor will sum up his case, the defence barrister/solicitor then sums up his.
In a magistrates court the magistrates will then retire to make a decision or if in a Crown court the judge will give his summing up.
The judges summing up is designed to advise the jury on the circumstances in which they should either convict (find guilty) or acquit (find not guilty) the defendant, the judge must be careful not to use inappropriate words that may influence the decision of a jury, if this happens, any conviction maybe overturned on appeal.
If the defendant is found not guilty he will be free to go straight away, however if he is convicted he will either be sentenced then or the judge may delay sentencing to await further information, such as social enquiry reports.
However long the defendant spent in prison awaiting trial will be removed from the sentence.

NB. Witnesses are not allowed to sit in court during the hearing, they have to sit outside and be called in, therefore any defendant pleasing guilty, as they will be giving evidence themselves they will not be in the court room for the whole duration of the trial.

Chapter 19 - After Court

19.1 - Notice Of Conviction

If your case was successful and you have secured a conviction, you will need to obtain a 'notice of conviction' from the court. You can then put this on your records and record the convictions as appropriate. Some offences are recordable and will be held on the nationally at CRB, HSE, PNC etc. However some offences, such as minor licensing breaches, are not held nationally, therefore you will usually have your own arrangements in your own organisations or local authority, such as recording on the premises/persons files. It is good to share this with other local authorities, in neighbouring areas. However when sharing information you need to adhere to the DPA and have data sharing protocols in place (see appendix 8). However once someone has been convicted this is public information and is therefore allowed to be in the public domain.

There is a need for a national database to hold none police/none recordable convictions (such as offences under the licensing act 2003) but as yet there is nothing in place.

19.2 - The Right of Appeal

Everyone has the right to appeal, irrelevant of whether they pleaded guilty or not guilty. An appeal against sentence or conviction on a question of fact goes to the Crown Court, it is then heard based on why the defendant was found guilty and if the decision was right or not, rather than it being a re-trial, if it is found that the decision should be re-assessed it will go back to the magistrates court to be re-heard (in most cases, depending on the circumstances of the case).

Where as an appeal against a conviction on a question of law alone goes to the Divisional Court of the Queen's Bench Division in the high court.

To appeal from the magistrates to the crown court, the defendant must appeal, in writing, within 21 days from the date of the decision setting out the grounds of appeal on; a. the clerk of the convicting court, and b. the prosecutor. The appellant may appeal to the crown court for an appeal period to be extended, or apply to the convicting court or the high court (as applicable), to be released on bail pending the appeal hearing, in certain circumstances, or they may abandon the appeal, if they notify the convicting court not less than two clear days before the hearing.

The crown court can confirm, reverse, or vary the magistrates decision or remit the matter with its opinion to a court acting for the same place as the court which have the decision or make an order which the court thinks just, and thereby exercise any power which the magistrates' court may have exercised

Appeals against a crown court decision are passed up to the high court, and if they can not be resolved or are appealed further then up to the house of lords, appeals from the commonwealth go to the judicial committee of the Privy Council.

With regards to specific licensing appeals; offences such as plying for hire are criminal matters and will take the form of a criminal appeal, where as most other licensing matter appeals are quasi-judicial, rather than judicial. This is because such hearings are neither criminal nor civil but instead are a repeat of the exercise which was conducted by the local authority and as such, the court exercises the same quasi-judicial functions as the local authority.

Therefore the appeals will take place as a 'hearing de novo' (a new hearing, almost as if the first hearing didn't take place), as established in the case of *Stepney Borough Council v Joffe*, during which the court can hear new evidence that might have arisen as well as any additional factors, also they take account of any local authority policies and there is no burden of proof. With regards the presentation the rules of evidence are not as strict, for instance hearsay evidence is admissible and the order in which parties present themselves can change. Strictly speaking it is the magistrates decision how they want it to be heard although in most normal cases the appellant gives their account first where as in licensing cases the local authority normally goes first in order for the case to be understood. The other fundamental difference with licensing appeals, as established in *Bradford City Council v Booth*, is that even if the Local Authority looses the case they shouldn't have to pay costs, as long as they acted reasonably and honestly. This is because otherwise councils would fear bringing court proceedings in case they were hit with heavy costs, therefore in the interest of justice Local Authorities are exempt from paying the usual costs if they loose a case.

Appeals against licensing decisions can take two forms, that of statutory right of appeal or that of judicial review. There are two different approaches to statutory appeals, depending upon whether the Local Government (Miscellaneous Provisions) Act 1979 has been adopted or not. Where the Act has been adopted (i.e. most Local Authorities outside of London) there are statutory rights of appeal to the magistrates court, against a refusal to grant or re-new a licence or against a decision to suspend or revoke the licence, or against any additional conditions that have been added to the licence. Except an appeal against a refusal to grant a hackney carriage proprietors licence which will go to the crown court, although again an appeal against refusal to re-new a licence or against a decision to suspend or revoke the licence, or against any additional conditions that have been added to the licence will go to the magistrates court. This is covered in the Public Health Act 1936, sections 300-302 by virtue of section 77 of the Local Government (Miscellaneous Provisions) Act 1979, furthermore by virtue of the Act there is a further appeal, as of right to the Crown Court.

The Local Government (Miscellaneous Provisions) Act 1979, has the affect *'to stay any action pending the determination of the appeal'* – therefore the licence will remain in force, pending the appeal. Therefore licensing authorities will not take action regarding a licence until the time period for appealing against a decision, which is 21 days, has expired. If the decision of the magistrates is then appealed to the Crown Court, by virtue of the Crown Court Rules 1982, the time limit to appeal is 21 days from the date of the magistrates decision, again the effect of any action is stayed until the expiry of that time. Unless the local authority decide to take civil proceedings under section 222 of The Local Government (Miscellaneous Provisions) Act 1979.

Within Greater London, a right of appeal against refusal to grant or suspension or revocation of the licence lies to the magistrates' court by virtue of the Transport Act 1985, s 17.

The decision-making process of the local authority can be challenged, by way of judicial review of the local authorities decision, but the local authority has to first take a decision, as demonstrated in the case of *R v Halton Borough Council, ex p Poynton*. Moreover, judicial review is not appropriate when there is a statutory right of appeal, as upheld in *R v Blackpool Borough Council, ex p Red Cab Taxis Ltd*.

19.3 - Final Paperwork

Any additional paperwork, such as notices to injured parties should be attached to the Case File. It is also worth attaching a copy of any invoice as this will certainly make future audit easier.

19.4 - Storage

All documents relating to the investigation must be securely stored (See also Chapter 12.8). This hard copy storage must follow the same protocols as those required for digital and evidential storage. For a Local Authority or Police Force this will invariably be a vault type storage within secure confines. For private enterprise it may require the purchase of a safe or other similarly secure storage facility.

Under the freedom of information act all public bodies are also required to have a data sharing protocol. A data sharing protocol is a formal agreement between organisations that are sharing personal data. It explains why data is being shared and sets out the principles and commitments organisations will adopt when they collect, store and disclose personal information about members of the public.

Protocols also explain when information can be shared. Without such formal agreements, public organisations may find themselves falling short of common standards. Also, there may be confusion over responsibilities - both within and between organisations.

The Data Protection Act says that information should be kept for no longer than is necessary. The Act does not specify what a 'necessary' period should be for particular information. Each case would be considered on its own merits. If an organisation is obliged to retain data for a given length of time under any other laws, this should be taken into consideration. Depending on the data and what it is being used for you may need to keep it for a minimum time. a case may be reviewed long after the judge has passed final sentence. It will depend on the case in question, the legislation breached, seriousness of the offence and the sentence. As a rule of thumb look at the deadline for an appeal on the case, once this has passed you may not need the data again. Your organisation should have a protocol of record retention but on average it is usually between 5-10 years.

19.5 - Case Review/Feedback/De-brief

Any case, successful or not, must be reviewed. There is something to be learned from the outcome of all cases, whether procedural or technical. Ideally the case should be reviewed alongside any other officers who participated and your legal representatives (if relevant). Sharing information will allow to you to improve on efficiency, and efficiency will save money. See Appendix section for a suggested Case Review Form.

Final word

We've seen in the previous chapters how the laws in Great Britain have evolved over a great period of time, evolving in an almost organic way to reach the stage we now find them. This evolution of the law has often come at great cost and against a background of civil unrest, uprising and war, and all of these are invariably accompanied by hardship, famine and personal loss. The enforcement of this law has also evolved in the same way. Gone are the days when a feudal Baron would send three or four heavily armed knights to extract tolls or fines from the populace. As modern day enforcement officers, we must never lose sight of the importance of this evolution. The law has grown up with a single aim; that of protecting the population of this country against tyranny and oppression. The law is not personal. It does not make distinction based on religious or sexual preference, or on basis of ethnicity. The law of the country is applicable to every citizen of the country equally. You may hear it said, and quite often, that the law is not equal. That there are those who are treated more equally than others, perhaps based on wealth or influence. If this is the case it is the fault of no one but the citizens of this country for allowing it to be so. We are all of us responsible for allowing or preventing the actions of the society in which we share. Therefore, as enforcement officers, but also as citizens who may one day have to answer questions from the other side of the dock, please remember the time and historical significance of that which you are choosing to serve. Please remember that the law of this nation and the continued goodwill of the people of this nation toward that law, rests in your hands. You are the frontline; the face of the court. Make sure it is a fair face. An open face, and understanding face. If you are enforcing the law it is important for you to be an upstanding citizen and abide by the law yourself so that your actions and motives can not be called into question.

Appendices

Appendix 1

Conducting Operations - Best Practice & Initiatives

Plying for hire

A licensed private hire vehicle that takes passengers 'for hire or reward' who have not pre booked is Illegally plying for hire, contrary to section 45 of the 1847 Town Police Clause Act - Max. penalty Level 4

Section 143A Road Traffic Act 1988 makes having insufficient insurance an offence (max. penalty level 5).

Section 165 (a) Serious Organised Crime and Police Act 2005 - Police powers to remove vehicle from the highway, if in breach of Section 143A Road Traffic Act 1988.

Points to prove;
- The journey took place
- The journey was paid for
- The journey was not pre booked

Case Law

Substantial case law has shown that vehicles, in full view of the public are therefore inviting custom, and therefore shouldn't be picking customers up off the street, even if the street is private property – Eastbourne Borough Council v Stirling[2001] RTR 7.

In the case of Vant v Cripps [1963] 62LGR, it was ruled that the vehicle was on display and therefore inviting the travelling public into believing that the vehicle was available for immediate hire.

Moreover the courts appear, when looking at the location of the vehicle to also consider the intentions of the private hire driver and whether they were attempting to mislead the public into thinking they were available for immediate hire. This was apparent in the case of Ogwr v Baker [1989] COD concerns, when the driver had his vehicle in the street and took a fare but said that at the time his vehicle was on display he had stopped for a hot dog, he was acquitted of illegally plying for hire but later found guilty on appeal, similar principals were also applied to the case of Milton Keynes Borough Council v Barry (1984), where the court looked at the position of the vehicle and how long they had been waiting as evidence of wrongdoing. This was also confirmed in case of Nottingham City Council v Woodings [1994] RTR 72, in this case the driver parked outside a public house and then went into use the toilet, after which he was approached by two plain clothed officers, who he told that he was available for hire. In his judgement Rose LJ ruled: "In my judgement when the defendant parked the marked car in the street, for the purpose of going to the toilet, he was not plying for hire, and when he came out of the toilet he was not plying for hire. But when, having sat in the driver's seat, he told prospective passengers that he was free to carry them, at that stage bearing in mind where the car was and what the car looked like, he was plying for hire."

In conclusion the main principals seem to be the location that the vehicle is in, the time spent in that location, and the likely intentions of the driver.

Possible plying for hire offences;
- If driver X drove a Hackney carriage he would not be able to ply for hire on any area that had waiting restrictions, if he did he could be illegally plying for hire;
- A private (unlicensed) vehicle that takes passengers for hire or reward is also illegally plying for hire.
- A private hire licensed vehicle that takes passengers 'for hire or reward' who have not pre – booked, is also illegally plying for hire.

The legal framework governing private hires that illegally ply for hire i.e. take passengers, for hire or reward that have not pre-booked, is as follows;

Only Hackney carriages can ply for hire, it is an offence to ply for hire, without a hackney carriage proprietor's licence under Section 45 of the 1847 Town Police Clause. Section 75)1) 1976 Local Government (miscellaneous provisions) Act, gives powers to enforce within a controlled zone.

Furthermore if a driver, in a vehicle other than a Hackney Carriage, illegally plys for hire their insurance will not cover them for such activities, section 143A Road Traffic Act 1988 makes having insufficient insurance an offence and section 165 (a) Serious Organised Crime and Police Act 2005 (Police powers to remove vehicle from the highway on confirmation of section 143 under the act as no insurance details showing on vehicle, (or driver unable to confirm insurance).

All evidence gathered will be in accordance with Police and Criminal Evidence Act 1984.

In order to prove an offence of plying for hire a journey must take place, and this journey must be for hire or reward, therefore we must prove money has changed hands and a journey has taken place.

However substantial case law has shown that vehicles, in full view of the public are therefore inviting custom, and therefore shouldn't be picking customers up off the street, even if the street is private property – Eastbourne Borough Council v Stirling[2001] RTR 7.

Then in the case of Vant v Cripps [1963] 62LGR, it was ruled that the vehicle was on display and therefore inviting the travelling public into believing that the vehicle was available for immediate hire.

Moreover the courts appear, when looking at the location of the vehicle to also consider the intentions of the private hire driver and whether they were attempting to mislead the public into thinking they were available for immediate hire. This was apparent in the case of Ogwr v Baker [1989] COD concerns, when the driver had his vehicle in the street and took a fare but said that at the time his vehicle was on display he had stopped for a hot dog, he was acquitted of illegally plying for hire but later found guilty on appeal, similar principals were also applied to the case of Milton Keynes Borough Council v Barry (1984), where the court looked at the position of the vehicle and how long they had been waiting as evidence of wrongdoing. This was also confirmed in case of Nottingham City Council v Woodings [1994] RTR 72.

In this case the driver parked outside a public house and then went into use the toilet, after which he was approached by two plain clothed officers, who he told that he was available for hire. In his judgement Rose LJ ruled: "In my judgement when the defendant parked the marked car in the street, for the purpose of going to the toilet, he was not plying for hire, and when he came out of the toilet he was not plying for hire. But when, having sat in the driver's seat, he told prospective passengers that he was free to carry them, at that stage bearing in mind where the car was and what the car looked like, he was plying for hire."

In conclusion the main principals seem to be the location that the vehicle is in, the time spent in that location, and the likely intentions of the driver.

Plying for hire is an offence contrary to section 45 of The 1847 Town Police Clauses Act (this is a summary only offence which carries a maximum level 4 fine and in the first instance will be heard in a magistrates court), also as most insurance companies only insure private hire vehicles for hire and reward with the clause 'to take pre-booked passengers only' the insurance would, in most cases not extend to insuring the vehicle for plying for hire and therefore as well as committing the offence of plying for hire they would be driving without valid insurance contrary to the Road Traffic Act 1988, section 143A, (this is a summary only offence which carries a maximum level 5 fine and in the first instance will be heard in a magistrates court). Therefore the evidence must proven beyond reasonable doubt in order to secure a conviction.

Therefore we have a set operation to target locations where we know plying for hire is prevalent where we control all factors as far as possible to ensure that the necessary evidence is used. We have set protocols to follow that have been risk assessed to ensure the operation is safe, and to ensure a consistent and fair approach, with regards to gathering evidence and securing prosecutions/taking enforcement action.

With regards to RIPA and licensed drivers if you are carrying out covert investigations, which is in he line of their normal courses of business i.e. taking a journey, it is not likely that you are going to gather personal or private information about the driver. Also you already have some information about the driver on file and as they are licensed by you and carrying a licensing job at the time, and obviously know you are in the vehicle and as they have also signed up to your terms and conditions, you should not need RIPA clearance. Unless you are targeting specific drivers, merely going to a location and undertaking journeys, from vehicles waiting in that area should not need RIPA clearance and with regards to issues of entrapment; as long as you only ask them if they will take you to a location and do not continue discussions if they say no then it is reasonable to expect that you need to do this, in order to be able to carry out a test purchase and is therefore not classed as entrapment.

This is stated in the House of Lords, opinions of the lords of appeal for judgment, made by Lord Nicholls of Birkenhead, Lord Mackay of Clashfern, Lord Hoffmann, Lord Hutton and Lord Scott of Foscote ON 25 OCTOBER 2001, in which Lord Nicholls of Birkenhead states that;

'In some instances a degree of active involvement by the police in the commission of a crime is generally regarded as acceptable. Test purchases fall easily into this category. In Director of Public Prosecutions v Marshall [1988] 3 All ER 683 a trader was approached in his shop in the same way as any ordinary customer might have done. In breach of his licence he sold individual cans of lager to plain-clothes police officers'.

More specifically he goes onto say that;

'In Nottingham City Council v Amin [2000] 1 WLR 1071 a taxi was being driven in an area not covered by its licence. The driver accepted plain-clothes police officers as fare paying passengers. Police conduct of this nature does not attract reprobation even though, in the latter case, the roof light on the taxi was not illuminated. The police behaved in the same way as any member of the public wanting a taxi in the normal course might have done. Indeed, conduct of this nature by

officials is sometimes expressly authorised by Act of Parliament. The statute creating an offence may authorise officials to make test purchases, as in section 27 of the Trade Descriptions Act 1968.

Thus, there are occasions when it is necessary for the police to resort to investigatory techniques in which the police themselves are the reporters and the witnesses of the commission of a crime. Sometimes the particular technique adopted is acceptable. Sometimes it is not. For even when the use of these investigatory techniques is justified, there are limits to what is acceptable. Take a case where an undercover policeman repeatedly badgers a vulnerable drug addict for a supply of drugs in return for excessive and ever increasing amounts of money. Eventually the addict yields to the importunity and pressure, and supplies drugs. He is then prosecuted for doing so. Plainly, this result would be objectionable. The crime committed by the addict could readily be characterised as artificial or state-created crime. In the absence of the police operation, the addict might well never have supplied drugs to anyone.'

In order to carry out test purchase journeys, it is crucial to go to a location which is a prevalent area for PHV to illegally tout for business and two officers approach vehicles in that area (ideally that have been sitting their for a while and look like they may be plying –, once the undercover officers approach the vehicle (its always at least two officers, usually 2 police officers and a council officer, sometimes 3 or 4 – Its best to have a few officers and swap them around in the night so they don't get spotted as test purchases, obviously it could be dangerous if a driver works out who they are) and ask them if they will take them to a location (which we have pre-arranged). Once their journey has commenced they make a call or send us a text to say they are on their way. We already have an unmarked car waiting in that location, and a marked Police car nearby but out of sight (If the Police car is spotted it can be dangerous as the driver may panic and drive off to an unknown destination with the officers in the car). For safety purposes, chose a cul-de-sac as the destination so that the vehicle can't speed off with the passengers in, if it spots the police car (alternate the location for each operation so that the drivers don't identify us). Once the passengers alight the vehicle, approach the vehicle in high visibility uniform and alert the Police in the marked car (they can usually see from their position as well). Identify yourself and ask the driver to switch off the engine and step out of the car. Ensure that the driver does not use their engine to alert other drivers. The Police then carry out vehicle and insurance checks, and call in the recovery vehicle to impound the car (if appropriate), meanwhile the lead reception officer cautions and interviews the driver, you may want to have special forms designed specifically for this operation, this will help us produce our statement and will be signed by the driver to use as evidence at court.

Also fill in a in a producer form for the driver to produce his insurance. At this time check no further offences have taken place, i.e. check the driver is wearing a badge, has a first aid kit and fire extinguisher, and that the car is roadworthy etc. While lead officer one is doing this the second officer will phone the operator to confirm where the driver should be (at this stage the driver should not be able to overhear this conversation). This officer along with a colleague will then need to visit the operators office to pick up the booking dockets and secure them as evidence (It is a requirement of the operators licence for the operator to keep accurate and clear records of all bookings, the fact that there will be no booking for this journey will be evidence that the driver shouldn't have been in that location).

The passengers at this time will be sitting in the unmarked car, out of the sight of the driver, as they also have taxi tagging forms to be filled in.

Steps to take to organise a taxi tagging covert operation;

1. Speak to police re: availability of officers and resources.

Resources needed;
- Unmarked car with 1 police officer
- Marked car with 2 police officers (1 receiving officer)
- 2 Officers to be test purchase passengers to undertake the test journeys (from the police or volunteers) 1 of which to be a lead officer.
- Recovery truck – To impound any vehicles that illegally ply for hire and therefore have insufficient insurance.

2. Plan for the operation - Decide upon the location to undertake test purchase and the destination.

Mark these on a map to be given to the driver of the marked and unmarked car (also pass around at the briefing).

Decide on signal once the target vehicle is on route to the stop destination i.e. text message or phone call.

Dress code;
- Reception team = uniformed Police officers (in high visibility jackets), Local Authority staff in black trs and high vis jacket and boots to protect feet.
- Passengers = casual/undercover dress but something warm as they may be outside in the cold for a long time.

1. Confirm dates and availability & collect some petite cash to use in the operation.

2. Prior to the operation conduct a briefing with the police and local authority staff; the brief should include relevant legislation, the plan for the operation, who will take the lead in each team, what the locations will be, what vehicles to look out for, and safety information and what to do if anything goes wrong. Everyone to know the date and synchronise watches (so that the forms and statements should be correct).

3. On the evening insure that you take;
    - Working watch
    - Mobile phone
    - Pace book and ID
    - Clip boards
    - Plastic folders to put completed forms in
    - Labels (for folders)
    - Spare pens
    - Forms & producer documents
    - Carbon paper
    - Torches

4. After the evening give everyone involved a photocopy of their forms and get them to fill in a S9 Statement.

Then prepare file for prosecution, as appropriate;

To prepare the prosecution file you would need to ensure you have all the evidence; all officers statements and the booking dockets for that driver.
You would then need to use the template as shown in appendix 2. Ensuring that the memorandum to Prosecute includes full summary of the case, with particular facts to be drawn out in the statement of fact and summons.

If other exhibits are attached as part of the evidence log, ensure they are marked at

Obtain dates to avoid for all witnesses where possible for the next 4 months at least, unless this is a significant matter whereby it is anticipated a trial may take several days, in which case obtain dates for the next 6 – 8 months.

If an interpreter will be required, notification will be needed of the language service we will be using, an interpreter may be required for service of documents, (the court will provide an interpreter for all court proceedings).

Any previous warnings given to the driver and/or any previous convictions should be included in the prosecution case. Searches should also be made with the Police National Computer DVLA printout should have been obtained for the file.

An Evidence Log , Decision Log, and Schedule of Sensitive Material will need to be completed in accordance with the Criminal Procedure and
Investigations Act 1996. The Schedule of Sensitive Material will need to describe the item and the reason why it is sensative and therefore the of the reason for non disclosure, if there is no sensative material this will need to be indicated. Anything that is relevant and not sensitive should be put in the Schedule of Non-sensitive Material, again in accordance with the Criminal Procedure and Investigations Act 1996. All of which should be signed off by the disclousre officer. All witness statements must be completed on a section 9 form, with the s.9 CJA 1976...pre-amble at the top of the statement, age of witness: over 18, if under 18 please state age only, occupation and contact details on the back. Exhibits must be properly labelled and exhibited in the officers statement, if photographed, these need to be properly exhibited and if the exhibits are placed in any safe place, a statement of continuation regarding to whom if was passed to and where is located should be provided. In most taxi tagging cases the exhibits will be the forms and producer forms and photocopies of relevant entires in officers pace note books, signed by the officer (the original note book will be kept by the officer and taken to court with them). Any photographs should be colour photographs, with at least 4 copies of each, these will be for the defendant, /solicitor/court clerk/bench /Council's counsel. Tapes will need to be transcribed and the transcripts exhibited, the working copy of the tape along with the sealed master copy will need to be taken to court, for the trial.

Planning a specific operation to prove plying for hire

1. Gather evidence to see where illegal plying is most prevalent & times and days (Police INTEL, CCTV, Complaints etc.)
2. Get resources;
Resources needed;
Unmarked car with 1 police officer
Marked car with 2 police officers (1 receiving officer)
2 Officers to be test purchase passengers to undertake the test journeys (from the police or volunteers) 1 of which to be a lead officer.
Recovery truck – To impound any vehicles that illegally ply for hire and therefore have insufficient insurance.
3. Formulate a plan for the operation - Decide upon the location to undertake test purchase and the destination & mark these on a map to be given to the driver of the marked and unmarked car (also pass around at the briefing & decide on signal once the target vehicle is on route to the stop destination i.e. text message or phone call.
4. Confirm dates and availability & collect some petite cash to use in the operation and gather equipment etc.
5. Prior to the operation conduct a briefing with the police and local authority staff;

The brief should cover;
- The relevant legislation
- The plan for the operation;

Aim.
Targets - what the locations will be & what vehicles to look out for.
Team allocation & who will take the lead in each team.
Procedure / overview.
Safety information and what to do if anything goes wrong.
Communication and call signs.

6. On the evening insure that you take;
   a. Working watch
   b. Mobile phone
   c. Pace book and ID
   d. Clip boards
   e. Plastic folders to put completed forms in
   f. Labels (for folders)
   g. Spare pens
   h. T1 & T1A Forms & producer documents
   i. Carbon paper
   j. Torches
   k. Maps
7. After the evening give everyone involved a photocopy of their forms and get them to fill in a S9 Statement.
8. De-brief & Evaluate
9. Prepare file for prosecution, as appropriate;

Ensure you have all the evidence; all officers statements and the booking dockets for that driver.

Once you have proved that the journey was not pre-booked you can show that the insurance would have been invalid. Therefore you have to obtain a copy of the insurance document to check the driver was actually insured (otherwise the offence will become a more serious offence of driving without insurance).

Complete a memorandum to Prosecute includes full summary of the case, with particular facts to be drawn out in the statement of fact and summons.

Obtain dates to avoid for all witnesses where possible for the next 4 months at least, unless this is a significant matter whereby it is anticipated a trial may take several days, in which case obtain dates for the next 6 – 8 months.

If an interpreter will be required, notification will be needed of the language service we will be using, an interpreter may be required for service of documents, (the court will provide an interpreter for all court proceedings).

Any previous warnings given to the driver and/or any previous convictions should be included in the prosecution case. Searches should also be made with the Police National Computer DVLA printout should have been obtained for the file.

An Evidence Log, Decision Log, and Schedule of Sensitive Material will need to be completed in accordance with the Criminal Procedure and Investigations Act 1996.

The Schedule of Sensitive Material will need to describe the item and the reason why it is sensitive and therefore the of the reason for non disclosure, if there is no sensitive material this will need to be indicated. Anything that is relevant and not sensitive should be put in the Schedule of Non-sensitive Material, again in accordance with the Criminal Procedure and Investigations Act 1996. All of which should be signed off by the disclosure officer. All witness statements must be completed on a section 9 form, with the s.9 CJA 1976…pre-amble at the top of the statement, age of witness: over 18, if under 18 please state age only, occupation and contact details on the back.

Exhibits must be properly labelled and exhibited in the officers statement, if photographed, these need to be properly exhibited and if the exhibits are placed in any safe place, a statement of continuation regarding to whom if was passed to and where is located should be provided. In most taxi tagging cases the exhibits will be the T1 and producer forms and photocopies of relevant entries in officers pace note books, signed by the officer (the original note book will be kept by the officer and taken to court with them). Any photographs should be colour photographs, with at least 4 copies of each, these will be for the defendant, /solicitor/court clerk/bench /Council's counsel. Tapes will need to be transcribed and the transcripts exhibited, the working copy of the tape along with the sealed master copy will need to be taken to court, for the trial.

Operation Calibre

What is Tackling underage drinking in parks?

Calibre is a local authority and joint partnership response, specifically targeting open spaces and play areas, with the intention of disrupting and deterring the purchase possession and consumption of alcohol by minors.

Tackling underage drinking in parks is part of the alcohol miscue campaign and links directly into the crime reduction stagy and the community safety plan for reduction of crime within priority 5, ASB and as the new ASBO officer Liam will be passing the info of operation calibre up to the next JAG meeting on our behalf. Highlighting the following aims;

OP Tackling underage drinking in parks is a joint LA Police operation, which sets out to identify areas in which underage drinking occurs, and then to target with specific four five action.
1 Entering parks with a high viz operation to detect and confiscate alcohol.
2.To trace the point of sale and collect Intel.
3 To advise the congregated of the continued Police presence as in reaction to group drinking ,and the consequences of failure to abide by the law.
4 To visit the identified outlets, for formal warning /caution /prosecuting, dependant on evidence quantity of seizure
5 To also target anyone buying alcohol on behalf of minors and for FPNs to be issued for this.

How does it work?

Officers meet at the Police station, which includes Police officers, PCSOs, members of the community team – environmental crime officers and licensing enforcement officers. After the briefing they split down into teams so that all council officials team up with at least one police officer or PCSO and therefore have radio contact via the Police radios. Depending on officer availability we aim to get enough teams to cover each entrance/exit to the park. We approach the park from each entrance/exit at the same time, with the park rangers van going in first and everyone following, this way when minors see the park rangers they will associate them with having Police back up and will hopefully be more responsive to the park rangers when they are carrying out there normal patrols.

If adults are found buying alcohol and giving it to minors, the Police officers issue an £80 fixed penalty notice to them.

Minors are stopped & searched (by the Police) – Any drinks checked to see if they contain alcohol (sometimes the minors conceal alcohol in soft drink containers) large groups of youths are dispersed and any alcohol if confiscate and decanted. The alcohol found is then traced to where it was purchased – this is done by asking the youths where they purchase the alcohol, looking at the labels (certain brands may be unique to a particular premises), checking the batch numbers of the bottles.

If no minors are in the park we check for bottles to get an idea of what is being consumed in the parks.

We tend to run the operations during the school holidays and during key dates where it is likely there will be more underage drinkers such as the announcement of the GCSE results.
We also work on any intel from the public, the asbo line, PCSOs observations, feedback from park rangers, from councillors etc.

<u>Calibre</u>

All meet at Police station and carry out short briefing 20mins prior to start of opp.

1.   Explain what the opp is;

Tackling underage drinking in parks is part of the alcohol miscue campaign and links directly into the crime reduction stagy and the community safety plan for reduction of crime within priority 5, ASB and as the new ASBO officer Liam will be passing the info of operation calibre up to the next JAG meeting on our behalf. Highlighting the following aims;

OP Tackling underage drinking in parks is a joint LA Police operation, which sets out to identify areas in which underage drinking occurs, and then to target with specific four five action.
1 Entering parks with a high viz operation to detect and confiscate alcohol.
2.To trace the point of sale and collect Intel.
3 To advise the congregated of the continued Police presence as in reaction to group drinking ,and the consequences of failure to abide by the law.
4 To visit the identified outlets, for formal warning /caution /prosecuting, dependant on evidence quantity of seizure
5 To also target anyone buying alcohol on behalf of minors and for FPNs to be issued for this.

2. Explain the process

High vis presence, officers working in teams and approaching the park from each entrance/exit at the same time, with the park rangers van going in first and everyone following.

PCs to issue FPN if we find anyone supplying alcohol to anyone under 18.

Minors stopped & searched – Any drinks checked, disperse any drinkers and confiscate alcohol, trace the origins of the alcohol and speak to the off licences involved & lisening enf. To take the lead on this and act according to evidence

If adults are found buying alcohol and giving it to minors, FPNs should be issued.

2.   Allocate team and assign entrances & agree timings. A 'spotter' covert car may be used to go ahead of the group and look for areas where there are youths. Teams can then be radioed in.

3.   Hand out maps

Appendix 2

Checking driving licences

Eligibility to drive in the UK.

It is important to note that although anyone with a full EU license can drive in the UK if the full EU license, rather than being issued in an EU country i.e. the person taking their test there, was transferred in an EU country, other than the UK from a foreign license to an EU one, it will not be classed in the UK as a full EU license and they may only drive in the UK for a year, unless they re-do a test in the EU.
i.e. Even if they have a full EU licence, unless they passed a test in the EU they will not be able to drive on it, in the UK, for over a year. They will have to apply for a full UK driving licence and do a driving test, unless they re-do their driving test in another EU country. To see if the license is a transferred one rather than a license that originated in the EU have a look on the back of the license and there should be a country code, this shows where the license originated from.

How can I check Driving Licenses?

Do not accept licenses, other than those stated in the list of valid identity documents. English, Welsh and Scottish driving license numbers contain information about the applicant's name, sex and date of birth. This information is written in a special format but can be gleaned and matched against the information provided by the applicant.
Please note that the date of birth on English, Welsh and Scottish driving licenses, issued before 1977, is not recorded as a separate entry on the license. The date of birth must be deciphered from the driving license number.

For example the format of the number for Christine Josephine Robinson, born 2 July 1975

```
R O B I N   7 5 7 0 2 5   C J 9 9 9 0 1
N N N N N   Y M M D D Y   I I C C C C
```

N = 1st five letters of the surname (if the surname begins MAC or MC it is treated as MC for all).
Y = YEAR of birth.
M = MONTH of birth (In the case of a female, the number represented by the first M will have the value 5 added to the first digit e.g. a female born in November (i.e. 11) would display '61' in the MM boxes) or if born in February (i.e. 02) would display '52').
D = DAY of month of birth.
I = Initial letter of the first two forenames - if only one, then 9 will replace the second letter. If the license indicates that the applicant has a middle name, ensure that one has been provided in Section A.
C = Computer generated.

Please note, for Northern Ireland driving licenses the license number is in a different format. The license number is unique to the driver and the 'name' or 'date of birth' validation, as shown above, cannot be used.

How do I check for indicators of fraud?
Always check for signs of tampering when checking identity documents. Documents should be queried if they display any signs of damage, especially in the areas of personal details such as the name and the photograph. The following table of guidelines should help you look out for any suspicious signs when authenticating documents.

Photo driving license;

Examine the license for evidence of photo tampering or any amendment of the printed details.

Old style driving licence (no photograph)
Remove the document from the plastic wallet and check that it is printed on both sides. It should have a watermark visible by holding the licence up to the light and there should be no punctuation marks in the name or address. The 'Valid To' date should be the day before the bearer's 70th birthday (unless the bearer is already over 70). The 'Valid To' date can therefore be cross-referenced with the applicant's date of birth.

Appendix 3 -

General codes;

Police warrant numbers numbers;

6 = PCSO
7 or 8 = Civilian
Highest number = 2000

Ethnicity codes -

IC1 – White European
IC2 – Dark European
IC3 – Afro-Carribbean
IC4 – Asian (Indian, Bangladeshi or Pakistani)
IC5 – Oriental
IC6 – Arab/North African
IC0 – Unknown ethnicity

However, although the above are useful to know, you should be aware that even police will often not use the above codes. Always use the most succinct information to convey the message. It is no good wasting time with lengthy explanations when the suspect may be fleeing rapidly!

Appendix 4 -

Data Protection Request

CONFIDENTIAL

DATA PROTECTION ACT 1984, section 28(3)
DATA PROTECTION ACT 1998, section 29(3)

TO:	
FOR THE ATTENTION OF:	
POSITION:	

I am making enquiries that are concerned with:

(tick box)	
☐	**The prevention or detection of crime** <State below the legislation under which the alleged offence has been committed>:..
☐	**The prosecution of offenders**
☐	**You are required to produce this information by law under the following legislation:**

I confirm that the personal data requested is needed for those purposes and failure to provide the information will, in my view, be likely to prejudice those matters.

DETAILS OF PERSON:

NAME:	Date of Birth:
Address:	

INFORMATION REQUIRED:

THIS REQUEST SHOULD BE TREATED AS CONFIDENTIAL

Name:		Position:	
Telephone:			
E-Mail:		Number of pages	

Appendix 5

Alert level codes – Here is an example of alert codes you could use;

Black – Full scale emergency - to be used in full scale emergencies, potential terrorist attack, fire arms, riot etc.
Red – Emergency
Amber – Potential problem.
Green – Incident concluded.

Radio procedure;

Phonetic alphabet	
A	Alpha
B	Bravo
C	Charlie
D	Delta
E	Echo
F	Foxtrot
G	Golf
H	Hotel
I	India
J	Julliet
K	Kilo
L	Lima
M	Mike
N	November
O	Osca
P	Pappa
Q	Qubec
R	Romeo
S	Sierra
T	Tango
U	Uniform
V	Victor
X	Xray
Y	Yankee
Z	Zulu

Appendix 6
ENVIRONMENTAL VISUAL AUDIT (EVA)

What is an environmental visual audit?

An EVA is a visual scan of a particular area, to identify particular problems. It is about visiting an area, where there may be problems or potential problems and conducting a visual check. It involves checking neighborhoods for those things which may encourage criminal damage and anti-social behavior. Looking for damaged property, which gives the impression that the locality isn't cared for because the damage hasn't been repaired, looking for fly tipping and litter, overgrown vegetation and graffiti and all sites where these are found will be recorded.

Conducting the audit

The area being audited should be a size that is manageable; too large an area may be difficult to improve. An Environmental Visual Audit is a visual audit of a part of a neighbourhood. The audit can be used as a diagnostic tool in any problem solving process.

The audit process has three parts:

- A physical audit - a walkabout - where the team looks for signs of disorder and so-called 'background noise'. The team should be looking for 'Signal Crimes' i.e. graffiti, groups of youths congregating, poor lighting, signs of deprivation, etc. Notes should be taken, which can provide an accurate picture of the area.

A public perception survey to gather local opinions of the area.

- Collation of statistics on calls received, reported crime and detections for the area.

- An action plan is then drawn up by the team, which usually requires collaboration from the partner agencies. This material can then be used by the local officer(s) to acquaint them with the local area, and to feed back to the local Neighbourhood Panel about actions that are being taken to address their issues and problems. The auditing process is also a clear demonstration of the gap between local perceptions and the reality, which can be used to address perceptions and provide reassurance.

Stage two of the process involves a repeat of the process at regular interval, perhaps every six-months and review of the action plans, usually at six-weekly intervals.

The audit can be a general one, link to existing work on improving an area, or to look at a specific problem. It may, for instance, be as a result of complaints by the public about a particular area. It can be done with the police and council alone to look at a set issue. However it is god to involve the public to bring partners and communities together. EVA's work better to support activity around community safety and cohesion, when the community is involved.

It is recommended that the audit process involves a team of between four and eight people, including a police officer, local councillor, local CDRP or Community Safety Partnership representative, volunteers and local residents (Neighbourhood panel members). Consider using local businesses, such as shops and also schools to help with the process in and around their locations. By getting the community involved it will give them a better understanding and respect for their environment, this may also present additional funding opportunities.

It is a good idea to do 2 audits at different times of the day, perhaps one in the day and one at night as this will provide a more accurate picture of the area. However when doing the repeat EVA later on, to check the progress, be sure to conduct it at roughly the same times as the first EVA in order that you are comparing like with like.

The benefits of conducting EVA's

Conducting EVA's helps the service with its communication strategy and engagement work with the local community.

As well as the EVA you may want to include public meetings and events, postcards and flyers and local surgeries and suggestion boxes.

Organising and implementing the public perception surveys and making sure that a wide section of the community is engaged. For instance, on an analysis of a public perception survey showed that none of the respondents were under age 25 - yet one of the major issues identified was youth nuisance. By organising a focus group at the local high school the concerns of the younger members of the community were incorporated into the process. So it is worth thinking outside the box to ensure all members of the community are engaged.

By using different methods of engagement, such as web-based surveys to reach busy professionals and placing kiosks in supermarkets and even in pubs, the public perception surveys will reach beyond the public who typically respond to postal surveys. A wide range of methods will be used to gather information from the whole community.

It gives the community the chance to tell your local policing team, local authority and other partner agencies about the issues causing most concern in your neighbourhood and which ones you want dealt with as a priority. Once the community aggress on the priorities, all agencies can work with a common aim to address these problems.

What happens in the street, estates and public open space is the major factor in shaping peoples perception of the areas they live in. Enviro-crime - litter, fly-tipping, graffiti, nuisance cars, dog fouling, vandalism and noise nuisance - shapes perceptions. Its presence encourages a spiral of decline (broken window effect). This can undermine the community and the efforts of public agencies. There is a clear link from litter to more serious environmental crime. Left unchecked, dirty streets and neighborhoods affect the perception of the local community, which can lead to anti-social behaviors and eventually serious crime.

If we step outside our front door into a safe, well cared for residential area, with clean well maintained streets and open spaces, not dominated graffiti, dog fouling and vandalism, it has a positive impact on our daily life. We have made significant progress in improving our residential environments in recent years and levels of public satisfaction are rising. But we have to sustain the momentum of this improvement and visual audits will go some way to further improving our environment.

Tools for conducting the EVA

Equipment you will need;

Template EVA forms, similar to the ones below, a map of the area and a camera.

EVA templates

Template design1;

Date	
Name(s) of Auditors	
Location	
Name of organisation*	

*For example, Neighbourhood Watch, Housing Association. Where auditor is a community member, this can be left blank or filled in with 'resident' / 'community member'.

Please indicate if any of the following are a problem in your area,
keeping a tally of occurrences:

SOCIAL DISORDERS	
Homeless people	
Blankets / clothing left in public places	
People begging	
Emergency litter (e.g. glass and drug paraphernalia)	
Groups hanging around:	
Youths	
Adults	
Mixed	
Stray or unleashed dogs	
Signs of outdoor sexual activity / public urination	
Other local problems (please state):	

Please indicate if any of the following are a problem in you area,
keeping a tally of occurrences:

PHYSICAL DISORDER	
Poor street lighting	
Graffiti:	
Tag	
Racist	
Painted over graffiti	
General	
Litter / rubbish lying around	
Vandalised telephone boxes	
Vandalised buildings	
Damaged bus shelters	
Dog fouling	
Damaged / abandoned / burnt out vehicles (include location and registration number)	
Other local problems (please state):	

DRUGS AND SUBSTANCE MISUSE PROBLEMS	
Drug houses / premises	
Public sales of drugs	
Use of drugs substances in public	
Physical signs of drug / substance use *(aerosol cans, glue containers, syringes, ampoules)*	
TRAFFIC AND PARKING ISSUES	
Broken traffic lights	
Broken / missing street signs	
Obstructive parking *(e.g. on pavements / grass verges (include location and road name))*	
Speeding / reckless driving / running red lights	
Other local road traffic related problems *(e.g. state of road repair)*	

Please provide any **specific additional detail** around the problems noted:

Can you make any suggestions as to **actions** which should be taken to address these problems?

Can you make any suggestions as to how these problems could be **prevented**?

Can you make a note of any **comfort factors** you have seen? (These are things which make you feel safe / reassured.)

Template design 2;

The above template can be completed with a map, certain areas of the map known to have problems can be highlighted and numbered. This can then be checked and the location number logged in the map reference section.

Map ref	Road address	Issue/fault	Further details/pic ref (copy picture in)	Fill in who action was reported to/tick when complete
1	Whitehall street	Graffiti on electricity box	Electricity box ref; SSE1157/ the graffiti is racist.	Officer B to arrange cleaning.

Template design 3;

Visual Audit

Date:	
Names of Auditors:	
Location:	
Ownership details:	

Insert Photograph (If available)

Please tick if problem in area:

Graffiti	☐
Litter	☐
Overflowing bins	☐
Emergency Litter (glass and drug paraphernalia)	☐
Dog Fouling	☐
Damage (fencing, lighting columns, broken windows etc)	☐
Lighting Levels	☐
Fly-posting	☐
Availability of missiles (bricks, accumulations in ready access)	☐
Overgrown vegetation	☐

Please detail below the specific problems:

Please detail below any prevention suggestions:

Please detail follow up action taken:

Here is an example of a completed EVA

Ref No	IDENTIFIED ISSUE	RECOMMENDED ACTION	LEAD OFFICER & OTHER AGENCIES	PROPOSED ACTION BY LEAD AGENCY & TIMESCALE
	South Car Park			
1	Displaced kerb in South Car Park being used for skateboarding over	Remove displaced kerbs and re-instate new ones where needed	Phase 1 Landowner	Done
2	Retaining wall in South Car Park adj to footpath leading to Over Minnis Coping stones removed.	Make wall safe and secure by footpath	Phase 1 Landowner	Not done Timescale required
3	Parking areas ill defined in South Car Park	Lines to be re-painted	Phase 1 Landowner	Done
4	Dead vegetation in planting bays in South Car Park to be looked at as fire risk in summer	Planting to be looked at	Phase 1 Landowner	NOT DONE Timescale required
5	Light ball fitting by Village Hall Sign nearly falling off	Light needs re-fitting	Village Association	Done
6	South Car Park drain grills missing	Grills to be replaced	Phase 1 Landowner	NOT DONE Timescale required
7	Landscaping is poor	Landscaping to be redone on South Car Park	Phase 1 Landowner	NOT DONE Timescale required
	Studio Car Park			
8	Flooding in Studio Car Park lack of proper drainage - floods a lot of the parking bays	Review drainage for car park and amend as necessary	Phase 1 Landowner	• Action needed re flooding in disabled parking bays & timescale required
9	Fencing in Studio Car park damaged with gaps above a drop to the street below	Fence needs replacing urgently	Phase 1 Landowner	Done

Ref No	IDENTIFIED ISSUE	RECOMMENDED ACTION	LEAD OFFICER & OTHER AGENCIES	PROPOSED ACTION BY LEAD AGENCY & TIMESCALE
71	Graffiti throughout the Centre	All graffiti to be reported to Sevenoaks District Council's Contact Centre 01732 227000	SDC	Graffiti removed 25 June & 1 July 2008 & March 2009
72	Lack of signage in car park	Rules and information signs for car park	Phase 1 Landowner	NOT DONE Timescale required
73	CCTV system needs upgrading	West Kent Police to work with caretaker and Sevenoaks District Council to offer advice on surveillance issues	West Kent Police Sevenoaks District Council	Done
74	Reports of Anti-Social Behaviour (ASB)	Police Neighbourhood Team to deploy where necessary to address ASB and report any individuals to the ASB Task Group	West Kent Police	Police action ongoing, regular reviews by ASB group
75	Public toilets closed and causing residents difficulty	Public toilets to be re-opened	SDC	Done

Appendix 7 - Personal Behaviours

The operation of transactional analysis.

Transactional analysis is the analysis of the communication between two people. In the 1950's Eric Berne developed theories of transactional analysis stating that verbal communication is at the centre of human social relationships and psychoanalysis and that when two people encounter each other one will speak to the other. The initial speaker he referred to as the Transaction stimulus and The response from the person receiving this stimulus was referred to as a Transaction Response. Therefore communication occurs between at least two people and requires one person to initiate communication and another a response. According to the PAC model founded by Eric Berne, there are three main ego states, Parent, Adult and Child. The parent ego state encompasses our learning and attitude from when we were young, therefore this is our 'Taught' concept of life. The child ego state encompasses our internal reactions and feelings and this is therefore our 'Felt' concept of life. The adult ego state encompasses our ability to think and determine actions based on the facts, this is therefore our 'Thought' concept of life. The ego states are individual to each person's own experiences, therefore what they have experienced in the past will effect how they respond to the Transactional stimulus. A negative past experience may be triggered by the Transactional stimulus and therefore bring about an irrational reaction to the Transactional stimulus. Understanding these ego states may help us to analyze how or why people react to the way we communicate with them in a certain way.

Our adult ego state allows us to keep control over our parent and child ego states. The relevance this has to how we communicate is that depending on the Transactional stimulus and how this is given will determine our feelings and which ego state this puts us into, and therefore how we respond. Something can trigger a shift from one ego state to another, therefore the way a person is spoken to will affect how they respond.

It is important to be aware of this and to determine how the other person may react to what you say. The ego states that the Transactional stimulus is given in and the ego state that the Transactional response is received i.e. how you speak to someone and how they respond to you will determine the manner of the communication. Using the parent ego state as a means of communication involves carrying out Transactional stimulus or Transactional response (i.e. initiating the communication or responding) as if to be authorative, whereas communicating in the child ego state is to communicate in a submissive manner over the other person.

In order that the interaction is set at the right mode, the approach should be one of adult to adult. Communicating in the parent ego state may be perceived as over aggressive or patronising, whereas communicating within the child ego state could be perceived as not concerned, uninterested, unable to understand or lenient.

Furthermore in face to face conversation the message is transmitted;
7% by the words used and their meaning
23% by the tone of voice
70% by none-verbal communication

Beware of body language and tone when speaking to people, also be aware that when you are on the phone they can't see your body language and it is likely that what you say could be misinterpreted so it is important to think carefully about the words you use, this principle applies even more so when you send a letter or e-mail as in these forms of communication all the emphasis is on the words.
This is true across all cultures, no matter what language is spoken, non verbal communication will always have more impact than the words used.

There are two elements to conflicts, the problem itself and the emotions that surround it, to deal with the problem effectively we also need to deal with emotions and that means being able to communicate effectively.

It is also important to get the balance right and not be too negative when pointing out negative issues, if you get the balance right you will appear to be more objective and people are more likely to be willing to listen to you and will take what you say seriously.

Communication failures are typically caused when people are addressing each other in different ego states. Typically people prefer others to communicate in a way that matched their style of communication and may feel that others are being deliberately awkward when they do not match their style of communication.

Furthermore Berne went on to say that to read the real communication requires both surface and non-verbal readings, its not just what's said but the way its said, the tone used and the accompanying body language. Messages may get misinterpreted and communication could therefore fail when the body language and / or tone contradicts what is being said.

Moreover he elaborates that people require recognition, attention or responsiveness that one person gives another. This can be positive or if they can not gain positive recognition they will seek negative recognition in order to get the attention they crave.

This could explain why people act in a negative way when they do not receive the response they require or feel that they are not being listened to.

It is important to effectively listen to people, this means actually hearing and understanding what the other person means and giving them feedback or some sort of evidence to show that you listening. Listen to what they say, ask questions to clarify what they say and get the necessary information to help solve their problem, or at least understand what their issues are. Then paraphrase and summarise what they have said to ensure that you have understood it correctly. Try and empathise and show you understand but without actually agreeing (in some circumstances it may be inappropriate to agree with them, but you can still empathise). If you can, solve their problem.

Be aware of the attitude cycle, if they think that you are being too assertive or aggressive with them they may become aggressive, as people often mirror each others behaviour, therefore you can get stuck in a cycle where things spiral out of control. Also your dealings with someone in the past may cloud your judgement and inhibit your from understanding the current issues effectively.

Obviously if someone is showing warning signs of aggression than communication may be failing and you may need to remove yourself from the situation before it becomes dangerous.

Communication skills and team dynamics;
We need communication skills in order to respond to everyone around us, as a enforcement officer / investigator not only do we need to communicate effectively when carrying out investigations and enforcement activities but we also need to communicate effectively with our colleagues and teams that we work in.

Meredith Belbin studied team-work for many years, and named nine typical team roles that people in a team tend to adopt, the team dynamics will depend of the roles adopted by each member of the team.

The roles he identified are as follows;

1. Shaper	Challenges the team to improve.
2. Implementer	Puts ideas into action.
3. Completer Finisher	Ensures thorough, timely completion.
4. Coordinator	Acts as a chairperson.
5. Team Worker	Encourages cooperation.
6. Resource Investigator	Explores outside opportunities.

7. Plant	Presents new ideas and approaches.
8. Monitor-Evaluator	Analyzes the options.
9. Specialist	Provides specialized skills.

You obviously need the right mix of roles for the team to function properly, as the whole point of a team is that everyone has different skills that they can offer the team and therefore between you, you should be equipped with more skills and therefore be more able to complete a project than you would on your own. However the team dynamics can fall down if there are too many of one type of team role and not enough of another.

If team members have similar weakness, the team as a whole may tend to have that weakness. If team members have similar team-work strengths, they may tend to compete (rather than co-operate) for the team tasks and responsibilities that best suit their natural styles.

Therefore by understanding your team role within a particular team, you can develop your strengths and manage your weaknesses as a team member, and so improve how you contribute to the team. Also if you know everyone's roles you can put them into set teams that work more efficiently, although this isn't always practicable.

It is often about getting other people involved by asking their opinions so that they feel part of the project and motivating them by selling them the benefits and showing them how successful the project could be.

Also when you work hard on a project and make it a success it encourages people to want to work on future projects with you.

- Be mindful of how you speak to someone, the tone you use and how they may perceive it. If they think you are being aggressive they will be aggressive so you will need to lighten the tone and calm them down, perhaps show some empathy and sympathise with their position but stand your ground by explaining what you position is and why but also accepting theirs, then try and meet a compromise, or by gently persuade them into your way of thinking, as appropriate.

- If you start off with a mild manner you can up your game but if you are too assertive or aggressive it is very hard to come down from that, the other person may perceive you as rude and the situation could easily get out of control.

- The way you talk to people affects how they view you and how they react to you. You must give respect to get respect. Even if you have a valid point if your tone is loud and aggressive people won't listen to you. It is much more affect to stay calm, and then if you are a calm person when you do become more assertive it will have more of an affect, habitual use of strong language means that when it is truly needed it will have less of an affect, the same senior as if you cry wolf too often.

- In order to communicate with people you need to listen, often we think we are listening but really we are concentrating on the next thing that we are going to say and don't take in, or understand what the other person is saying. Hearing but not understanding is the root cause of most communication problems. Poor communication causes many problems, especially in business if the customer is understood the affects can be disastrous. Remember the message is not just in the words but also in the body language, and the tone used. As well as listening you need to ensure that you understood exactly what they said, when you are investigating a case it is important that you don't make assumptions, let your own opinions get in the way or put words in peoples mouths. In order to listen effectively and understand what someone is saying you should.

L – Listen

A - Ask questions if you need to clarify anything
P – Paraphrase and summarise the main points of what they said
S – Say back to them & confirm your understanding is correct.

- When communicating it may help the communication flow if you mirror the other person as it will make the other person feel more at ease and feel like they are being understood. Also use non verbal communication to influence the listener – when the tone of voice lowers at the end of the sentence, it can be perceived by the listener as a command, especially if accompanied by appropriate body language, such as leaning forward and a palm down gesture, this is more likely to get the other person to follow through on your command.

This technique is often referred to as pacing and this is a good technique to calm people down as it appeals to their sub conscious, once you are effectively pacing and calming them down you can then try leading to steer the communication in the way that you want, and put your agenda in. You may not be successful at first with your lead and may need to continue pacing, and then try and plug for a lead a bit later on;

Pace
↓
Pace
↓
Pace
↓
Lead

- To reassure people and make them feel that you are listening to them and understanding them and perceive them as important, increase the use of eye contact, smiling and other positive facial expressions, head nodding open gestures and posture. It is also good to mirror/pace someone's behaviour/body language (as appropriate) if they have a different cultural background and you are unsure as to what is expectable and what isn't in communication i.e. in western cultures we expect eye contact where as other cultures may not use if so much and may find it offensive so look at what they do. Don't make assumptions or form opinions just stick to facts. i.e. just because they avoid eye contact this doesn't mean they are guilty, this could just be a cultural difference.

- Understand that everyone is different and will communicate differently, different cultures also have different behaviours that are acceptable, in some cultures it is rude not to give eye contact where as in other cultures it is rude to do so, recognizing and understanding different cultures will make you better at communication, you should always try and understand someone else's culture and the rules in that culture so that you don't offend them, people will respect you more for doing this. This is very important if you have a guest coming from abroad, or who has a different cultural background, or you are going abroad – get reading up on the culture. Often there can be a cycle of behaviour based on how someone perceives someone's behaviour to be, (rather than what it actually is) and reacts to this, an example of this is that, often older people may see younger people as rude because they don't understand their culture, they may react to this perceived rudeness, with rudeness which will leave the other person angry and they then may be rude back, which would then re-enforce the other persons opinion that they were rude in the first place, however if they discussed the issue instead of being rude back the other person may understand them, see they are not actually rude and foster relations with them.

- Always look at things from someone else's view and treat them fairly and with respect, don't treat someone how you would not expect to be treated, irrespective of what you think they have or haven't done.

Appendix 8

1. Summary of the Information Commissioner CCTV Code of Practice July 2000

1.1 Disapplication
This Code is not intended to apply to:
- Targeted and intrusive surveillance activities covered by RIPA
- Surveillance by employers of their employees to ensure compliance with their employment contracts
- Home security
- Broadcast media use of cameras and similar equipment

1.2 Initial assessment procedures
Establish person(s) or organisation(s) legally responsible for the scheme
Establish the purpose of the Scheme (First and Second data Protection Principle)
Ensure this is notified to the Information Commissioner
Establish and document security and disclosure policies

1.3 Siting the cameras
The equipment should be sited such that it only monitors those spaces intended to be covered (First and Third Data Protection Principles)
Operators must be aware that they are only able to use the equipment in order to achieve the purpose(s) for which it has been installed (First and Second Data Protection Principles)
Signs should be placed so that the public are aware that they are entering a zone covered by surveillance equipment (First Data Protection Principle)
The signs should contain the following information:
- Identity of the person or organisation responsible for the scheme
- The purposes of the scheme
- Details of whom to contact regarding the scheme

In exceptional and limited cases, such as prevention and detection of crime, signs may be dispensed with where to do otherwise would prejudice this

1.4 Quality of the images
Ensure the equipment performs properly
If tapes are used, ensure that they are of good quality (Third and Fourth Data Protection Principles)
The medium on which the images have been recorded should not be used when the quality of the images has deteriorated (Third Data Protection Principle)
If an automatic facial recognition system is used to match images captured against data base of images, then both sets of images should be clear enough to ensure an accurate match (Third and Fourth Data Protection Principles)
Users should assess whether it is necessary to carry out constant real-time recording (First and Third Data Protection Principles)

1.5 Processing the Images
Images should not be retained for longer than is necessary (Fifth Data Protection Principle).
If the images are retained for evidential purposes, they should be retained in a secure place to which access is controlled (Fifth and Seventh Data Protection Principle).
On removing the medium on which the images have been recorded for use in legal proceedings, the operator should ensure that they have documented:
- The date on which the images were removed from the general system for use in legal proceedings
- The reason why they were removed from the system
- Any crime incident number to which the images may be relevant
- The location of the images

Access to the recorder images should be restricted to a manager or designated member of staff who will decide whether to allow requests for access by third

parties in accordance with the user's documented disclosure policies (Seventh Data Protection Principle)
All operators should be trained in their responsibilities under this Code of Practice i.e. they should be aware of:
. The user's security policy e.g. procedures to have access to recorded images
. The users disclosure policy
. Rights of individuals in relation to their recorded images
(Seventh Data Protection Principle)

1.6 Access to and disclosure of images to third parties
Access to recorded images should be restricted to those staff who need to have access in order to achieve the purpose(s) of using the equipment (Seventh Data Protection Principle)
All access to the medium on which the images are recorded should be documented
Disclosure of the recorded images to third parties should only be made in limited and prescribed circumstances ie compatible with reason(s) or purpose(s) of the scheme (Second and Seventh Data Protection Principles)
If it is decided that images will be disclosed to the media …the images of the individuals will need to be disguised or blurred so that they are not readily identifiable (First, Second and Seventh Data Protection Principles)

1.6 Access by data subjects
Individuals should …be provided with a leaflet which describes the types of images which are recorded and retained, the purposes for which those images are recorded and retained, and information about the disclosure policy in relation to those images (Sixth Data Protection Principle)
All subject access requests should be dealt with by a manager or designated member of staff
If third party images are not to be disclosed, the manager or designated member of staff shall arrange for the third party images to be disguised or blurred (Sixth Data Protection Principle)

1.7 Other rights
All staff must be aware of the manager or designated member of staff who is responsible for responding to requests from an individual to:
. Prevent processing likely to cause substantial and unwarranted damage to that individual
. Prevent automated decision taking in relation to that individual

1.8 Monitoring compliance with this code of practice
A manager or designated member of staff should undertake regular reviews of the documented procedures to ensure the provisions of this Code are being complied with (Seventh Data Protection Principle)

2. Summary of the Information Commissioner's Office CCTV Additional Guidance 1 February 2004
[In light of the *Durant* case], whether or not you are covered will depend on how you use your CCTV system.
If you can answer 'no' to the following 3 questions, you will not be covered by the DPA:
. Do you ever operate the cameras remotely in order to zoom in or out or point in different directions to pick up what particular individuals are doing?
. Do you ever use the images to try to observe someone's behaviour for your own purposes such as monitoring staff members?
. Do you ever give the recorded images to someone other than a law enforcement body such as the police?
The activities of more sophisticated CCTV systems (i.e. used to focus on the activities of particular people) will still be covered by the DPA, but not some of the images they record. The simple rule of thumb is that you have to decide whether the image you have taken is aimed at learning about a particular person's activities.

Data Matching –

What is Data Matching?

1.1. For the purposes of this code of practice, data matching is defined as a process by which data held for one purpose are taken and compared electronically with data held for other purposes with the aim of establishing any inconsistencies, anomalies or duplications in the data. Depending on the circumstances, this will involve the comparison of data held for different purposes on the same computer; held for the same or different purposes on different computers and, in particular circumstances, against data held by other local authorities or government departments (eg during benefit fraud investigation).

1.2. As a procedure, data matching is not new to local government, even though many who use it many not be aware or consider that that is what they are actually doing. Any procedure, which requires the comparison of one set of data against another, is in effect a data matching exercise. In the majority of cases such comparisons are carried out in order to determine the level of service to be provided to an individual. What is new is the use of the technique in fraud prevention/detection whereby whole populations of data are matched against each other with a view to identifying potential fraud. The use of data matching for this purpose has implications for personal privacy and, unless properly controlled, could result in public authorities accidentally breaching the law.

2. Scope of the Code of Practice

2.1. This code of practice has been prepared in the knowledge that local authorities are making increasing use of data matching techniques in the provision of services and for the purpose of local fraud detection. Data matching is also used by the Audit Commission and other agencies (especially the Benefits Agency) to compare data provided by local authorities participating in national fraud initiatives. The purpose of the code is to provide a framework within which authorities can apply data matching techniques while complying with the requirements of the Data Protection Act.

2.2. The code recognises that the issues surrounding the use of data matching in service provision and local fraud prevention are not the same as those raised by the provision of personal data for the purposes of national fraud initiatives. As a result, the two are treated as separate, though related, purposes throughout the code.

3. The privacy issue

3.1. The use of data matching, especially for the purposes of fraud prevention/detection requires a delicate balancing act between the individual's right to privacy, as set out in the Data Protection Act, and the local authority's duty to protect the public purse. Although the latter may be paramount in the eyes of the local authority, it must be recognised that the majority of applicants for benefits, goods or services are honest and have no intention of committing any offence. In addition, information provided by individuals is often provided on the understanding that it will be treated in confidence and not used for any other purpose or given to any other organisation. Yet individuals may find that data they have provided is being shared with others as though they have been guilty of an offence. The Data Protection Commissioner has reported that many commentators have expressed fears that, not only could the use of data matching constitute a breach of confidence but that it could 'reverse the normal rules of evidence and presumption of innocence' and raises fears of its potential as a means of conduction a mass surveillance of the population. If conflict between these separate rights and consequent accusations of unwarranted intrusions into private lives are to be avoided it is essential that procedures are introduced which limit those conducting data matching exercises to the sharing of personal data for the purposes of identifying possible cases of fraud and for these purposes alone.

3.2. Local authorities are, also, statutory bodies and as such use of data is restricted to what is allowed by the statutes governing such use. To use or disclose the data for any other purpose would be outside the authority's powers and the authority would be acting 'ultra vires'. Before participating in a data matching exercise, authorities must ensure that they have the necessary powers to do so. In the case of any national campaign authorities must also be sure that those carrying out the data matching are acting within their legal powers and are not asking for data over and above that necessary for the campaign and that, in addition, the intention is not to use the data for purposes other than those provided by the statute.

3.3. In the absence of legislation covering the use of data matching, codes of practice, such as that described here, are essential. An important aspect of such codes must be the reconciliation of the local authorities' right to protect the public purse and the rights of the individual as set out in the Data Protection Act and to have information about him/her treated in confidence. This code of practice has been prepared with that aim in mind. Its application should not, however, be limited to the exchange of personal data in the interests of fraud prevention initiatives. It has been designed, therefore, to allow it to be adapted to other uses of data matching, which should also be conducted according to the requirements of the code of practice.

Appendix 9

Some Legislation that you may find useful;

The Crime and Disorder Act 1998 is intended to reduce the general level of crime and disorder in society, through the introduction of several changes to the criminal justice system (*e.g.* strategies, powers and court orders).

The Act covers diverse areas, such as crime and disorder strategies, youth crime, racially-aggravated offences, sexual or violent offenders. It also introduces various police powers.

Section one of the act introduces a wide range of measures for preventing crime and disorder and enables a magistrates' court to make an 'anti-social behaviour order' against an individual whose behaviour has caused harassment, alarm or distress. A breach of such an order is an offence.

Also section 17 of the Crime and Disorder Act 1998 imposes an obligation on every police authority, local authority and other specified bodies, such as fire and rescue, the primary care trust, the county council etc, to consider crime and disorder prevention/reduction in the exercise of their functions.

This not only means that when any policies are written the impact on crime and disorder as a result of the policy needs to be looked at, but local authorities, as well as other public bodies have a real obligation to actively find ways to reduce crime and disorder.

The objectives of the act are to bring together different partners from the public sector to work alongside private organisations and the voluntary sector to work on a local level to tackle specific issues in their community thus making their communities a safer place to work and live and a community where people want to move to and invest in.

This is done through the establishment of a community safety partnership / crime and reduction partnerships (CDRP), who are required to look at issues in their area and put together a community safety strategy and translating high-level strategic priorities into local action plans for delivery, to meet the objectives set out in the strategy.

In the review of the Crime and Disorder Act 1998 (Review – Jan 2006), it states a vision 'for an intelligence led, problem-solving and outcome oriented approach to community safety enabling all partners to collaborate and target their efforts where they are most needed', it recognises that that effective delivery relies on good decision making, which are based on good information, from real time intelligence and data via improved information sharing. It also goes onto say how local people should be engaged in collective action and actively involved (by use of volunteering work, focus groups etc.)

By legislation placing the responsibility on public authorities to reduce crime and disorder and making funding available it means many schemes can take place that perhaps didn't before. It encourages all partners to get involved and work together, partners can pool together skills, resources and powers to get things done in a much more productive way.

Recent amendments to the Crime and Disorder Act require there to be a strategic drugs and alcohol plan, which for most licensing authorities is closely related to the managing of their night time economy.

There are various funding streams, including funding via the Home Office 'Safer Stronger Communities Fund'.

Crime (Sentences) Act 1997

The act aimed to limit the freedom which judges exercised over sentencing by introducing a range of mandatory sentences covering crimes such as murder and domestic burglary.

Sentences can be halved if they are 4 years and under, they can also get extra time off for good behaviour, therefore a 4 year sentence could be reduced to 1 but if its over 4 years they have to serve a certain amount of their sentence.

Section 63 of the **Criminal Justice and Public Order Act 1994** gives police powers to tackle raves during the night which are in progress or which are being planned in the open air. These include a power to direct people to leave the land, to prevent people travelling in the direction of a rave, and to confiscate sound equipment used in connection with the rave.

Criminal Justice and Police Act 2001

Section 19 of the Criminal Justice and Police Act 2001 empowers a constable or local authority to serve a closure notice on a person having control of, or responsibility for, any premises that are being, or have been used within the last 24 hours, for the sale or consumption of alcohol on or in the vicinity of the premises, without a liquor licence. Where such a closure notice is served it must also be served on any other occupier of the premises whose access may be impeded if the part involved in the unlicensed sale of alcohol was to be closed. PREMISES include any land or other place (whether enclosed or otherwise);

Each responsible authority will be notified as soon as possible that a closure notice under section 19 has been issued.

Following any serious incident involving an unlicensed activity, the relevant enforcement agencies will participate in a de-brief. Information on preventative operations will be discussed and best practice and areas of weakness identified, All information/evidence surrounding an event will be shared with a view to taking decisions on prosecution or future licensing applications.

Section 20 of the Criminal Justice and Police Act 2001 enables a constable or local authority to apply for a closure order by complaint from magistrates (between 7 days and six months after the service of the closure notice) in relation to premises on which a closure notice has been served. A complaint cannot be laid where the police or local authority is satisfied that the unlicensed sale of alcohol has ceased and there is no reasonable prospect of it re-starting.

Misuse of Drugs Act

This is the main piece of legislation covering drugs and categorizes drugs as class A, B and C.

These drugs are termed as controlled substances, and Class A drugs are those considered to be the most harmful.

Offences under the Act include

- Possession of a controlled substance unlawfully
- Possession of a controlled substance with intent to supply it
- Supplying or offering to supply a controlled drug (even where no charge is made for the drug)
- Allowing premises you occupy or manage to be used for the purpose of drug taking

Drug trafficking (supply) attracts serious punishment including life imprisonment for Class A offences.

To enforce this law the police have special powers to stop, detain and search people on 'reasonable suspicion' that they are in possession of a controlled drug.

Classification under the Act

Class A drugs

Include: Ecstasy, LSD, heroin, cocaine, crack, magic mushrooms (if prepared for use) amphetamines (if prepared for injection)

Penalties for possession: Up to seven years in prison or an unlimited fine. Or both

Penalties for dealing: Up to life in prison or an unlimited fine. Or both

Class B drugs

Include: Amphetamines, Methylphenidate (Ritalin), Pholcodine

Penalties for possession: Up to five years in prison or an unlimited fine. Or both

Penalties for dealing: Up to 14 years in prison or an unlimited fine. Or both

Class C drugs

Include: Cannabis, tranquilisers, come painkillers, GHB (Gamma hydroxybutyrate

Penalties for possession: Up to two years in prison or an unlimited fine. Or both

Penalties for dealing: Up to 14 years in prison or an unlimited fine. Or both

Drugs Act 2005

The new Act brings about new police powers to test for class A drugs and more

Aims of Drugs Act

- Increase the effectiveness of the Drug Interventions Program by getting more offenders into treatment.
- Introduce a new civil order that will run alongside ASBOs for adults to tackle drug related anti-social behavior.
- Enhance Police and Court powers against drug offenders.
- Clarify existing legislation in respect of magic mushrooms.

Content of Drugs Act

- Test drug offenders on arrest, rather than on charge.
- Require a person with a positive test to undergo an assessment by a drugs worker.
- Provide for an -intervention order- to be attached to ASBOs issued to adults whose anti-social behavior is drug related, requiring them to attend drug counseling.
- Allow a court to remand in police custody for up to a further 192 hours those who swallow drugs in secure packages, to increase the likelihood of the evidence being recovered.
- Allow a court or jury to draw adverse inference where a person refuses without good cause to consent to an intimate body search, x-ray or ultrasound scan.
- Create a new presumption of intent to supply where a defendant is found to be in possession of a certain quantity of controlled drugs.

- Require courts to take account of aggravating factors - such as dealing near a school - when sentencing.
- Amend the Anti-Social Behaviour Act 2003 to give police the power to enter premises, such as a crack house, to issue a closure notice.
- Amend the Misuse of Drugs Act 1971, making fungi containing the drugs Psilocin or Psilocybin (-magic mushroom') a class A drug.
- Repeal section 38 of the Criminal Justice and Police Act 2001.

Other drug laws

Drug legislation since 1968.

Medicines Act 1968

This law governs the manufacture and supply of medicine. There are three categories:

- Prescription Only drugs can be sold by a pharmacist if prescribed by a doctor
- Pharmacy medicines may be sold by a pharmacist without prescription
- General sales list medicines may be sold without a prescription in any shop

Possession of Prescription Only medicines without a prescription is a serious offence. Drugs such as amyl nitrite, GHB and ketamine are regulated under the Medicines Act.

Drug Traffickers Offences Act 1994

- Gives police the power to seize the assets and income of anyone who is found guilty of drugs trafficking, even if that income isn't related to the trafficking of drugs.
- It also makes it illegal to manufacture of sell equipment for the preparation or use of controlled drugs.
-
  Crime and Disorder Act 1998

- Makes it legal to force offenders who are convicted of crime committed in order to fund their drug habit into getting drug treatment.

It also allows for them to be tested for drug misuse.

Gambling Act 2006

Gambling is;

- Gaming

- Betting

- Lotteries

- Can include casino games
- Game of both chance and skill
- Game with some chance that can be eliminated by superlative skill
- Game presented as involving elements of chance
- BUT is not a sport
- Does not need other participants in the game
- Same definition as for gaming
- A player plays and has a chance of winning a prize and

- Whether or not he risks losing anything at the game
- Prize can be for money or money's worth and includes prizes by organiser of game or winning from the money staked
- Does not involve playing or staking against a bank, and
- the chances are equally favourable to all participants.
- it is immaterial-

- how a bank is described, and
- whether or not a bank is controlled or administered by a player

- Spread bets
- Betting: prize competitions
- Pool betting
- "betting" means making or accepting a bet on-

    - the outcome of a race, competition or other event or process,

    - the likelihood of anything occurring or not occurring, or

    - whether anything is or is not true.
- Guessing (including predicting using skill or judgement) any of the matters relevant to ordinary betting
- Requirement to pay to participate but not stake a bet in the normal way AND
- Wins a prize (or enters a class with a chance to win a prize) if guess is accurate or more accurate than other guesses
- pool betting if made on terms that all or part of winnings-

    - shall be determined by reference to the aggregate of stakes paid or agreed to be paid by the persons betting,
    - shall be divided among the winners, or
    - shall or may be something other than money.
- Simple lotteries
- Complex lotteries
- Non-commercial society
- Local authority lottery
- External lottery manager for non-commercial society
- External lottery manager for local authority lottery
- National Lottery

Exempt lotteries –
- Incidental to non-commercial event
- Private lottery
- Customer lottery
- Small society lottery
- Works lottery
- Residential lottery

Simple lotteries are an arrangement where:

- Persons are required to pay to take part in the arrangement
- One or more prizes are allocated to one or more members of a class AND
- The prizes are allocated on a process which relies wholly on chance

In addition, a complex lottery is arranged so:

- the prizes are allocated by a series of processes, and
- the first of those processes relies wholly on chance
- Operating licences
- Personal licences

- Premises licences
- Permits
- Occasional notices/permissions
- Exceptions

Licensing objectives

- Preventing gambling from being a source of crime or disorder, being associated with crime or disorder or being used to support crime

- Ensuring that gambling is conducted in a fair and open way, and

- Protecting children and other vulnerable persons from being harmed or exploited by gambling

Enforcement

- Warning
- Add/remove/amend conditions
- Suspend (specifically or indefinitely) or revoke due to:

    - conduct inconsistent with objectives
    - breach of conditions
    - failure to co-operate with review
    - licensee unsuitable (integrity, competence and financial circumstances inc. of connected persons)

	Maximum Stake	*Maximum Prize*
A	Unlimited*	Unlimited*
B1	£2	£4000
B2	£100 (in £10 multiples)	£500
B3A	£1	£500
B3	£1	£500
B4	£1	£250
C	50p	£35
D	10p/30p	£5 cash/£8 prizes

- Casino
- Bingo
- General betting (not pool betting)
- Pool betting
- Betting intermediary
- Gaming machine operating: adult gaming centre
- Gaming machine operating: family entertainment ctr
- Gaming machine technical
- Gaming software
- Lottery

Gambling exemptions
- Exempt lotteries
- FEC gaming machine permits
- Limited prize machines
- Clubs and miners' welfare institutes
- Premises with alcohol licences
- Prize gaming (by permit and exception)
- Private gaming and betting

Non-commercial gaming

GAMING MACHINES STAKES & PRIZES		
	Maximum Stake	Maximum Prize
A	Unlimited*	Unlimited*
B1	£2	£4000
B2	£100 (in £10 multiples)	£500
B3A	£1	£500
B3	£1	£500
B4	£1	£250
C	50p	£35
D	10p/30p	£5 cash/£8 prizes

	Betting shops	Bingo	AGC	Licensed FEC	Unlicensed FEC	Members Club etc	Pubs with permit	Pubs without permit
A								
B1								
B2	Maximum of 4 in B2 to D	Max 4 in B3 or B4	Max 4 in B3 or B4					
B3A						Max 3 in B3A to D		
B3								
B4								
C		No limit in C or D	No limit in C or D	No limit in C or D				Max 2 in C or D
D					No limit in D		As stated on permit	

GAMBLING ACT 2005
POWERS OF ENTRY

	POLICE		GAMBLING COMMISSION ENFORCEMENT OFFICER		LOCAL AUTHORITY AUTHORISED PERSON	
	Assess applications	Compliance or enforcement	Assess applications	Compliance or enforcement	Assess applications	Compliance or enforcement
Family entertainment centres	✓	✓	✓	✓	✓	✓
Alcohol-licensed premises	X	✓	✓	✓	✓	✓
Prize gaming permit	✓	✓	✓	✓	✓	✓
Clubs	✓	✓	✓	✓	✓	X
GA 2005 premises licence	✓	*	✓	*	✓	*
Registered society lottery	X	X	✓	✓	✓	✓
Temporary use notices	✓	✓	✓	✓	✓	✓

All
Summary of the terms and conditions of the premises licence shall be displayed in a prominent place within the premises. (mandatory premises licence condition - SI 2007 / 1409)
Premises licence shall be kept on the premises and available on request by police, enforcement officer or authorised local authority officer. (Gambling Act 2005 Section 185)
The layout of the premises shall be maintained in accordance with the plan. (mandatory premises licence condition - SI 2007 / 1409)
The premises shall not be used for the sale of tickets in a private lottery or customer lottery or the sale of tickets in any other lottery in respect of which the sale of tickets on the premises is otherwise prohibited. (mandatory premises licence condition - SI 2007 / 1409)
A notice stating that no person under the age of 18 is permitted to enter the premises shall be displayed in a prominent place at every entrance to the premises. (mandatory condition - SI 2007 / 1409)
No customer shall be able to access the premises directly from any other premises in respect of which a premises licence or the following types of permit have effect: • unlicensed family entertainment centre gaming machine permit • club gaming or club machine permit • alcohol licensed premises gaming machine permit (mandatory premises licence condition - SI 2007 / 1409)
Any ATM made available for use on the premises shall be located in a place that

requires any customer who wishes to use it to cease gambling at any gaming machine in order to do so. (mandatory condition - SI 2007 / 1409)
No alcohol shall be permitted to be consumed on the premises at any time during which facilities for gambling are being provided on the premises. A notice to this effect shall be displayed at every entrance to the premises in a prominent place. (mandatory premises licence condition - SI 2007 / 1409)
No gambling on Christmas Day. (Gambling Act 2005 Section 183)
Protection of Children & Young Persons - Offence if invite, causes or permit a person under 18 to gamble. (Gambling Act 2005 Section 46)
Offence if invites or permit a person under 18 from entering premises where an AGC premises licence has effect. (Gambling Act 2005 Section 47)
An offence if employ a person under 18 to provide facilities for gambling. (Gambling Act 2005 Section 51)
An offence if employ a person under 18 to perform any function on the premises where gaming machines are sited or in connection with a gaming machine. (Gambling Act 2005 Section 54)
An offence if employ a person under 18 to perform any function on the premises where a casino, betting, or AGC premises licence have effect and where the gambling activity is being carried on. (Gambling Act 2005 Section 55)
Employment offences – An offence if employ a person under 16 to perform any function on the premises when bingo is being provided. (Gambling Act 2005 Section 53)
Additional premises licence conditions attached by the licensing authority: *(NB. Where a condition is attached to a premises licence to require door supervisors, if the Private Security and Industry Act 2001 means that they must be SIA registered then that also becomes a condition of the premises licence. (Gambling Act 2005 Section 178))*

Adult Gaming Centres

Hours of operation – there are no statutory restrictions on opening hours for AGCs but individual premises may have different hours as conditions attached by the licensing authority.

Gaming machines permitted: 4 Category B3 and B4 (i.e. 4 of either B3 or B4 of a mix of both) and any numbers of Categories C and D. (Gambling Act 2005 Section 172 and SI 2007 / 2158)

Category B3 = £1 stake / £500 prize
Category B4 = £1 stake / £250 prize
Category C = 50p stake / £35 prize
Category D = 10p cash or 30p non-money stake / £5 cash or £8 non-money prize
(SI 2007 / 2158)

Licensing officers may also wish to familiarise themselves with the requirements of SI 2007 / 2319 and SI 2007 / 2320 which include requirements that gaming machines display what category it is, the name and telephone number for assistance with problem gambling, that the machine is not to be used by child / young person unless is a category D and also provisions that no machines should be made available which can accept credit or debit cards.

Family Entertainment Centres

Where category C gaming machines are made available for use on the premises, then the gaming machines must be:
- separated from the rest of the premises by a physical barrier to prevent access other than via an entrance designed to be the entrance

- supervised at all times to ensure children or young persons do not enter the area

- arranged so that the area can be observed by persons responsible for supervision, or closed circuit television which is monitored

The gaming machines area must also have a notice at the entrance stating that no person under the age of 18 is permitted to enter the area. (mandatory premises licence condition - SI 2007 / 1409)

No alcohol shall be permitted to be consumed on the premises at any time during which facilities for gambling are being provided on the premises. A notice to this effect shall be displayed at every entrance to the premises in a prominent place. (mandatory premises licence condition - SI 2007 / 1409)

Hours of operation – there are no statutory restrictions on opening hours for FECs but individual premises may have different hours as conditions attached by the licensing authority.

Gaming machines permitted: any number of Category C and / or D (Gambling Act 2005 Section 172 and SI 2007 / 2158)

Category C = 50p stake / £35 prize
Category D = 10p cash or 30p non-money stake / £5 cash or £8 non-money prize
(SI 2007 / 2158)

Licensing officers may also wish to familiarise themselves with the requirements of SI 2007 / 2319 and SI 2007 / 2320 which include requirements that gaming machines display what category it is, the name and telephone number for assistance with problem gambling, that the machine is not to be used by child / young person unless is a category D and also provisions that no machines should be made available which can accept credit or debit cards.

Bingo

Where children and/or young persons are permitted by the licence holder to enter the premises, and category B or C gaming machines are made available for use on the premises, then the gaming machines must be:
- separated from the rest of the premises by a physical barrier to prevent access other than via an entrance designed to be the entrance

- supervised at all times to ensure children or young persons do not enter the area

- arranged so that the area can be observed by persons responsible for supervision or closed circuit television which is monitored

The gaming machines area must also have a notice at the entrance stating that no person under the age of 18 years is permitted to enter the area. (mandatory premises licence condition - SI 2007 / 1409)

Where there is a charge for admission there must be a notice of the charge displayed in a prominent place at the principal entrance to the premises. (mandatory premises licence condition - SI 2007 / 1409)

A notice setting out any other charges in respect of the gaming (except prize gaming) shall be displayed at the main point where payment for the charge is to be made. Such a notice must include the cost (in money) of each game card or set of game cards, payable by an individual ion respect of the game of bingo, and the amount that will be charged by way of a participation fee. There should also be in the notice a statement that all/part of the participation fee may be waived at the discretion of the person charging it. This notice can be displayed in electronic form. (mandatory premises

licence condition - SI 2007 / 1409)
The rules of each type of game that is available (other than gaming machines) shall be made available to customers within the premises by either displaying a sign, making leaflets or other written material available, or running an audio-visual guide prior to any game commencing. (mandatory premises licence condition - SI 2007 / 1409)
Hours of operation – No facilities for gambling shall be provided on the premises between midnight and 9am, apart from gaming machines (default premises licence condition - SI 2007 / 1409)
An offence if employ a person under 18 to perform any function on the premises where gaming machines are sited or in connection with a gaming machine. (Gambling Act 2005 Section 54)
Gaming machines permitted: 4 Category B3 and B4 (i.e. 4 of either B3 or B4 of a mix of both) and any numbers of Categories C and D. (Gambling Act 2005 Section 172 and SI 2007 / 2158) Category B3 = £1 stake / £500 prize Category B4 = £1 stake / £250 prize Category C = 50p stake / £35 prize Category D = 10p cash or 30p non-money stake / £5 cash or £8 non-money prize (SI 2007 / 2158) *Licensing officers may also wish to familiarise themselves with the requirements of SI 2007 / 2319 and SI 2007 / 2320 which include requirements that gaming machines display what category it is, the name and telephone number for assistance with problem gambling, that the machine is not to be used by child / young person unless is a category D and also provisions that no machines should be made available which can accept credit or debit cards.*
Betting shop
The premises shall not be used for any purpose other than for providing facilities for betting apart from anything permitted under the Gambling Act 2005 and having an ATM, permitted visual/sound apparatus and permitted publications. (mandatory condition - SI 2007 / 1409)

No apparatus for making information or other material available in the form of sounds or visual images may be used on the premises, except for apparatus used for the following purposes:
   a) Communicating information about, or coverage of, sporting events, including-
   (i) information relating to betting on such an event; and
   (ii) any other mater of information, including an advertisement, which is incidental to such an event;
   b) Communicating information relating to betting on any event (including the result of an event) in connection with which betting transactions may be or have been effected on the premises.
(mandatory condition – SI 2007 / 1409)

No publications, other than racing periodicals or specialist betting publications, may be sold or offered for sale on the premises. (mandatory condition - SI 2007 / 1409)
No music, dancing or other entertainment shall be provided or permitted on the premises, save for entertainment provided via the sound / visual apparatus referred to above. (mandatory condition - SI 2007 / 1409)
A notice setting out the terms on which customers are invited to bet on the premises shall be displayed in a prominent place on the premises to which customers have unrestricted access. (mandatory premises licence condition - SI 2007 / 1409)
Hours of operation – No facilities for gambling shall be provided on the premises between the hours of 10pm on one day and 7am on the next day. (default premises licence condition - SI 2007 / 1409)
Protection of Children & Young Persons - Offence if invite, causes or permit a person under 18 to gamble. (Gambling Act 2005 Section 46)

Offence if invites or permit a person under 18 from entering premises where an AGC premises licence has effect. (Gambling Act 2005 Section 47)
An offence if employ a person under 18 to provide facilities for gambling. (Gambling Act 2005 Section 51)
Employment offences – An offence if invites, cause or permit a person under 16 to participate in football pools. (Gambling Act 2005 Section 57)
Gaming machines permitted: total of 4 gaming machines which can be Category B2, B3, B4, C and D (i.e. 4 of either Category or a mix up to a total of 4). (Gambling Act 2005 Section 172 and SI 2007 / 2158) Category B2 = £100 stake / £500 prize Category B3 = £1 stake / £500 prize Category B4 = £1 stake / £250 prize Category C = 50p stake / £35 prize Category D = 10p cash or 30p non-money stake / £5 cash or £8 non-money prize (SI 2007 / 2158) *Licensing officers may also wish to familiarise themselves with the requirements of SI 2007 / 2319 and SI 2007 / 2320 which include requirements that gaming machines display what category it is, the name and telephone number for assistance with problem gambling, that the machine is not to be used by child / young person unless is a category D and also provisions that no machines should be made available which can accept credit or debit cards.*
<center>Tracks</center>
The terms on which a bet may be placed must be displayed in a prominent place within the premises to which customers wishing to use facilities for betting have unrestricted access. (mandatory condition - SI 2007 / 1409)
The premises licence holder shall make arrangements to ensure that betting operators who are admitted to the premises for the purpose of accepting bets- (a) will be operating under a valid operating licence; and (b) are enabled to accept such bets in accordance with- (i) the conditions imposed under sections 92 (general betting operating licence) or 93 (pool betting operating licence) of the 2005 Act, or (ii) an authorisation under section 94 (horse-race pool betting operating licence) of that Act.
The premises licence holder shall make arrangements to ensure that reasonable steps are taken to remove from the premises any person who is found to be accepting bets on the premises otherwise than in accordance with the 2005 Act. (mandatory condition - SI 2007 / 1409)
The licence holder shall ensure that any part of the tracks which, prior to 1st September 2007, were made available for betting operators (or their assistants) will continue to be so. (Horseracing converted tracks only). (mandatory condition - SI 2007 / 1409)
The charge for admission to an existing betting area for providing facilities for betting shall not exceed five times the cost of the highest charge paid by members of the public (for betting operators) or the highest charge paid by member of the pubic (for the betting operator's assistant). All betting operators and betting operators' assistants will be charged the same for admission to the same part of the track. No other charged may be made and the charges must only cover reasonable costs. (Horseracing converted tracks only) (mandatory condition - SI 2007 / 1409)
The premises licence holder shall provide a place on the premises where betting operators and betting operators' assistants may provide facilities for betting. This does not apply to converted licences until 1st September 2012. (Horseracing tracks only) (mandatory condition - SI 2007 / 1409)
A totalisator on the premises shall only be operated at a time when the public are admitted for the purpose of attending dog races and no other sporting events are taking

place on the premises, and for the purpose of effecting betting transactions on the dog races taking place on the premises. (Dog tracks only)
At any time when the totalisator is being used, no betting operator or betting operator's assistance shall be excluded from the premises for the reason that s/he proposes to negotiate bets on the premises. There must also be space made available where the betting operators and their assistants can conveniently accept and negotiate bets in connection with the dog races running on the premises that day. (Dog tracks only) (mandatory premises licence condition - SI 2007 / 1409)
Hours of operation – No facilities for gambling shall be provided on the premises between the hours of 10pm on one day and 7am on the next, except where there is a sporting event taking place on the premises. Where there is a sporting event taking place on the premises then gambling may take place at any time that day. (default premises licence condition - SI 2007 / 1409)
Gaming machines permitted: If the track holds a Pool Betting Operating Licence then can have a total of 4 gaming machines which can be Category B2, B3, B4, C and D (i.e. 4 of either Category or a mix up to a total of 4). (Gambling Act 2005 Section 172 and SI 2007 / 2158) Category B2 = £100 stake / £500 prize Category B3 = £1 stake / £500 prize Category B4 = £1 stake / £250 prize Category C = 50p stake / £35 prize Category D = 10p cash or 30p non-money stake / £5 cash or £8 non-money prize (SI 2007 / 2158) *Licensing officers may also wish to familiarise themselves with the requirements of SI 2007 / 2319 and SI 2007 / 2320 which include requirements that gaming machines display what category it is, the name and telephone number for assistance with problem gambling, that the machine is not to be used by child / young person unless is a category D and also provisions that no machines should be made available which can accept credit or debit cards.*

GAMBLING ACT 2005 OFFENCES

	Prosecuting Authority	PENALTY*
PROVIDING GAMBLING FACILITIES		
Providing gambling facilities without licence/permit (s 33)	Gambling Commission	51 weeks' imprisonment and/or level 5 fine
Any person using premises to provide gambling facilities (s 37)	Gambling Commission/Licensing Authority	51 weeks' imprisonment and/or level 5 fine
Manufacturer, supply, install or adapt gambling software without operating licence (s 41)	Gambling Commission	51 weeks' imprisonment and/or level 5 fine
Cheat, attempt to cheat, or assisting another person to cheat at gambling (s 42)	Gambling Commission	51 weeks' imprisonment and/or level 5 fine 2 years on indictment
Invite another person to join chain-gift scheme or participation in promoting a scheme (s 43)	Gambling Commission	51 weeks' imprisonment and/or level 5 fine
CHILDREN AND YOUNG PEOPLE		
Invite, cause or permit child or young person to gamble, including intentional distribution of advertising documentation with intent to encourage gambling (s 46) NB the defences to this and reasonable belief	Gambling Commission	51 weeks' imprisonment and/or level 5 fine Level 3 fine if by young person
Gambling by young person where not permitted (eg allowed to use Cat D machine) (s 48)		Level 3 fine
Young person enters certain premises offering gambling facilities (eg betting office) (s 49)	Gambling Commission	Level 3 fine
Young person providing facilities for gambling (s 50)	Gambling Commission	Level 3 fine
Employing young person to provide gambling facilities (s 51)	Gambling Commission	51 weeks' imprisonment and/or level 5 fine
Employing child/young person to provide lottery/football pools gambling facilities (s 52)	Gambling Commission	51 weeks' imprisonment and/or level 5 fine

		Level 3 fine if young person
Employing child for any purposes when bingo provided or gambling provided in accordance with club gaming permit or club machine permit (s 53)	Gambling Commission	51 weeks' imprisonment and/or level 5 fine Level 3 fine if young person
Employing child/young person in connection with provision of category A – D machines on licensed premises (s 54)	Gambling Commission	51 weeks' imprisonment and/or level 5 fine Level 3 fine if young person
Employing child/young person in respect of casino, betting premises or adult gaming centre (s 55)	Gambling Commission	51 weeks' imprisonment and/or level 5 fine Level 3 fine if young person
Invite, cause or permit child to take part in non-exempt lottery (s 56)	Gambling Commission	51 weeks' imprisonment and/or level 5 fine Level 3 fine if young person
Invite, cause or permit child to take part in football pools (s 57)	Gambling Commission	51 weeks' imprisonment and/or level 5 fine Level 3 fine if young person
Failure to comply with operating licence condition to return stake to child or young person (s 58)	Gambling Commission	51 weeks' imprisonment and/or level 5 fine Level 3 fine if young person

OPERATING LICENCES		
Failing without reasonable excuse to notify Commission of change of circumstances (s 101)	Gambling Commission	Level 2 fine
Licensee failing without reasonable excuse to produce operating licence when requested by constable or enforcement officer (s 108)	Gambling Commission	Level 2 fine
Operating licence holder failing to notify without reasonable excuse GC as soon as reasonably practicable of conviction of offence (s 109)	Gambling Commission	Level 2 fine
Failing to notify court on conviction for relevant offence of being operating licence holder (s 109)	Gambling Commission	Level 2 fine
Failing without reasonable excuse to produce records relating to operating licensed activities or information about licensed activities (s 122)	Gambling Commission	Level 2 fine
PERSONAL LICENCES		
Failure without reasonable excuse to produce personal licence to constable or enforcement officer (s 134)	Gambling Commission	Level 2 fine
Personal licence holder failing to notify without reasonable excuse GC as soon as reasonably practicable of conviction of offence (s 138)	Gambling Commission	Level 2 fine
Failure to act in accordance with terms and conditions of personal licence (s 139)		51 weeks' imprisonment and/or level 5 fine
PREMISES LICENCES		
Failure of premises licence holder without reasonable excuse to keep premises licence on premises and to make available for inspection by constable, enforcement officer or authorised person (s 185)	Gambling Commission/Licensing Authority	Level 2 fine
Failure to notify without reasonable excuse the licensing authority of a change of residential address or other specified details on the premises licence (s 186)	Gambling Commission/Licensing Authority	Level 2 fine
Premises licence holder fails without reasonable excuse to prominently display temporary use notice or make available for inspection to constable, customs and excise officer or authorised officer (s 229)	Gambling Commission/Licensing Authority	Level 2 fine
MACHINES		
Making a machine available for use without licence/permit (s 242)	Gambling Commission/Licensing Authority	51 weeks' imprisonment and/or level 5 fine
Making a machine available for use in contravention of regulations under s 240 (s 242)	Gambling Commission	51 weeks' imprisonment

		and/or level 5 fine
Manufacture, supply, install, adapt, maintain, repair gaming machine without operating licence or as sale of scrap or sale of previously licensed property (s 243)	Gambling Commission	51 weeks' imprisonment and/or level 5 fine
Supply, install or maintain a machine contrary to regulations under s 241 (s 243)	Gambling Commission	51 weeks' imprisonment and/or level 5 fine
Supply, install or make available gaming machine allowing payment by a credit card (s 245)	Gambling Commission	51 weeks' imprisonment and/or level 5 fine
LOTTERIES		
Promoting a non-exempt lottery without an operating licence (s 258)	Gambling Commission/Licensing Authority	51 weeks' imprisonment and/or level 5 fine
Facilitating a non-exempt lottery (s 259)	Gambling Commission/Licensing Authority	51 weeks' imprisonment and/or level 5 fine
Misusing profits of lottery (s 260)	Gambling Commission/Licensing Authority	51 weeks' imprisonment and/or level 5 fine
Misusing profits of exempt lottery (s 261)	Gambling Commission/Licensing Authority	51 weeks' imprisonment and/or level 5 fine
Breach of small society lottery condition	Gambling Commission/Licensing Authority	51 weeks' imprisonment and/or level 5 fine

BINGO ETC		
Failing without reasonable excuse to inform Gambling Commission of high turnover bingo period (s 275)	Gambling Commission	Level 3 fine
Misusing profits for non-specified purpose of non-commercial prize gaming (s 301)	Gambling Commission	51 weeks' imprisonment and/or level 5 fine
Holder of operator licence failing without reasonable excuse to produce authorisation (s 316)	Gambling Commission	Level 2 fine
OBSTRUCTING ENFORCEMENT OFFICER ETC		
Obstructing or failing to cooperate without reasonable excuse with constable, enforcement officer or authorised person seeking to exercise powers under Part 15 (s 326)	Gambling Commission/Licensing Authority	Level 3 fine
Without reasonable excuse providing false or misleading information to Gambling Commission or licensing authority for a purpose connected with the Act (s 342)	Gambling Commission/Licensing Authority	51 weeks' imprisonment and/or level 5 fine
ADVERTISING OF GAMBLING		
Contravention of regulations relating to advertising (s328)	Gambling Commission	51 weeks' imprisonment and/or level 5 fine
Knowingly advertising unlawful gambling without reasonable belief (s 330)	Gambling Commission	51 weeks' imprisonment and/or level 5 fine
Advertising foreign gambling facilities (s 331)	Gambling Commission	51 weeks' imprisonment and/or level 5 fine

PERMITS		
Failure to comply with a forfeiture order or co-operate with steps to comply (s 345)	Gambling Commission	51 weeks' imprisonment and/or level 5 fine
Occupier of premises failing without reasonable excuse to produce family entertainment centre gaming machine permit to constable, enforcement officer or authorised officer (sch 10, para 20)	Gambling Commission/Licensing Authority	Level 2 fine
Fail without reasonable excuse to produce club gaming permit or club machine permit on request of constable or enforcement officer	Gambling Commission	Level 2 fine
Fail without reasonable excuse to have to have club gaming permit/club machine permit varied as soon as practicable upon a change of circumstances (sch 12, para 15)	Gambling Commission	Level 2 fine
Failure without reasonable excuse to produce licensed premises gaming machine permit on request of constable, enforcement officer or authorised officer	Gambling Commission/Licensing Authority	Level 2 fine
Failure to produce without reasonable excuse prize gaming permit on request of constable, enforcement officer or authorised officer	Gambling Commission/Licensing Authority	Level 2 fine

The Fireworks (Safety) Regulations 1997 –
Fireworks for use by the public must meet British Standards BS7114
Fireworks must not be sold to under 18s
Caps, cracker snaps and party poppers must not be sold to under 16.
Fireworks that fly erratically and large powerful display fireworks can not be sold to members of the public.

The Fireworks Regulations 2004
- Prohibit the supply of fireworks louder than 120 decibels
- Prohibit anyone under 18 possessing fireworks , and anyone except professionals from possessing display fireworks.
- Section 9 & 11 Prohibit the sale of fireworks to the public from unlicensed traders except for;

The Chinese new year, and the proceeding 3 days.
Diwali and the proceeding 3 days.
15th October – 10th November
26th – 31st December.
A licence is needed to supply all year round.
- Fireworks can not be used at night (11pm – 7am) except;

Until 1am on the night of the Chinese New Year
Until 1am on the night of Diwali
Until 1am on New Years Eve
Until midnight on 5th November
(6 months in prison and £5000 fine, enforced by the Police)

Control of Explosives Regulations 1991
It is an offence to keep fireworks (except those for private use) on premises that have not been registered for this purpose (individuals can store fireworks, for private use, in a safe place, for up to 14 days).

Explosives Act 1875
Throwing or setting off fireworks in the street is an offence
Police – fine up to £5000

Intoxicating Substances (Supply) Act 1985

- Makes it an offence for a retailer to sell solvents to anyone under the age of 18, knowing that they are being purchased to be abused. However please not that it doesn't make it illegal to own or buy solvents.

Licensing act 2003;

SECT.	DESCRIPTION OF OFFENCE	OFFENDER(S)
32 (6)	Failure to notify licensing authority of change in name or address of premises licence holder or designated premises supervisor	Premises licence holder
39 (2)	Failure to notify existing premises supervisor that premises licence has been varied to replace them, or that such application has been refused	Premises licence holder
40 (5)	Failure to provide premises licence (or statement of reasons for failure to do so) to licensing authority within 14 days of direction following premises supervisor giving notice of intention to cease	Premises licence holder
45 (4)	Failure to notify designated premises supervisor of application for transfer of premises licence with interim effect or of actual transfer (where applicant and premises supervisor not same person)	Applicant for transfer of premises licence
48 (5)	Failure to notify premises supervisor of interim authority notice	Interim authority holder
55 (3)	Failure to produce premises licence at request of licensing authority for amendment	Premises licence holder
56 (4)	Failure to keep premises licence or certified copy at premises	Premises licence holder
56 (4)	Failure to display summary of premises licence or certified copy and notice specifying nominated person	Premises licence holder
56 (5)	Failure to produce premises licence or certified copy to constable or authorised person for examination	Premises licence holder Nominated Person
58 (5)	Obstruction of authorised person entering premises to inspect premises re: grant of licence, provisional statement, variation or review	Any person
80 (6)	Failure to give notice of change of name or alteration of rules of club	Secretary of club
81 (6)	Failure to give notice of change of registered address of club	Secretary of club
91 (3)	Failure to produce club premises certificate for amendment within 14 days of request from licensing authority	Secretary of club
92 (5)	Failure to produce club premises certificate (or certified copy) at premises in custody or control of nominated person	Secretary
92 (6)	Failure to display at premises summary of club premises certificate (or certified copy) and a notice stating position held by nominated person	Nominated person
92 (9)	Failure to produce club premises certificate (or certified copy) to constable or authorised person for examination	Nominated person
94 (6)	Obstruction of authorised person trying to enter premises for purposes of inspection prior to grant, variation or review of CPC	Any person
106 (3)	Obstruction of authorised officer from inspecting temporary event premises to assess impact upon crime prevention objective	Any person
107 (4)	Failure to display copy of temporary event notice; keep notice in custody of premises user (or nominated person at premises); or display notice of who nominated person is	Premises user
107 (8)	Failure to produce temporary event notice to authorised officer	Premises user Nominated

			person
121 (2)	Failure to notify licensing authority of conviction for relevant offence or foreign offence as soon as reasonably practicable during grant or renewal application period		Applicant for personal licence
125 (4)	Failure to notify licensing authority of change of name or address of personal licence holder		Personal licence holder
126 (6)	Failure to notify court of personal licence or 'notifiable event' when being dealt with for relevant offence		Personal licence holder
130 (4)	Failure to notify licensing authority of conviction for relevant or foreign offence		Personal licence holder
132 (5)	Failure to produce personal licence within 14 days to licensing authority to be updated		Personal licence holder
133 (4)	Failure to produce personal licence to authorised person or a constable whilst on premises to make or authorise sale or supply of alcohol		Personal licence holder
134 (1)	Knowingly allow or carry on or attempt to carry on unauthorised licensable activity		Any person (but exceptions – see s134(2)
135 (1)	Unauthorised exposure for sale by retail of alcohol		Any person
136 (1)	Unauthorised possession of alcohol with intent to sell or supply in club (Consider PND)		Any person
138 (1)	Allowing disorderly conduct on licensed premises		Any person authorised to prevent conduct
139 (1)	Sale or supply (or attempt) or allow sale or supply of alcohol to person who is drunk (Consider PND)		Any person in capacity to prevent
140 (1)	Obtain or attempt to obtain alcohol for consumption on relevant premises by drunk person (Consider PND)		Any person
141 (1)	Failure to leave licensed premises or attempt to enter premises following request from constable or authorised person		Any drunk or disorderly person
142 (1)	Keeping unlawfully imported goods on relevant premises		Any person authorised to prevent
143 (1) (2) (3)	Sale/supply of alcohol to under 18 (Consider PND)		Any person or a club
144 (1) (3)	Allowing sale/supply of alcohol to under 18 (Consider PND)		Any person authorised to prevent
145 (1) (2)	Sale/supply of liquor confectionary to under 16		Any person or a club
146 (1) (3) (4)	Purchase/supply (or attempt purchase/supply) of alcohol by or on behalf of under 18
Purchase/supply (or attempt purchase/supply) of alcohol for consumption on relevant premises by under 18 (Consider PND)		Under 18 or person purchasing on behalf of
147 (1) (2)	Consumption on relevant premises of alcohol by under 18 or knowingly allowing the consumption to occur		Under 18 or person in capacity to prevent
148 (1)	Delivering alcohol sold or supplied on relevant premises to under 18		Person working on

		(Consider PND)	premises
	148 (2) (4)	Allowing anybody else to deliver alcohol sold or supplied on relevant premises to under 18 (Consider PND)	Person working on premises in capacity to prevent delivery
	149 (1)	Sending an under 18 to obtain alcohol sold or supplied on relevant premises for consumption off the premises	Any person
	150 (1)	Allowing on relevant premises an -18 to sell or supply alcohol	'Responsible person' – see 150(4)
	153 (1)	Sale of alcohol in or from moving vehicle	Any person
	154 (5)	Sell or attempt to sell or allow sale of alcohol on train contrary to prohibition order	Any person
	155 (1)	False statement in connection with licensing application	Any person
	157 (4)	Keeping premises open, or allowing premises to be kept open in breach of a closure order in respect of an identified area	Manager, prem. licence holder, DPS or prem. user (temp event)
	158 (6)	Permit premises to be open in contravention of a closure order for specified premises	Any person
	162 (7)	Permit premises to be open in contravention of magistrates' closure order	Any person
	165 (8)	Permit premises to open in contravention of magistrates' closure order pending reconsideration of conditions	Any person
	174 (4)	Obstructing entry of a constable or authorised person entering premises to investigate whether licensable activity is being carried out in accordance with an authorisation	Any person
	Sch 8, para 10 (1)	(Transitional offence) – false statement in connection with application for conversion of existing licence under para 2	Any person
	Sch 8, para 22 (1)	(Transitional offence) – false statement in connection with application for conversion of existing club certificate under para 14	Any person

Noise legislation;

Councils have a range of powers to tackle noise nuisance from licensed premises:

The Environmental Protection Act 1990
- Places a duty on local authorities to investigate complaints of noise nuisance made by residents of their area.
- Places a duty on local authorities to serve an abatement notice where it is satisfied that a statutory nuisance exists or is likely to occur or recur.
- Failure to comply with the abatement notice may result in prosecution in the Magistrates' Court; the penalty for business or trade premises is a fine of up to £20,000.
- Power to take the necessary steps to abate the noise if an abatement notice is not complied with, including seizure of noise-making equipment.
- Power to recover any reasonable expenses incurred and to place a charge on the property.
- Power to seek an injunction where proceedings for a contravention of an abatement notice would not afford an adequate remedy.

The Noise Act 1996 (as amended by the Clean Neighbourhoods and Environment Act 2005)
- The Clean Neighbourhoods and Environment Act 2005 amended the Noise Act 1996, which deals with night-time (11pm-7am) noise, to apply to licensed premises.
- Power to serve warning notices if officers are satisfied that the noise, if measured from within a complainant's dwelling, would or might exceed the permitted level.
- Power to issue fixed penalty notices of up to £500 if the warning notice is not complied with.
- Failure to comply with a warning notice may, alternatively, result in prosecution in the Magistrates' Court; the penalty for licensed premises is a fine of up to £20,000.
- Power to seize noise-making equipment if a warning notice is not complied with.

The above powers apply to noise from premises, the definition of which includes land. Therefore, the actions outlined above could be taken when noise is created by people congregating outside, but within the curtilage of the premises e.g. roof terraces, beer gardens, street side tables as part of the premises etc.

Whether noise created by people congregating on the street might amount to a statutory nuisance has not yet been tested in the courts, however, the widely held view is that the definition of "premises" does not cover noise made in streets (outside the curtilage of the premises) or public places (not including those parts of premises such as street side tables licensed and approved by planning and highways).. This is supported by the encyclopaedia of environmental law, which states in relation to statutory nuisance of noise emitted from premises that: "The noise must be emitted from a premises. In a case decided under s.58 of COPA, the word "premises" was held not to cover noise made in streets or public places (see Tower Hamlets London Borough Council v Manzoni and Walder (1984) J.P. 123..." Although the case relates specifically to the use of amplification devices on the highway, this would suggest that local authorities could not take statutory nuisance action in circumstances where noise is generated on the street.

Closure of noisy permises

Noise Nuisance
There is no set definition of Public nuisance caused by noise, it is a question of interpretation for the courts and will depend upon the circumstances of the case, therefore senior police officers are required to judge reasonably whether the noise is causing a nuisance, the noise in question must be emitted from the licensed premises.

'Both the police and the courts have the power to order the temporary closure of licensed premises in specified circumstances. The existing powers afforded to the police, courts and local authorities under the Public Entertainment Licences (Drug misuse) Act 1997, Licensing Act 1964, ss 179A-179K and 188, and the criminal Justices and Police Act 2001 will be repealed. Thus the code for closure orders set out in LA 2003, Part 8 is now the only source of police, local authority or judicial powers. The same applies to premises in respect of which a temporary event notice has effect, but the closure powers do not apply to clubs with a premises certificate.' – *Kerry Barker & Susan Cavender (2003).*

General closure

A Magistrate's Court can implement a closure order in areas where there may be disorder as a preventative action in advance of any possible disorder. Premises that are situated at or near to the area of concern may be required to close for up to 24 hours.

It is an offence knowingly to keep open premises to which a general closure order relates. The offence can be committed by either a manager of the premises kept open, the holder of the premises licence, the designated supervisor, or, in the case of a temporary event, the premises user.

Specific closure order
Section 161 of the 2003 Act provides that a senior police officer of the rank of inspector or above may make an order closing individual premises covered by the premises licences or a temporary event notice for up to 24 hours where disorder is taking place or is likely to take place imminently or a nuisance is being caused by noise emanating from the premises. The premises may be closed with immediate affect for up to 24 hours. After 24 hours the police must seek a judicial review if they wish to extend this, (unless the court will not have determined whether to exercise its power by the end of the closure period as long as the conditions for an extension are satisfied).

If the premises are allowed to re-open they may be given a caution and can be re-closed for an indefinite period if they cause a noise nuisance again.
-Department for Culture and Media Studies Guidance

Local authorities can ask the licensee to modify what they are doing or close the event but can't close the premises. However under The Environmental protection Act 1990, local authority enforcement officers have the power to confiscate noisy equipment, therefore there may be no need to close the premises also voluntary co-operation such as closing doors and windows, or requiring customers to remain inside if effective in reducing the noise will eliminate the need for premises closure. In addition the Noise Act 1996. The police also have further powers under the Anti –Social Behaviour Act 2003.

"Liaisons with local government enforcement officers with existing powers for controlling noise nuisance would therefore be beneficial. It will ultimately be for senior police officers to decide, in the circumstances of any case, whether it is appropriate for them to deploy these powers, which are likely ultimately to lead to the review of the premises licence for the premises affected with the possibility of a licensing authority determining that it is necessary for the promotion of licensing objectives to take steps in relation to that licence, which may include its revocation."
-Department for Culture and Media Studies Guidance

Public order act

Offences under s5 of the Public Order Act 1986

Section 5 makes it a criminal offence to use threatening, abusive, insulting words or behaviour or disorderly behaviour within the hearing or sight of a person likely to be caused harassment, alarm or distress by that behaviour. There must be a victim present at the scene for this offence to be made out.

Disorderly behaviour includes:

- causing a disturbance in a residential area;
- persistently shouting abuse or obscenities at passers-by;
- rowdy behaviour in a street late at night;
- using slogans or language that cause distress.

Threatening, abusive or insulting words or behaviour includes:

- threats or abuse directed at individuals carrying out public service duties;
- throwing missiles;
- minor violence or threats of violence;
- incidents between neighbours that do not justify a charge of assault;
- an individual who is picked on by a gang where the behaviour does not justify an assault charge.

Before the police have the power to arrest a person for this offence, the offender must first be warned about the behaviour and can only be arrested if the behaviour is repeated. The offence is a summary only offence punishable by a Level 3 fine in the magistrates' court or a penalty notice for disorder (PND) where appropriate.

Police and Criminal Justice Act 2001.

The closure orders under section 19 of the Criminal Justice and Police Act 2001 do not apply to off-licences. but only to on-licences, despite being amended by the Licensing Act 2003.

This Act applies to the no drinking zone – if they carry on drinking when asked not to by a police officer they can get a fine of up to £500 & a conviction.

Police and Magistrates Courts Act 1994

Requires police forces to attain objectives set for them by the home secretary, limiting the ability of chief constables to set out the priorities for their force.

Sunday Trading Act 1994 - Large shops over 3000 sq ft cannot open on Easter Sunday. Easter Monday is a normal working day. On other Sundays large shops can open for up to 6 hours, between 10 am and 6 pm.

Private Security Industry Act 2001
- *Engaging in Licensable conduct without a licence S3(1)*
- *Employing unlicensed person in licensable conduct S5(1)*
- *Occupier of land permitting unlicensed wheel clamper to operate S6(1)*
- *Contravening licence conditions S9(4)*
- *Wrongly claiming SIA Approved Contractor status S16(2)*
- *Contravening terms of Approved Contractor status S17(2& 3)*
- *Obstructing SIA to exercise power of entry/ or failure to comply with requirements S19(5)*
- *Intentionally or recklessly making a false statement to the SIA S22(1).*

- **Individual support orders** – These are for anyone 10-17 years old. They are usually issued with ASBO, it gives them positive instructions rather than negative i.e you will attend x,y,z (where as an ASBO is you will not do X,Y,Z). These are issued by the youth offending team.
- **Intervention orders** – Similar to the above but for 18 year olds (drugs related).
- **Education welfare** - £50 FPNs if parents take kids out of school i.e. go on holiday during term time.
- **Section 27 Violent Crime Reduction Act 2006- Dispersal Zones** – Must be authorised by a Police superintendent or above, the local authority must agree to it. Once in place 2 or more people either causing or likely to cause asb can be asked to be removed from an area and not return for up to 48 hours. Anyone under 16 should be taken home, under **Child protection legislation**. In order to enforce the dispersal zone, it must be enforced by a Police constable (not a PCSO), they must be in uniform. They can ask anyone 16+ to leave the area, to move to another locality and not return for a max of 48 hours. They must provide a written notice setting out the location to avoid and the prescribed time limit. The notice can be amended and reduced at a Police station i.e. another officer may allow them to come back into an area to go into work once they have sobered up, although it can be extended above 48 hours. They can tell a group to move but each person must have a separate written notice. It may specify the route that they have to take and the mode of transport i.e if they are really drunk they maybe told that they can't go on public transport and have to walk, as the legislation includes public places, including public transport. It is an offence to refuse to comply, Breach of direction (i.e. coming back into an area that they have been asked to leave). There is no right of appeal, they can only challenge it if they have been taken to court for preaching the notice. Officers can't stop someone accessing an area where they live/work or need to go to for a genuine reason.

- Disorder on/removal from licensed premises will be dealt with under the **Licensing Act 2003**. Although if someone repeatedly tries to get onto licensed premises they can be moved on under the Section 27 Violent Crime Reduction Act 2006- Dispersal Zone powers.

- **Section 59 Police Reform Act** covers the seizure of vehicles causing alarm or distress, or is likely to cause harm, harassment or distress. They must receive a warning before the vehicle is seized. It also allows a vehicle to be seized if it contravenes section 3 of the Road Traffic Act (driving without due care and attention – driving without reasonable consideration to other road users including pedestrians – this could include driving through a puddle to splash pedestrians) or contravening section 34 of the Road Traffic Act – driving on common land ie. Using mini motos on parks. Section 59 (2) states that a Police officer doesn't have to witness the offence in order to take enforcement action, as long as they have sufficient evidence. Section 59 (3) prescribes the power to stop, and if previously warned, seize the vehicle. The warning lasts up to 12 months. An officer can go into a garage to seize the vehicle if they believe that the offence has been committed, although they can't go into the house. They have the power to use reasonable force to seize the vehicle. A PCSO has this power, but does not have the power to enter the premises without a police constable. The vehicle has to be a mechanically propelled one but the engine does not have to be running for an offence to be committed. (The requirements to have a vehicle on the road are that it must be; insured, registered, taxed, a helmet must be worn in the case of bikes and the driver must have a valid driving licence).

Trading standards & fraud legislation

- Fraud Act 2006 (Conspiracy)

- Consumer Protection from Unfair Trading Regulations 2008

Town and Country Planning Act 1990

Section 215 (s215) of the Town & Country Planning Act 1990 (the Act) provides a local planning authority (LPA) with the power, in certain circumstances, to take steps requiring land to be cleaned up when its condition adversely affects the amenity of the area. If it appears that the amenity of part of their area is being adversely affected by the condition of neighbouring land and buildings, they may serve a notice on the owner requiring that the situation be remedied. These notices set out the steps that need to be taken, and the time within which they must be carried out. LPAs also have powers under s219 to undertake the clean up works themselves and to recover the costs from the landowner.

The use of s215 by LPAs is discretionary and it is therefore up to the LPA to decide whether a notice under these provisions would be appropriate in a particular case, taking into account all the local circumstances. LPAs will need to consider, for example, the condition of the site, the impact on the surrounding area and the scope of their powers. In some circumstances s215 notices may be used in conjunction with other powers, for example, repair notices in respect of listed buildings or dangerous structure notices.

Town and Country Planning Act 1990

A breach of planning control is defined in the Town and Country Planning Act 1990 as "the carrying out of a development without the required planning permission, or failing to comply with any condition or limitation subject to which planning permission has been granted".

Examples of breaches of planning control
- Building work, engineering operations and material changes of use that is carried out without the benefit of planning permission.
- Development that has planning permission but is not carried out in accordance with the approved plans.
- Failure to comply with conditions or the terms of a legal agreement attached to a permission or consent.
- Demolition within a conservation area without conservation area consent, when it is required.
- Works carried out to a "listed" building, which affect the historic character or setting, without Listed Building consent being granted.
- Removal of, or works carried out, to protected trees and hedgerows without consent being granted or proper notification being given.
- Advertisements, which require express, consent under the Advertisement Regulations, but are displayed without consent being granted.
- Fly posting.
- Failure to comply with the requirements of a planning legal notice e.g. enforcement, discontinuance, stop notice.

The Highways Act 1980

This deals with many highways offences, including causing an obstruction on the highway and is a great peiece of legislation to use, if taxis are forming an illegal rank.

Appendix 10 - Statement template

STATEMENT OF WITNESS

*(Criminal Procedure Rules, r 27.1(1);
Criminal Justice Act 1967, s. 9, Magistrates' Courts Act 1980, s.5B)*

STATEMENT OF: _____

Age of witness: (if over 18 enter "Over 18") _____

Occupation of witness: _____

This statement consisting of…. page(s) each signed by me, is true to the best of my knowledge and belief and I make it knowing that, if it is tendered in evidence, I shall be liable to prosecution if I have wilfully stated in it anything that I know to be false or do not believe to be true.

Dated the _____ day of _____ _____ Signed: _____

Appendix 11 - Statement template

REPORT OF CONTRAVENTION

Date report submitted:		Last date for informations:	
		Case ref. №:	

Report of:	(Investigating officer)	**Investigating officers:**	
Officer in charge:		**Disclosure officer:**	

Defendant(s):	1. 2. 3. 4. 5.	Date of birth:	Unknown

Address(es) for service:	1. 2.

Legislation: ....

Details of offence(s): .....

Date of offence(s): ....

Place of offences: ....

Previous convictions: ...

Documents attached:
- **Infringement report** .... ☐
- **Schedule of witnesses** .... ☐
- **Schedule of witnesses dates** .... ☐
- **Schedule of exhibits** .... ☐
- **Statement of costs** .... ☐
- **Schedule of CPIA non-sensitive** .... ☐
- **Schedule of CPIA sensitive** .... ☐
- **Declaration by disclosure officer** .... ☐
- **Witness Statements** .... ☐

Legal proceedings are / are not recommended

Date   Signed

INFRINGEMENT REPORT

Introduction

(i.e. Background history – first complaint that came in on..., from then on chronology of events including the date the summons was served).

On the (date), ...received a complaint reference number........... regarding ....

On the ...., obtained a warrant of entry search and seizure for ....Computers and Documents were seized by .... Standards Evidence seized is detailed in the 'premises search book' & '..........property log' detailed in the statements of ....

At the time of the seizure ......(date) it was agreed between .... the 'lead officer' and the company secretary on the ....premises at the time of the seizure, namely a .... and his solicitor (also present) namely ......of ....Solicitors LLP, that a 'search and sift' exercise would take place at ....on............. It was agreed that .... would be present to oversee the exercise in the spirit of procedural cooperation. Ordinarily, a 'search and sift' notice would be tendered to the responsible person at the time of the execution of the warrant and seizing of evidence but this was postponed upon 'mutual agreement' to jointly conduct the said operation. This was a break from recognised investigative procedures and may be raised by the defendants. I agreed to break no sealed evidence bags until .... arrived on ....date).... At ....(time & date)..... on .... in (full address of the location), I broke open evidence bags and seals in front of .... and a colleague .... facilitating a cooperative 'search and sift' exercise. Documents agreed to be of <u>no</u> evidential value were returned to .... The matter was conducted amicably.

On the ....(date)........., the ....(defendant/company name).......... seized computers were delivered to .... by .... for downloading onto discs for subsequent examination by investigating officers. On the ....(date)......., a signed endorsed copy of the warrant executed at .... in .... was also returned to

……….Court. On …….(date), the computers were collected from ………in Leatherhead by ………... etc.

Other agencies also prosecuting? – Give details of these.

Summary of the investigation

Brief overview of case, i.e.

In the initial prosecution file already provided namely …….. criminal offences are outlined against ………(defendants name). The offences were committed by ……………… in ………….. Execution of a warrant of entry and seizing and detaining of computers and documentation was conducted on ………….. against ……………...in ……….(location).

The reason for such action was to establish whether the 'Limited Company' and its 'directing minds' were aware and encouraging the alleged criminal offences committed by ……… 'sales staff' in consumers homes.

Etc.

Details relating to the defendant(s) explanation of the alleged offence(s) *(State "none" if appropriate)*:

Details relating to any doubt regarding any admission or confession by the defendant(s) *(State "none" if appropriate)*:

How does the defendant satisfy the statutory defence?

In this protracted investigation no due diligence procedures and or practices by …..(Defendant)……… would seem to provide a statutory defence.

Mitigating circumstances that they have mentioned….

Observations

Background information i.e. other authorities who have prosecuted, number of complaints, impact this has had, documents found and their significance etc.

Conclusion

Recommendations

i.e. prosecution / none prosecution

Signed:

Name:

Job Title:

Date:

SCHEDULE OF WITNESSES

| 1. | Name:
 ....
 Job title:
 ....
 Address:
 ....
 Telephone N$^{os.}$: .... | Da y: | e-mail: .... |

| 2. | Name:
 ....
 Job title:
 ....
 Address:
 ....
 Telephone N$^{os.}$: ....
 ....
 .... | Da y: Ev e: | e-mail: .... |

| 3. | Name:
 ....
 Job title:
 ....
 Address:
 ....
 Telephone N$^{os.}$: ....
 ....
 .... | Da y: Ev e: | e-mail: .... |

| 4. | Name:
 ....
 Job title:
 ....
 Address:
 ....
 Telephone N$^{os.}$: ....
 ....
 .... | Da y: Ev e: | e-mail: .... |

| 5. | Name:
 .... |

Job title:		
....		
Address:		
....		
Telephone Nos.:	Day:	e-mail: ....
....	Eve:	
....		

DATES TO AVOID

Case name & Year   ▓ Confirmed unavailability

January   1 2 3 4 5 6 7 8 9 10 11 12 13 14 15 16 17 18 19 20 21 23 24 25 26 27 28 29 30 31

February   1 2 3 4 5 6 7 8 9 10 11 12 13 14 15 16 17 18 19 20 21 23 24 25 26 27 28 29

March   1 2 3 4 5 6 7 8 9 10 11 12 13 14 15 16 17 18 19 20 21 23 24 25 26 27 28 29 30 31

April   1 2 3 4 5 6 7 8 9 10 11 12 13 14 15 16 17 18 19 20 21 23 24 25 26 27 28 29 30

May   1 2 3 4 5 6 7 8 9 10 11 12 13 14 15 16 17 18 19 20 21 23 24 25 26 27 28 29 30 31

June   1 2 3 4 5 6 7 8 9 10 11 12 13 14 15 16 17 18 19 20 21 23 24 25 26 27 28 29 30

July   1 2 3 4 5 6 7 8 9 10 11 12 13 14 15 16 17 18 19 20 21 23 24 25 26 27 28 29 30 31

August   1 2 3 4 5 6 7 8 9 10 11 12 13 14 15 16 17 18 19 20 21 23 24 25 26 27 28 29 30 31

September   1 2 3 4 5 6 7 8 9 10 11 12 13 14 15 16 17 18 19 20 21 23 24 25 26 27 28 29 30

October   1 2 3 4 5 6 7 8 9 10 11 12 13 14 15 16 17 18 19 20 21 23 24 25 26 27 28 29 30 31

November   1 2 3 4 5 6 7 8 9 10 11 12 13 14 15 16 17 18 19 20 21 23 24 25 26 27 28 29 30

December   1 2 3 4 5 6 7 8 9 10 11 12 13 14 15 16 17 18 19 20 21 23 24 25 26 27 28 29 30 31

Following year

January   1 2 3 4 5 6 7 8 9 10 11 12 13 14 15 16 17 18 19 20 21 23 24 25 26 27 28 29 30 31

February   1 2 3 4 5 6 7 8 9 10 11 12 13 14 15 16 17 18 19 20 21 23 24 25 26 27 28 29

March   1 2 3 4 5 6 7 8 9 10 11 12 13 14 15 16 17 18 19 20 21 23 24 25 26 27 28 29 30 31

April   1 2 3 4 5 6 7 8 9 10 11 12 13 14 15 16 17 18 19 20 21 23 24 25 26 27 28 29 30

May   1 2 3 4 5 6 7 8 9 10 11 12 13 14 15 16 17 18 19 20 21 23 24 25 26 27 28 29 30 31

June   1 2 3 4 5 6 7 8 9 10 11 12 13 14 15 16 17 18 19 20 21 23 24 25 26 27 28 29 30

July   1 2 3 4 5 6 7 8 9 10 11 12 13 14 15 16 17 18 19 20 21 23 24 25 26 27 28 29 30 31

August   1 2 3 4 5 6 7 8 9 10 11 12 13 14 15 16 17 18 19 20 21 23 24 25 26 27 28 29 30 31

September   1 2 3 4 5 6 7 8 9 10 11 12 13 14 15 16 17 18 19 20 21 23 24 25 26 27 28 29 30

October   1 2 3 4 5 6 7 8 9 10 11 12 13 14 15 16 17 18 19 20 21 23 24 25 26 27 28 29 30 31

November   1 2 3 4 5 6 7 8 9 10 11 12 13 14 15 16 17 18 19 20 21 23 24 25 26 27 28 29 30

December   1 2 3 4 5 6 7 8 9 10 11 12 13 14 15 16 17 18 19 20 21 23 24 25 26 27 28 29 30 31

Officer & Witness dates to be avoided:

;

SCHEDULE OF EXHIBITS

	Exhibit Reference	Item	Person producing exhibit	Current Location
01.				
02.				
03.				
04.				
05.				
06.				
07.				
08.				
09.				
10.				
11.				
12.				
13.				
14.				
15.				
16.				
17.				
18.				
19.				
20.				
21.				
22.				
23.				
24.				
25.				

NOTE

List here any consistencies in evidence i.e. ammendments in statements & why etc.

Attorney General's guidelines on the disclosure of unused material (Practice Note [1982] 1 All ER 734)

Editing single statements

(III.24.3)There are two acceptable methods of editing single statements.

(a)By marking copies of the statement in a way which indicates the passages on which the prosecution will not rely. This merely indicates that the prosecution will not seek to adduce the evidence so marked. The original signed statement to be tendered to the court is not marked in any way. The marking on the copy statement is done by lightly striking out the passages to be edited so that what appears beneath can still be read, or by bracketing, or by a combination of both. It is not permissible to produce a photocopy with the deleted material obliterated, since this would be contrary to the requirement that the defence and the court should be served with copies of the signed original statement. Whenever the striking out/bracketing method is used, it will assist if the following words appear at the foot of the frontispiece or index to any bundle of copy statements to be tendered: 'The prosecution does not propose to adduce evidence of those passages of the attached copy statements which have been struck out and/or bracketed (nor will it seek to do so at the trial unless a notice of further evidence is served).'

(b) By obtaining a fresh statement, signed by the witness, which omits the offending material, applying the procedure in paragraph III.24.2.

STATEMENT OF COSTS

Matter Initiated by: **Complaint / Routine Inspection / Other** *(delete as appropriate)*

Hourly Rate @ …….. per hour: *(based on LACORS recommended hourly rate)*

* cost £ = Total officer hours x hourly rate

Date	Reason	Time (hrs)	№ of Officers	Total Officer Hours	Cost * (£)
	Investigation				
	Preparation of Report				
	Pace Interview				
	Disclosure CPIA				
	Disbursements *(see below)*				
	Other				
	Totals:				

List of Disbursements: *(attach copies of receipts/invoices to this report).*

		£
1.	i.e. Accommodation for officers whilst on duty, computer forensics etc.	
2.		
3.		
	Total of Disbursements: *(enter value in main table above)*	

Request for forfeiture:

Description of items	№ of items

Total Costs:

	£
Legal Fees Unknown =	
Total Trading Standards Costs: =	

SCHEDULE OF NON-SENSITIVE UNUSED MATERIAL
CRIMINAL PROCEDURE & INVESTIGATIONS ACT 1996

Investigating Officer:

Officer in Charge:

Defendant(s):

The Disclosure Officer believes that the following material, which does not form part of the prosecution case, is **non-sensitive**:

	Full Description of Material	**Location** *F = submitted with file;* *O = retained by Officer.*

Continuation Sheet: Yes ☐ No ☐

I am the Officer responsible for disclosure in the above Investigation. I certify that I do not believe any of the listed material is sensitive.

Signed Disclosure Officer: _____ **Name:** _____ **Date:** _____

Schedule of Non-sensitive Unused Material
(Continuation Sheet)

	Full Description of Material	**Location** *F = submitted with file; O = retained by Officer.*

Schedule of Sensitive Unused Material
Criminal Procedure & Investigations Act 1996

Investigating Officer:

Officer in Charge:

Defendant(s):

The following material does not form part of the prosecution case. The Disclosure Officer believes that it is **Sensitive Material**.

If "none", state **NONE** under item 1.

	Full Description of Material and Reason Why Sensitive **(If too sensitive to list, advise the Prosecutor separately).**	**Location** *F = submitted with file;* *O = retained by Officer.*
	None	

Continuation Sheet: Yes ☐ No ☐

I am the Officer responsible for disclosure in the above investigation. I believe that the material listed above is **Sensitive**.

Signed Disclosure Officer: _____   Name: S Pearson   Date: 9/4/2010

Declaration by Disclosure Officer

I certify that to the best of my knowledge and belief, all material which has been retained and made available to me has been revealed to the prosecutor in accordance with the duties imposed by the Criminal Procedure and Investigations Act Code of Practice, with which I have complied.

Signed:

Name:

Job Title:

Date:

Signed……………………………….. Date…………………………….

……………………………..

Appendix (12) – Leading questions

Cognitive Psychology, 1975, 7, 550-572.

Leading Questions and the Eyewitness Report
Elizabeth F. Loftus[1]
University of Washington

A total of 490 subjects, in four experiments, saw films of complex, fast-moving events, such as automobile accidents or classroom disruptions. The purpose of these experiments was to investigate how the wording of questions asked immediately after an event may influence responses to questions asked considerably later. It is shown that when the initial question contains either true presuppositions (e.g., it postulates the existence of an object that did exist in the scene) or false presuppositions (e.g.. postulates the existence of an object that did not exist), the likelihood is increased that subjects will later report having seen the presupposed object. The results suggest that questions asked immediately after an event can introduce new — not necessarily correct — information, which is then added to the memorial representation of the event, thereby causing its reconstruction or alteration.

1 Although current theories of memory are derived largely from experiments involving lists of words or sentences, many memories occurring in everyday life involve complex, largely visual, and often fast-moving events. Of course, we are rarely required to provide precise recall of such experiences — though as we age, we often volunteer them — but on occasion such recall is demanded, as when we have witnessed a crime or an accident. Our theories should he able to encompass such socially important forms of memory. It is clearly of concern to the law, to police and insurance investigators, and to others to know something about the completeness, accuracy, and malleability of such memories.

2 When one has witnessed an important event, one is sometimes asked a series of questions about it. Do these questions, if asked immediately after the event, influence the memory of it that then develops? This paper first summarizes research suggesting that the wording of such initial questions can have a substantial effect on the answers given, and then reports four new studies showing that the wording of these initial questions can also influence the answers to different questions asked at [begin page 561] some later time. The discussion of these findings develops the thesis that questions asked about an event shortly after it occurs may distort the witness' memory for that event.

Answers Depend on the Wording of Questions 3 An example of how the wording of a question can affect a person's answer to it has been reported by Harris (1973). His subjects were told that "the experiment was a study in the accuracy of guessing measurements, and that they should make as intelligent a numerical guess as possible to each question" (p. 399). They were then asked either of two questions such as, "How tall was the basketball player?", or, "How short was the basketball player?" Presumably the former form of the question presupposes nothing about the height of the player, whereas 1This research was supported in part by a grant to the author by the United States Department of Transportation, Urban Mass Transportation Administration. The manuscript has benefited enormously from the comments of Dedre Gentner, Geoffrey Loftus, Duncan Luce, and Steve Woods. Several undergraduates contributed ideas and/or other assistance in connection with this research: Diane Altman, Helen Burns, Robert Geballe, John Palmer, and Steven Reed. Requests for reprints should be sent to Elizabeth F. Loftus, Department of Psychology, University of Washington, Seattle, WA 98195.

C:\rsm\y520\readings\loftus75\loftus75.fm 2 the latter form involves a presupposition that the player is short. On the average, subjects guessed about 79 and 69 in. (190 and 175 mm), respectively. Similar results appeared with other pairs of questions. For example, "How long was the movie?", led to an average estimate of 130 min, whereas, "How short was the movie?" led to 100 min. While it was not Harris' central concern, his study clearly demonstrates that the wording of a question may affect the answer.

4 The phenomenon has also been demonstrated in two other contexts: past personal experiences and recently-witnessed events.

Past Personal Experiences
5 In one study (Loftus, unpublished), 40 people were interviewed about their headaches and about headache products under the belief that they were participating in market research on these products. Two of the questions were crucial to the experiment. One asked about products other than that currently being used, in one of two wordings:
(1a) In terms of the total number of products, how many other products have you tried? 1? 2? 3?
(1b) In terms of the total number of products, how many other products have you tried? 1? 5? 10?

6 The 1/2/3 subjects claimed to have tried an average of 3.3 other products, whereas the 1/5/10 subjects claimed an average of 5.2; $t(38) = 3.14$, = .61, $p < .01$.

7 The second key question asked about frequency of headaches in one of two ways:

(2a) Do you get headaches frequently, and, if so, how often?
(2b) Do you get headaches occasionally, and, if so, how often?

8 The "frequently" subjects reported an average of 2.2 headaches/wk, whereas the "occasionally" group reported only 0.7/wk; $t(38) = 3.19$, = .47, $p <.01$. [begin page 562]

Recently Witnessed Events 9 Two examples from the published literature also indicate that the wording of a question put to a person about a recently-witnessed event can affect a person's answer to that question. In one study (Loftus, 1974; Loftus & Zanni, 1975), 100 students viewed a short film segment depicting a multiple-car accident. Immediately afterward, they filled out a 22-item questionnaire which contained six critical questions. Three of these asked about items that had appeared in the film whereas the other three asked about items not present in the film. For half the subjects, all the critical questions began with the words, "Did you see a . . ." as in, "Did you see a broken headlight?" For the remaining half, the critical questions began with the words, "Did you see the . . ." as in, "Did you see the broken headlight?"

10 Thus, the questions differed only in the form of the article, *the* or *a*. One uses "the" when one assumes the object referred to exists and may be familiar to the listener. An investigator who asks, "Did you see the broken headlight?" essentially says, "There was a broken headlight. Did you happen to see it?" His assumption may influence a witness' report. By contrast, the article "a" does not necessarily convey the implication of existence. 11 The results showed that witnesses who were asked "the" questions were more likely to report having seen something, whether or not it had really appeared in the film, than those who were asked "a" questions. Even this very subtle change in wording influences a witness' report.

12 In another study (Loftus & Palmer, 1974), subjects saw films of automobile accidents and then answered questions

about the accidents. The wording of a question was shown to affect a numerical estimate. In particular, the question, "About how fast were the cars going when they smashed into each other?" consistently elicited a higher estimate of speed than when "smashed" was replaced by "collided," "bumped," "contacted," or "hit." 13 We may conclude that in a variety of situations the wording of a question about an event can influence the answer that is given. This effect has been observed when a person reports about his own experiences, about events he has C:\rsm\y520\readings\loftus75\loftus75.fm 3 recently witnessed, and when answering a general question (e.g., "How short was the movie?") not based on any specific witnessed incident.

Question Wording and Answers to Subsequent Questions

14 Our concern in this paper is not on the effect of the wording of a question on its answer, but rather on the answers to other questions asked some time afterward. We will interpret the evidence to be presented as suggesting a memorial phenomenon of some importance. [begin page 563]

15 In the present experiments, a key initial question contains a *presupposition*, which is simply a condition that must hold in order for the question to be contextually appropriate. For example, the question, "How fast was the car going when it ran the stop sign?" presupposes that there was a stop sign. If a stop sign actually did exist, then in answering this question a subject might review, strengthen, or make more available certain memory representations corresponding to the stop sign. This being the case, the initial question might be expected to influence the answer to a subsequent question about the stop sign, such as the question, "Did you see the stop sign?" A simple extension of the argument of Clark and Haviland (in press) can be made here: When confronted with the initial question, "How fast was the car going when it ran the stop sign?", the subject might treat the presupposed information as if it were an address, a pointer, or an instruction specifying where information related to that presupposition may be found (as well as where new information is to be integrated into the previous knowledge). In the process the presupposed information may be strengthened. 16 What if the presupposition is false? In that case it will not correspond to any existing representation, and the subject may treat it as new information and enter it into his memory. Subsequently, the new "false" information may appear in verbal reports solicited from the subject.

17 To explore these ideas, subjects viewed films of complex, fast-moving events. Viewing of the film was followed by initial questions which contained presuppositions that were either true (Experiment 1) or false (Experiments 2-4). In Experiment I, the initial questions either did or did not mention an object that was in fact present in the film. A subsequent question, asked a few minutes later, inquired as to whether the subject has seen the existing object. In Experiments 2-4, the initial questions were again asked immediately after the film, whereas the subsequent questions were asked after a lapse of 1 wk.

Experiment 1

Method

18 One hundred and fifty University of Washington students, in groups of various sizes, were shown a film of a multiple- car accident in which one car, after failing to stop at a stop sign, makes a right-hand turn into the main stream of traffic. In an attempt to avoid a collision, the cars in the oncoming traffic stop suddenly and a five-car, bumper-to-bumper collision results. The film lasts less than 1 min, and the accident occurs within a 4-sec period.

19 At the end of the film, a 10-item questionnaire was administered. A diagram of the situation labeled the car that ran the stop sign as "A," and the cars involved in the collision as "B" through "F." The first question asked about the speed of Car A in one of two ways:

1. How fast was Car A going when it ran the stop sign?
2. How fast was Car A going when it turned right?

20 Seventy-five subjects received the "stop sign" question and 75 received the "turned right" question. The last question was identical for all subjects: "Did you see a stop sign for Car A?" Subjects responded by circling "yes" or "no" on their questionnaires.

Results and Discussion

C:\rsm\y520\readings\loftus75\loftus75.fm 4

21 Fifty-three percent of the subjects in the "stop sign" group responded "yes" to the question, "Did you see a stop sign for Car A?", whereas only 35% in the "turn right" group claimed to have seen the stop sign; (1) The wording of a presupposition into a question about an event, asked immediately after that event has

taken place, can influence the answer to a subsequent question concerning the presupposition itself, asked a very

short time later, in the direction of conforming with the supplied information.

22 There are at least two possible explanations of this effect. The first is that when a subject answers the initial stop

sign question, he somehow reviews, or strengthens, or in some sense makes more available certain memory representations

corresponding to the stop sign. Later, when asked, "Did you see a stop sign . . . ?", he responds on the basis of the strengthened memorial representation.

23 A second possibility may be called the "construction hypothesis." In answering the initial stop sign question, the

subject may "visualize" or "reconstruct" in his mind that portion of the incident needed to answer the question,

and so, if he accepts the presupposition, he introduces a stop sign into his visualization whether or not it was in

memory. When interrogated later about the existence of the stop sign, he responds on the basis of his earlier supplementation

of the actual incident. In other words, the subject may "see" the stop sign that he has himself constructed.

This would not tend to happen when the initial question refers only to the right turn.

24 The construction hypothesis has an important consequence. If a piece of true information supplied to the subject

after the accident augments his memory, then, in a similar way, it should be possible to introduce into memory

something that was not in fact in the scene, by supplying a piece of false information. For example, Loftus and

Palmer (1974, Expt. 2) showed subjects a film of an automobile accident and followed it by questions about

events that occurred in the film. Some subjects were asked "About how fast were the cars going when they

smashed into each other?", whereas others were asked the same question with "hit" substituted for "smashed."

On a retest 1 wk later, those questioned with "smashed" were more likely than those questioned with "hit" to

agree [begin page 565] that they had seen broken glass in the scene, even though none was present in the film. In

the present framework, we assume that the initial representation of the accident the subject has witnessed is modified

toward greater severity when the experimenter uses the term "smashed" because the question supplies a piece of new information, namely, that the cars did indeed smash into each other. On hearing the "smashed"

question, some subjects may reconstruct the accident, integrating the new information into the existing representation.

If so, the result is a representation of an accident in memory that is more severe than, in fact, it actually was. In particular, the more severe accident is more likely to include broken glass.

25 The presupposition that the cars smashed into each other may be additional information, but it can hardly be said to be false information. It is important to determine whether it is also true that false presuppositions can affect a witness' answer to a later question about that presupposition. Such a finding would imply that a false presupposition can be accepted by a witness, that the hypothesis of a strengthening of an existing memorial representation is untenable (since there should be no representation corresponding to nonexistent objects), and that the construction hypothesis discussed above is supported. Experiment 2 was designed to check this idea.

Experiment 2

Method

26 Forty undergraduate students at the University of Washington, again in groups of various sizes, were shown a 3-min videotape taken from the film *Diary of a Student Revolution.* The sequence depicted the disruption of a class by eight demonstrators; the confrontation, which was relatively noisy, resulted in the demonstrators leaving the classroom.

27 At the end of the videotape, the subjects received one of two questionnaires containing one key and nineteen filler questions. Half of the subjects were asked, "Was the leader of the four demonstrators who entered the classroom a male?", whereas the other half were asked, "Was the leader of the twelve demonstrators who entered the classroom a male?" The subjects responded by circling "yes" or "no."

28 One week later, all subjects returned and, without reviewing the videotape, answered a series of 20 new questions about the disruption. The subjects were urged to answer the questions from memory and not to make inferences. The critical question here was, "How many demonstrators did you see entering the classroom?"

Results and Discussion

29 Subjects who had previously been asked the "12" question reported having seen an average of 8.85 people 1 wk earlier, whereas those asked [begin page 566] the "4" question recalled 6.40 people, $t(38) = 2.50$, = .98, $p < .01$.

The actual number was, it will be recalled, eight. One possibility is that some fraction of the subjects remembered the number 12 or the number 4 from the prior questionnaire and were responding to the later question with that number, whereas the remainder had the correct number. An analysis of the actual responses given reveals that 10% of the people who had been interrogated with "12" actually responded "12," and that 10% of those interrogated with "4" actually responded with "4." A recalculation of the means, excluding those subjects in the "12" condition who responded "12" and those in the "4" condition who responded "4," still resulted in a significant difference between the two conditions (8.50 versus 6.67), $t(34) = 1.70$, $p < .05$. This analysis demonstrates that recall of the specific number given in the initial questionnaire is not an adequate alternative explanation of the present results.

30 The result shows that a question containing a false numerical presupposition can, on the average, affect a witness' answer to a subsequent question about that quantitative fact. The next experiment was designed to test whether

the same is true for the existence of objects when the false presupposition concerns one that did not actually exist.

31 Experiment 3

Method

32 One hundred and fifty students at the University of Washington, in groups of various sizes, viewed a brief videotape of an automobile accident and then answered ten questions about the accident. The critical one concerned the speed of a white sports car. Half of the subjects were asked, "How fast was the white sports car going when it passed the barn while traveling along the country road?", and half were asked, "How fast was the white sports car going while traveling along the country road?" In fact, no barn appeared in the scene.

33 All of the subjects returned 1 wk later and, without reviewing the videotape, answered ten new questions about the accident. The final one was, "Did you see a barn?" The subjects responded by circling "yes" or "no" on their questionnaires.

Results and Discussion

34 Of the subjects earlier exposed to the question containing the false presupposition of a barn, 17.3% responded "yes" when later asked, "Did you see a barn?", whereas only 2.7% of the remaining subjects claimed to have seen it; (1) = 8.96, $p < .01$. An initial question containing a false presupposition can, it appears, influence a witness' later tendency to report the presence of the nonexistent object corresponding to that presupposition. [begin page 567]

35 The last experiment not only extends this finding beyond the single example, but asks whether or not the effect is wholly due to the word "barn" having occurred or not occurred in the earlier session. Suppose an initial question merely asks about, instead of presupposing, a nonexistent object; for example, "Did you see a barn?," when no barn existed. Presumably subjects will mostly respond negatively to such questions. But, what if that same question is asked again some time later? It is possible that a subject will reflect to himself, "I remember something about a barn, so I guess I must have seen one." If this were the case, then merely asking about a nonexistent object could increase the tendency to report the existence of that object at some later time, thereby accounting for the results of Expt III.

Appendix 13

The following is crib sheets to follow that includes all the legal requirements when conducting a PACE Interview; Please note this is merely a crib sheet not a record of interview. If conducting an interview which is not tape recorded you will need to keep an accurate record using a specific note sheet or by making notes in your pace notebook.

Prior to interview
▪ Select dates and book interview location/room / Select officers to conduct the interview. ▪ Write to suspect (if not in custody)/witness (ask them to bring ID in the form of a passport and proof of NI number) & Confirm if they are attending ▪ Complete plan of interview and write/plan possible interview questions.
Interview preparation
Get tapes & Tape seal & PACE code of practise to take into the interview, along with the following forms; • Formal notice to person being interviewed. • Notice to person whose interview has been tape recorded. • Sheets for record of interview (in case tape recorder breaks).
The Interview format
Welcome; ▪ Introduce yourself to the suspect, ask if they need to go to the toilet, want a drink, check they are not feeling unwell (that if they may need medication they have it), double check that they don't need an interpreter, don't have to be somewhere else i.e. if they have children to collect from school if they are under arrest you may have to make arrangements for them, if not you may want to re-schedule the interview. ▪ Photocopy any documents they have brought and get them to confirm they are true copies.
Switch on tape machine on; This interview is being tape recorded and is taking place at………..<State location> & <interview room>. As we believe an offence may have been committed this interview is being conducted in accordance with Codes of Practice of the Police and Criminal Evidence Act 1984 A copy of the Codes of Practice is available should you wish to consult it. (Quote edition/ colour of the book) ☐ The date is…………………. ☐ The time is……………………. My name is ………………………………..and I am an Investigator for …………….. *Also present is (Other Investigator)……………………………………………………….* ☐ Could you please state your full name and address? ☐ What is your date and place of birth? & you National Insurance number (if appropriate).
*Also present is (Solicitor/Friend/translator etc)……………………………….. **[Issue form]** / If there is no solicitor present state that they are entitled to legal representation /If appropriate double check they don't need a solicitor.* *Please can you give your name, and in what capacity you are present here today?* ☐ Can you please confirm that there are just the   [NUMBER]   of us in the room?

☐ Do you agree that the tapes were unsealed and placed into the tape recorder in your presence?

At the end of the interview I will give you a notice explaining what will happen to the tapes and how you can apply for a copy.

Caution the suspect;
"I am now going to let you know what your rights are – this is sometimes referred to as a caution".
You do not have to say anything. But it may harm your defence if you do not mention when questioned something which you later rely on in court. Anything you do say may be given in evidence.

| ☐ Do you understand your rights? | ☐ Can you tell me what your understanding of your rights is? |

Explanation: – I'll explain your rights to you in a little more detail.

- You don't have to answer our questions, if you don't want to.

- If you are asked a question now, and you do not answer it, **which is your right**, and you are asked the same question in court and you answer it then, the court would wonder why you didn't answer now, when I asked you.

- That does not mean that the matter will go to court, however, anything you do say now could be repeated in court as evidence if the case does go to court.

☐ You are not under arrest.   ☐ You are free to leave at any time

☐ You may obtain legal advice in person or by phone.

☐ Do you wish to obtain Legal advice?

☐ Is there any reason why you don't want Legal Advice?

☐ If during the interview you feel that you would like to obtain legal advice then please let me know as we can suspend the interview

Issue copy of Rights

☐ Can you read and write English?   ☐ Do you have any difficulty in understanding English?

(If they say yes ask for the language and stop the interview in order to arrange for an interpreter).

☐ For the purpose of this interview are you feeling fit and well, and are you on any medication that could affect your ability to continue?

(If they say no ask whether or not they wish to stop so that they can consult with a doctor and come back on another day).

☐ Do you have any learning difficulties or psychiatric problems that we should be aware of that you may not have mentioned previously?

(If they say yes advise the defendant that it may be helpful if they have an appropriate adult attend with them and that they can bring along a friend or relative over the age of 18 who may be able to assist them with any difficulties with the language or understanding of the content of the interview.

We may ask you to provide further information with regards to your benefit claim. Which may be used to assess or re-assess your claim to Housing and/or Council Tax Benefit; this information may also be used in legal proceedings

We will be making notes during the interview.

As mentioned in the appointment letter we have had reason to conduct an investigation into your benefit claim with regard to **[mention allegation]**. This interview is now your opportunity to offer an explanation of the facts.

- ☐ Is there anything you want to say before we continue?

Questions to ask;
....

Comments/Notes:

End of Interview;

Summarise what has been said.

I will be drawing the interview to a close now. Do you wish to add anything or clarify anything that has been said?

- State for the tape that it's the end of the interview and the time tape stopped at.
- Seal tapes
- Issue notice to person whose interview has been tape recorded
- Explain what happens next

Seal and give copy to suspect

Put a note in PACE notebook to record the fact that the interview took place inc;
Time & date & details of who's present & the ID No of the tapes.

If during the interview you need to change the tapes;

Tape Change

Beep means 1 minute till tape ends.

That noise means the tapes are coming to an end. I'm going to suspend the interview to allow the tapes to be changed.

The time is now _____ and I am turning off the tape machine.

>>>>>>>>>>>>>>>>>>>>>>>SEAL TAPES>>>>>>>>>>>>>>>>>>>>>>>>>

>>>>>>>>>>>>>>>>>>>>>PUT IN NEW TAPES>>>>>>>>>>>>>>>>>>>>>>

The time is now _____.

This is a continuation of the interview with _____ on _____.

Let me remind you that you are still under caution. Would you like me to repeat the caution?

You do not have to say anything but it may harm your defence if you do not mention when questioned something which you later rely on in court. Anything you do say may be given in evidence.

I remind you that you are not under arrest. You are free to leave at any time.

If at any time you wish to obtain legal advice please tell me and I will suspend the interview.

Do you agree that we have not discussed the case while the tape machine was switched off?

Do you agree that no one entered or left the room while the tape machine was switched off?

Do you agree that the tapes we are using were unsealed in your presence?

Are you happy to continue with the interview?

If during the interview you need to take a break;

Interview break

I'm going to suspend the interview to allow a break for................

The time is now _____ and I am turning off the tape machine.

.... Turn machine off...

<Break>

..............................Turn machine on...

The time is now _____.

This is a continuation of the interview with ___<suspect name>_____on ___<date>____ <at location>.........
Also present are……………………………………..

Let me remind you that you are still under caution. Would you like me to repeat the caution?

You do not have to say anything but it may harm your defence if you do not mention when questioned something which you later rely on in court. Anything you do say may be given in evidence.

I remind you that you are not under arrest. You are free to leave at any time.

If at any time you wish to obtain legal advice please tell me and I will suspend the interview.

Do you agree that we have not discussed the case while the tape machine was switched off?

Do you agree that no one entered or left the room while the tape machine was switched off?

Do you agree that the tapes we are using were unsealed in your presence?

Are you happy to continue with the interview?

PACE Interview

Prior to interview
<ul><li>Select dates and book interview location/room / Select officers to conduct the interview.</li><li>Write to suspect (if not in custody)/witness (ask them to bring ID in the form of a passport and proof of NI number) & Confirm if they are attending</li><li>Complete plan of interview and write/plan possible interview questions.</li></ul>
Interview preparation
Get tapes & Tape seal & PACE code of practise to take into the interview, along with the following forms;<ul><li>Formal notice to person being interviewed.</li><li>Notice to person whose interview has been tape recorded.</li><li>Sheets for record of interview (in case tape recorder breaks).</li></ul>
The Interview format
Welcome;<ul><li>Introduce yourself to the suspect, ask if they need to go to the toilet, want a drink, check they are not feeling unwell (that if they may need medication they have it), double check that they don't need an interpreter, don't have to be somewhere else i.e. if they have children to collect from school if they are under arrest you may have to make arrangements for them, if not you may want to re-schedule the interview.</li><li>Photocopy any documents they have brought and get them to confirm they are true copies.</li></ul>
Switch on tape machine on; This interview is being tape recorded and is taking place at...........<State location> & <interview room>. As we believe an offence may have been committed this interview is being conducted in accordance with Codes of Practice of the Police and Criminal Evidence Act 1984 A copy of the Codes of Practice is available should you wish to consult it. (Quote edition/ colour of the book) ☐ The date is.................... ☐ The time is........................ My name is ....and I am an Investigator for .... *Also present is (Other Investigator)...* ☐ Could you please state your full name and address? ☐ What is your date and place of birth? & you National Insurance number (if appropriate).
*Also present is (Solicitor/Friend/translator etc)....................................... **[Issue form]** / If there is no solicitor present state that they are entitled to legal representation /If appropriate double check they don't need a solicitor.*
Please can you give your name, and in what capacity you are present here today? ☐ Can you please confirm that there are just the   [NUMBER]   of us in the room? ☐ Do you agree that the tapes were unsealed and placed into the tape recorder in your presence? At the end of the interview I will give you a notice explaining what will happen to the tapes and how you can apply for a copy.

Caution the suspect;
"I am now going to let you know what your rights are – this is sometimes referred to as a caution".

You do not have to say anything. But it may harm your defence if you do not mention when questioned something which you later rely on in court. Anything you do say may be given in evidence.

| ☐ | Do you understand your rights? | ☐ | Can you tell me what your understanding of your rights is? |

Explanation: – I'll explain your rights to you in a little more detail.

- You don't have to answer our questions, if you don't want to.

- If you are asked a question now, and you do not answer it, **which is your right**, and you are asked the same question in court and you answer it then, the court would wonder why you didn't answer now, when I asked you.

- That does not mean that the matter will go to court, however, anything you do say now could be repeated in court as evidence if the case does go to court.

☐ You are not under arrest. ☐ You are free to leave at any time

☐ You may obtain legal advice in person or by phone.

☐ Do you wish to obtain Legal advice?

☐ Is there any reason why you don't want Legal Advice?

☐ If during the interview you feel that you would like to obtain legal advice then please let me know as we can suspend the interview

Issue copy of Rights

☐ Can you read and write English? ☐ Do you have any difficulty in understanding English?

(If they say yes ask for the language and stop the interview in order to arrange for an interpreter).

☐ For the purpose of this interview are you feeling fit and well, and are you on any medication that could affect your ability to continue?

(If they say no ask whether or not they wish to stop so that they can consult with a doctor and come back on another day).

☐ Do you have any learning difficulties or psychiatric problems that we should be aware of that you may not have mentioned previously?

(If they say yes advise the defendant that it may be helpful if they have an appropriate adult attend with them and that they can bring along a friend or relative over the age of 18 who may be able to assist them with any difficulties with the language or understanding of the content of the interview.

We may ask you to provide further information with regards to your benefit claim. Which may be used to assess or re-assess your claim to Housing and/or Council Tax Benefit; this information may also be used in legal proceedings

We will be making notes during the interview.

As mentioned in the appointment letter we have had reason to conduct an investigation into your benefit claim with regard to **[mention allegation]**. This interview is now your opportunity to offer an explanation of the facts.

☐ Is there anything you want to say before we continue?

Questions to ask;
……………………………….

Comments/Notes:

End of Interview;

Summarise what has been said.

I will be drawing the interview to a close now. Do you wish to add anything or clarify anything that has been said?

- State for the tape that it's the end of the interview and the time tape stopped at.
- Seal tapes
- Issue notice to person whose interview has been tape recorded
- Explain what happens next

Seal and give copy to suspect

Put a note in PACE notebook to record the fact that the interview took place inc;
Time & date & details of who's present & the ID No of the tapes.

If during the interview you need to change the tapes;

Tape Change

Beep means 1 minute till tape ends.

That noise means the tapes are coming to an end. I'm going to suspend the interview to allow the tapes to be changed.

The time is now _____ and I am turning off the tape machine.

>>>>>>>>>>>>>>>>>>>>>>>SEAL TAPES>>>>>>>>>>>>>>>>>>>>>>>>>

>>>>>>>>>>>>>>>>>>>>>>PUT IN NEW TAPES>>>>>>>>>>>>>>>>>>>>>

The time is now _____.

This is a continuation of the interview with _____ on _____.

Let me remind you that you are still under caution. Would you like me to repeat the caution?

You do not have to say anything but it may harm your defence if you do not mention when questioned something which you later rely on in court. Anything you do say may be given in evidence.

I remind you that you are not under arrest. You are free to leave at any time.

If at any time you wish to obtain legal advice please tell me and I will suspend the interview.

Do you agree that we have not discussed the case while the tape machine was switched off?

Do you agree that no one entered or left the room while the tape machine was switched off?

Do you agree that the tapes we are using were unsealed in your presence?

Are you happy to continue with the interview?

If during the interview you need to take a break;

Interview break

I'm going to suspend the interview to allow a break for…………….

The time is now _____ and I am turning off the tape machine.

…………………………. Turn machine off……………………………………………………………..

<Break>

…………………………Turn machine on……………………………………………………………….

The time is now _____.

This is a continuation of the interview with ___<suspect name>_____ on ___<date>____ <at location>………
Also present are…………………………………………..

Let me remind you that you are still under caution. Would you like me to repeat the caution?

You do not have to say anything but it may harm your defence if you do not mention when questioned something which you later rely on in court. Anything you do say may be given in evidence.

I remind you that you are not under arrest. You are free to leave at any time.

If at any time you wish to obtain legal advice please tell me and I will suspend the interview.

Do you agree that we have not discussed the case while the tape machine was switched off?

Do you agree that no one entered or left the room while the tape machine was switched off?

Do you agree that the tapes we are using were unsealed in your presence?

Are you happy to continue with the interview?

Legal Rights Form

NOTICE TO PERSONS BEING INTERVIEWED

1. This interview is being conducted in accordance with the Code of Practice for the treatment and questioning of persons by Local Authority staff when investigating offences, which has been prepared in accordance with the Police and Criminal Evidence Act 1984.

2. The interview is to enable you to offer an explanation of the facts, though should evidence of an offence emerge, you may be prosecuted.

3. You do not have to say anything, but it may harm your defence if you do not mention when questioned something which you later rely on in court. Anything you do say may be given in evidence.

4. You are not under arrest or detained here; you may leave at any time during the interview. If the officer is conducting the interview in your home, you may ask him/her to leave.

5. You may have a solicitor and/or an interpreter with you, in which case this interview will be suspended until another interview can be arranged.

6. You may seek legal advice either in person or by telephone

7. Copies of the Codes of Practice are available if you wish to consult them.

'Interviews under Caution'

Information for friends or relatives accompanying someone who is being interviewed under caution.

We conduct 'Interviews under Caution' in accordance with the Police and Criminal Evidence Act (PACE) 1984. These rules allow a person being interviewed to have a legal representative with them. <u>There is no provision for friends or relatives to be present and we can exclude them if we wish</u>.

We can allow a person not connected with the investigation to attend 'Interviews under Caution' to provide moral support for the person being interviewed. This person can be a friend or a relative.

As you are accompanying someone who is attending a taped Interview Under Caution you will be asked to state your name and your relationship to the person being interviewed at the beginning of the tape recording e.g. Ms Jane Yellow, Mrs Yellow's daughter.

We must advise you that we are allowing you to be present for moral support only. You do not have the right to speak, offer advice or ask questions during the interview.

If you do try to take part in the interview we may feel it necessary to ask you to leave.

We ask you to agree to these conditions so that the interview can proceed un-interrupted.

Appendix 14

1. Memo to the solicitor
2. Content page
3. Case disposal & summary;

    - *Summary of case*

    - *Allegation including appropriate section of legislation*

    - *Particular points to be drawn out in Statement of Facts to be served with Summons*

    - *Date of alleged offences*

    - *Full Names of alleged offender*

    - *Addresses of alleged offenders*

    - *Dates of birth and physical description*

    - *Ethnic origin/gender*

    - *Place alleged offence occurred*

    - *How was offence notified/discovered*

    - *Name/address of complainant if applicable*

    - *Ethnic origin of complainant if applicable*

    - *Documents below are attached*

DOCUMENT	Name of person producing the document
Report of urgent authorisation of surveillance	
Authorisation forms to use directed surveillance/use of covert human intelligence source	
Application for renewal of directed surveillance/use of covert human intelligence source	
Cancellation of authorisation to use directed surveillance/use of covert human intelligence sources	
evidence log	
decision log	
Schedule of Relevant Non-Sensitive Material	
Schedule of Non-Sensitive Material not forming part of prosecution case	
Schedule of Sensitive Material	
Case Disposal Decision Record	
Section 9 witness statements (1)	
Section 9 witness statements (2)	
Interview transcripts	
Statutory notices (and proof of service where applicable)	
Others:	

4. Other exhibits attached/relevant to case:
5. Costs incurred to date
6. Dates of each witness to avoid for hearing.
7. Confirmation delegated matter and name of officer exercising delegated authority.
8. Will an interpreter be required in court, and if so, what language is needed?

CASE DISPOSAL RECORD

Reference Number / Investigation:

Officer in Charge of Investigation:

Contact details;

Investigator:

Disclosure Officer:

Full name of alleged offender(s):

Is the offender a business?

Offence(s): state Act/Regulation and section(s)/regulation(s) contravened:

Maximum penalty for each offence:

Mode of Trial: ☐ Summary ☐ Indictable

Has/have the offender(s) admitted guilt?

What are the mitigating factors?

Is there an independent witness or evidence as to the offender's liability?

Are there any special circumstances surrounding witnesses (e.g. age, illness etc)?

Are there any special circumstances surrounding any victims (e.g. death, serious injury/illness etc)?

Has the offender previously been cautioned or convicted for this or a similar offence? Give details

Are there any public interest reasons why a prosecution ought not to be brought?

Is there a statutory defence to the allegation or a reasonable cause for it to have been committed? If so, briefly outline what they are.

Can the case be disposed of by other means (e.g. refusal/revocation of a licence, service of statutory notice?) If so, which?

Why should prosecution be used instead of the means above?

Recommendation for……………..

Reasons:

Case Summary/Key Facts

Signed (investigator):   Date:

Reviewed by Disclosure Officer: Date:

☐ Agree ☐ Disagree

Reasons:

Signed:

EVIDENCE LOG

Investigation: Reference Number:

Officer in Charge of Investigation:
Investigator: Disclosure Officer:

Date, Time and Location	Events and Individuals Involved	Other Information	Material or Exhibits obtained	Investigator

DECISION LOG

Investigation: Reference Number:

Officer in Charge of Investigation:
Investigator: Disclosure Officer: ….

DATE/TIME	DECISION (eg to interview or not to interview offender/witness, serve/not serve notice etc)	DECISION TAKEN BY	DECISION REVIEWED BY

A Police prosecution file will normally consist of the following, where applicable:

MG 1 (or Local Authority equivalent)	File front sheet
(MG 2) "	Initial Witness Assessment
MG 4 "	Charges
(MG 5) "	Case Summary
(MG 6) "	Confidential Case File Information
(MG 6C) "	Schedule of non-sensitive unused material
(MG 6D) . "	Schedule of sensitive unused material
(MG 7) *	Remand application
(MG 8) *	Breach of Bail
MG 9 (or Local Authority equivalent)	Witness List
MG 10 "	Witness non-availability
MG 11 "	Witness Statements
(MG 12) "	Exhibit List
MG 15 "	Record/Transcript of Interview
(MG 18) "	Other Offences (taken into consideration)
(MG 19) "	Compensation claim
(MG 20) "	Further Evidence/Information Report

The forms in brackets are not normally needed until there is a not guilty plea, or until the case is transferred to Crown Court.

Forms marked * will only be used by the Police, not by Local Authorities.

The forms make up section 3 of the Manual of Guidance, which can be downloaded from: http://police.homeoffice.gov.uk/operational-policing/prosecution-manual-guidance

Events & Links

Useful conferences and exhibitions;

- IRRV (Institute of Revenues Rating & Valuation) Collection and Enforcement Conference.
- Annual Conference for the National Community Safety Network
- IFSEC 2008
- Retail Security 2008
- National Association of Licensing Enforcement Officers Annual Conference.

Printed in Great Britain
by Amazon